Public management

MANAGEMENT, WORK AND ORGANISATIONS

Series editors: **Gibson Burrell**, The Management Centre, University of Leicester
Mick Marchington, Manchester Business School
Paul Thompson, Department of Human Resource Management, University of Strathclyde

This series of new textbooks covers the areas of human resource management, employee relations, organisational behaviour and related business and management fields. Each text has been specially commissioned to be written by leading experts in a clear and accessible way. The books contain serious and challenging material, take an analytical rather than prescriptive approach and are particularly suitable for use by students with no prior specialist knowledge.

The series is relevant for many business and management courses, including MBA and post-experience courses, specialist masters and postgraduate diplomas, professional courses and final-year undergraduate courses. These texts have become essential reading at business and management schools worldwide.

Published

Emma Bell **Reading Management and Organization in Film**
Paul Blyton and Peter Turnbull **The Dynamics of Employee Relations** (3rd edn)
Sharon C. Bolton **Emotion Management in the Workplace**
Sharon Bolton and Maeve Houlihan **Searching for the Human in Human Resource Management**
Peter Boxall and John Purcell **Strategy and Human Resource Management**
J. Martin Corbett **Critical Cases in Organisational Behaviour**
Susan Corby, Steve Palmer and Esmond Lindop (eds) **Rethinking Reward**
Ian Greener **Public Management**
Keith Grint **Leadership**
Irena Grugulis **Skills, Training and Human Resource Development**
Damian Hodgson and Svetlana Cicmil **Making Projects Critical**
Marek Korczynski **Human Resource Management in Service Work**
Karen Legge **Human Resource Management**: anniversary edition
Patricia Lewis and Ruth Simpson (eds) **Gendering Emotions in Organizations**
Stephen Procter and Frank Mueller (eds) **Teamworking**
Alison Pullen, Nic Beech and David Sims **Exploring Identity**
Helen Rainbird (ed.) **Training in the Workplace**
Jill Rubery and Damian Grimshaw **The Organisation of Employment**
Harry Scarbrough (ed.) **The Management of Expertise**
Hugh Scullion and Margaret Linehan **International Human Resource Management**
Ruth Simpson and Patricia Lewis **Voice, Visibility and the Gendering of Organizations**
Adrian Wilkinson, Mick Marchington, Tom Redman and Ed Snape **Managing with Total Quality Management**
Colin C. Williams **Rethinking the Future of Work**
Diana Winstanley and Jean Woodall (eds) **Ethical Issues in Contemporary Human Resource Management**

For more information on titles in the Series please go to www.palgrave.com/business/mwo

Invitation to authors
The Series Editors welcome proposals for new books within the Management, Work and Organisations series. These should be sent to Paul Thompson (p.thompson@strath.ac.uk) at the Dept of HRM, Strathclyde Business School, University of Strathclyde, 50 Richmond St Glasgow G1 1XT

Series Standing Order
If you would like to receive future titles in this series as they are published, you can make use of our standing order facility. To place a standing order please contact your bookseller or, in case of difficulty, write to us at the address below with your name and address and the name of the series. Please state with which title you wish to begin your standing order.
Customer Services Department, Macmillan Distribution Ltd
Houndmills, Basingstoke, Hampshire RG21 6XS, England

Public management

A Critical text

Ian Greener

First published 2009 by
PALGRAVE MACMILLAN

Palgrave Macmillan in the UK is an imprint of Macmillan Publishers Limited, registered in England, company number 785998, of Houndmills, Basingstoke, Hampshire RG21 6XS.

Palgrave Macmillan in the US is a division of St Martin's Press LLC, 175 Fifth Avenue, New York, NY 10010.

Palgrave Macmillan is the global academic imprint of the above companies and has companies and representatives throughout the world.

Palgrave® and Macmillan® are registered trademarks in the United States, the United Kingdom, Europe and other countries.

ISBN-13: 978–0–230–20328–0
ISBN-10: 0–230–20328–0

This book is printed on paper suitable for recycling and made from fully managed and sustained forest sources. Logging, pulping and manufacturing processes are expected to conform to the environmental regulations of the country of origin.

A catalogue record for this book is available from the British Library.

A catalog record for this book is available from the Library of Congress.

10   9   8   7   6   5   4   3   2   1
18 17 16 15 14 13 12 11 10 09

Printed and bound in China

For Linda Jayne, who could have done much better

Contents

Acknowledgements

Thanks to Mick Marchington for asking me if I would be interested in writing the book, and to his series co-editors for letting me do it. Ursula Gavin has been a patient, understanding and encouraging editor, and the book's four reviewers offered a range of suggestions for improving the text for which I'm extremely grateful. A number of staff in my time at Manchester University helped shape my view of public management including Colin Talbot, Kieran Walshe, Damien Grimshaw, Jill Rubery, Anne Shacklady-Smith and Naomi Chambers. Steve Harrison continued to provide me with an example of what kind of academic I'd like to be when I grow up. Outside of Manchester I've had the fortune to talk about some of the ideas presented here with Martin Powell, Matthias Beck, Mark Exworthy, Alison Hann, Chris Nottingham, Calum Paton, Stephen Peckham, Russell Mannion and Martin Laffin. In my time at Durham, David Byrne and David Hunter have been a constant source of inspiration, and Tim Blackman and Simon Hackett understanding bosses. Bethany, Anna and Emily continue to remind me that I really ought to try and write less. Thanks to you all.

1

Introduction

Introduction

In an age when everyone is already suffering from information overload, anyone adding to the huge amount of writing on any topic must surely provide a good reason for doing so. There is a range of very good books on public management available, so if an author is to introduce a new text, this suggests that they must be clear what it provides for potential readers.

This book treats the subject of public management critically. What this means is not that it treats the topic of public management to a series of criticisms, although the book is critical (in this sense) in some areas of public management. Instead, it treats the ideas and topics that much of the writing on public management has tended to take for granted as problematic, and tries to work out what taking a careful look at them might mean for those researching the topic, as well as for those that actually have to manage public organisations. Its argument can be summarised fairly briefly, but needs a full book's length to explore in the depth needed. The book's argument is that thinking about or doing public management needs us to embrace a range of contradictions and tensions that are probably not resolvable. It suggests that the best we can do is to be aware of them and to understand the problems that are likely to occur from falling on one side of the argument rather than the other.

This is not the kind of upbeat, high-energy message that public managers might want to receive, as it suggests that they operate in complex environments where there may not necessarily be straightforward, right choices, but in their heart of hearts, they probably knew that already anyway. Public managers seeking simple answers should pick up the latest business bestseller from their local train station instead, but I am not sure such a simple approach can work. Those who want to try and deal with this complexity, and begin to try and get a handle on where public management came from, will probably get on far better with the book that follows.

The book's approach

The following chapters typically begin with a question. Each of these questions addresses a central problem in public management today, from whether public management is different to private management through to who should pay for public services, to how marketing can be used in public management. Each chapter then takes apart that question and works through what seems to be its relevant dimensions to come up with a range of tensions and difficulties that public managers must be aware of when they are working out their own position on it. This book does not give public managers a simple guide as to what the right answers are – in fact it would question whether there are any right answers. Instead it tries to make them aware of the problems that each of the various positions it explores has and to get managers and those researching public management to develop their own understandings. The book's conclusion then works through some of the more intractable contradictions in public management, derived from the chapters that proceed it, in the hope that by at least making the problems of the discipline explicit, public managers might be able to make more informed decisions about their practices in the future.

The book, chapter by chapter

Dealing with a complex and wide-ranging subject such as public management means that decisions need to be made about what to include and what to miss out. There is a logic in terms of the way this book is structured that will help the reader to work his or her way through, and so it is worth making this clear at the start.

The book begins by asking whether there is such a thing as public management in the first place, and suggests that this is, in itself, a difficult question to answer. It provides a range of different ways of thinking about what public management might mean, before concluding that, as long as the public find it useful to think about public management as being a subject in its own right, then we have a duty to work out what the implications of this are, and to do our best to explore what the dimensions of 'publicness' ought to be. The next three chapters of the book attempt to address this, exploring the stronger involvement of the state in public management; the history of public management as a subject that arose from ideas around public administration; and the way that public services are funded. These three chapters attempt to show that the nature of public management today has historical elements that need to be understood in order to understand what might be distinctive about public services, and to understand how they evolved to reach their present form today.

The next four chapters explore significant areas of reform in public services. They deal with the increased use of the market in public services; the use of the marketing approach in public services; the use of performance management in the public sector; and the question of the relationship between public professionals, public managers, and the public itself. These chapters deal with the way that reform programmes over the last 30 years have attempted to restructure public services, and presents new thinking and scholarship as to what the difficulties and limits of those reforms might be. They consider when these reforms might work, and when they might not, and the implications of this analysis for public managers.

Finally, the book's conclusion examines a range of tensions and contradictions suggested by the book's analysis, and works through them one by one to make clear the difficulties on both sides of each argument, inviting public managers to work out where they might stand in relation to them. Again, there are no easy answers here, but by at least making clear what the problems are, managers might be able to make better informed decisions that reflect the complex nature of contemporary public management.

Organising the book in this way means that a few topics, particularly public professionals and public finance, are discussed in more than one chapter. There is no easy way around this, as these topics are particularly pervasive in public management. In order to keep each chapter readable in itself, a little repetition therefore occurs, but the advantage of this is that it hopefully increases clarity for readers wanting to read the whole book.

On with the book

Before moving on with the book, a few more words about the way the material is organised. First, I have tried to keep academic references in the text to a minimum, but instead provided a section on further reading at the end of each chapter that attempts to give additional sources that those interested in the particular topic might like to consider to achieve greater depth on them. I hope this keeps the text relatively uncluttered and makes it more accessible, but at the same time makes it clear that the material in the text is based upon a decade of research, teaching and writing in the field.

Each chapter contains not only numerous examples in the text itself, but also an extended example that attempts to show greater depth in one aspect of the analysis of the chapter. These are presented at the end of the chapter to give the reader something tangible to hang the analysis and ideas presented in each topic area, but can be read alongside, after or even before the rest of the material in each chapter.

Having covered the book's intended contribution and the way the book is organised, it now moves on to what would seem a fairly fundamental question – is public management different from private management?

Part 1

The context of public management

2

Public and private management

Introduction

This chapter considers what seems a fundamental question for public management as both an activity and an academic discipline. It is also one that students might be asking who are enrolled on general management degrees of various kinds and are coming to public management for the first time. What exactly is public management, and is it any different from private sector management? Can public management be considered a subject in its own right, or is the job of public managers now pretty much the same as that of private managers? Is management pretty much the same thing whether conducted in the public or private sector (or in the 'third' sector, which involves charities and not-for-profit organisations)?

The chapter is structured as follows. First, it considers exactly what public management might mean, exploring particularly the role of public funding and public provision. It then goes on to explore arguments, particularly from economics, that there are such things as public goods and services that need to be treated differently from those on offer in private markets. Next it considers whether such a thing as a public service ethic can be used to justify the existence of the public sector, and so public management. After this, it moves on to examine what the now substantial research on public/private management differences has said about the differences between the two areas of management, a literature that largely suggests that there are relatively few differences of importance. This would seem to be something of a problem for the public management field (and for public management books!), but the book's response is that looking at organisations in terms of their mechanisms of production and reproduction allows us to draw up archetypes that allow us to measure varying degrees of 'publicness', whether the organisation under consideration is entirely publicly funded and provided, or perhaps located largely in the private sector. This takes the chapter to its conclusion, which suggests that public management is a category that continues to make a great deal of sense at a societal level, so is worth continuing with, but that it represents a particular mode of organising rather than an explicit link to funding or to ownership.

Funding and provision

At the risk of starting with a definition that is rather obvious in many respects, public management work is carried out by managers in public organisations. This begs the question of what a public organisation is. Public organisations are usually regarded as those where the state both pays for and provides services. Therefore, on the face of it, all we need to do to work out is distinctive about it, is to examine what the managers of public organisations do, compare it to the activities of other managers and see whether there is any difference. However, almost inevitably, things are a bit more complex than this.

One problem is that reforms in recent years have seen public services across the world change considerably (see the accounts in Osborne and McLaughlin, 2002, for example). Whereas in the past public organisations were relatively easy to identify, being both paid for by the government and provided by public employees, this may no longer be the case. Organisations paid for by the state may now be required to compete for both public and private contracts with private or not-for-profit organisations, blurring the previously clear distinction that public organisations were publicly funded. Equally, private organisations may find themselves delivering services in the areas that were formerly the province of public organisations, but with those services paid for from the public purse. Trying to identify whether an organisation or service is public or private has become considerably more difficult. Table 2.1 summarises the four types of organisation that are possible when considering their funding and provision.

In Table 2.1, cell (A) represents the classic type of public organisation – one that is funded and provided by the state. The extent to which this type of organisation exists in a particular country depends upon a variety of factors. Countries with strong labour interest groups tended to be more successful in moving the provision of key goods and services from the private to public sector (nationalisation), and countries with strong central governments, where well-organised political parties secured power, have often been able to significantly expand public provision in an economy. In the United Kingdom, with the labour movement growing in power in the early half of the twentieth century, and with an increasingly strong central state, the first majority Labour government elected in 1945 created through the nationalisation of public, private and not-for-profit hospitals, the National Health Service (NHS). The NHS was both publicly provided, in that the state was responsible for its running, and public employees staffed the service, and publicly

Table 2.1 Types of organisation according to funding and provision

	Public funded	Private funded
Public provided	(A) Entirely public	(B) Private funded/public provided
Private Provided	(C) Private provided, public funded	(D) Entirely private

funded, in that the state paid for nearly its entire cost (Powell, 1997). It is, in many respects, the archetypal public organisation.

Type (B) organisations, those that are privately funded but publicly provided, are less common, but the need for public organisations to attract private financing is becoming more and more important. The increased use of private financing can occur in a number of ways, but typically occurs where public organisations have a function that can also be marketed in the private marketplace, thereby putting them in competition with private organisations. Publicly run infrastructure services like road maintenance or property maintenance, which may have been brought into existence to support public services, may offer their services on the private market as well as continuing to be provided in public settings. In these circumstances, publicly provided organisations become privately as well as publicly funded, or even majority privately funded.

Type (C) organisations, those which are privately provided but publicly funded, occur where public funding mechanisms have been designed or reformed to create quasi-markets or 'mixed economies' where public and private organisations compete with one another for public contracts. In this environment, private providers of services with excess capacity, such as private hospitals or schools, may enter public markets to achieve greater utilisation or to attempt to expand. New private providers may also enter public markets, with infrastructure management firms (such as property management or engineering) reasoning that their skills are transferable, and so are movable between public or private sectors.

Finally, Type (D) organisations are those which are both privately financed and privately provided, and so apparently have little to do with public management. However, even these organisations may have elements of 'publicness' about them where the service was formerly a part of the public sector (where the service has been privatised), or where privatised firms sub-contract their services to public organisations. After utility firm privatisation (formerly nationalised firms running services such as electricity or gas), formerly public employees have sometimes found themselves re-employed as consultants by private organisations, performing much the same job as before but for a private rather than public organisation. Have they ceased to be public employees in this case? Is being a public employee or public manager therefore a label which is relatively easily cast-off as the result of a state decision to privatise a service, or is public management about something more than who owns and pays for a particular service?

Public organisations as those which provide public goods

An alternative way of thinking about public organisations is to say that they are those that provide public goods. Economists regard public goods or services as those that have specific characteristics. They claim that public goods exist where competition is not possible or where their provision is what they call 'non-excludable'. Each of these arguments will be dealt in turn.

Where the competitive market may not be best

It may not always be the case that the use of the competitive market is the most efficient way for goods or services to be delivered to the public. Transport by train is one example; there is likely to be only one train line between two points (or where there are many possible routes, one that is likely to be the shortest or most convenient), and, as most travellers are concerned first and foremost with the time of travel, it is hard to create a competitive environment easily (Greener, 2008). There may be a case, in the circumstance where competition does not appear particularly relevant to those who require the services, for public provision to occur; for the provision of train services to be granted a public monopoly.

Where competition is not practical, public provision might relieve concerns that exploitation might occur by allowing a private monopoly to occur or exist (Bozeman, 2002). Equally, where a particular good or service is regarded as being essential to the people or to the country, then competition may also not be the best way of proceeding. A government might decide that the provision of water, for example, is too important to leave to competitive forces, as it might risk members of the public potentially losing their supply where they are in uneconomic locations for private firms to supply them, and so the state becomes the monopoly provider to guarantee supply or minimum standards. The water supply also shares many of the characteristics of train lines in that none of us want several pipes coming in and out of our houses and to have to choose which supplier we want on any given day.

A particular government decides which industries are essential for their economy or public, however, will vary from place to place and are value-laden decisions. In many countries, industries including coal and steel have gone through the cycles of nationalisation and privatisation, depending upon which government has been in power, whereas in others the idea of nationalising industry would be unthinkable. Arguments about which industries should be within the public sector are not only a function of where you live, but also vary tremendously over time.

Non-excludable goods

Non-excludable goods are those that, because of their nature, cannot be charged to people individually. Street lighting is the classic example – if a person decides, in the absence of an alternative, to put a light outside of their house, then they cannot prevent others from sharing it. As such, despite not having paid for the lighting, others can receive its benefits. Areas such as street lighting create a problem in that some people might decide to try and rely upon others rather than spend any money themselves – they might try and 'free ride'.

Where goods are non-excludable, it makes sense to them to be publicly provided because in the absence of public provision they may be under-provided, or not provided at all. Again, street lighting is a good example – where it is not provided for the public sector there is a danger that it may not exist in some communities, and this, in turn, might lead to an increased incidence of social problems such as crime, as well as leading to more accidents.

Public managers with public goods

Public managers, according to the idea that some goods are intrinsically public in nature, are those that are in charge of goods or services that are either best organised out of a competitive environment or are non-excludable. This distinction is perhaps made most forcibly by the United States Economist J.K. Galbraith, who noted that, whereas the private sector has a tendency to produce goods of increasing triviality (electric toothbrushes being a favourite example), the public sector produces far more important services such as education (Galbraith, 1958). Galbraith was also extremely concerned that, because public goods tended to be under-provided in the United States, this would lead to 'private affluence and public squalor' with deleterious effects upon society such as increasing inequality between the rich and the poor. This is a particular problem where public schooling does not allow individuals to achieve, to a significant extent, equality of opportunity compared to those attending private schools.

Public goods in practice

The problem with defining public goods in strictly economic terms is the tendency of governments to make the decision of which services will be provided by the public sector on political grounds. It seems self-evident that achieving competition on train lines is a futile task, but that has not stopped governments from attempting it, creating elaborate structures of charging and counter-charging in the name of increasing efficiency, even though there is little logic in the argument of trying to create competition for competition's sake.

The non-excludability seems to work better as a barometer of which services are provided publicly and which not, but does tend to reduce the role of public services to fairly mundane (if essential) tasks. How else might we define what a public service is?

A public service ethic?

A less theoretical and more instinctive argument is often used in defence of public services, especially when they are under the threat of privatisation or from the increased use of markets. In these circumstances, public service advocates or professional groupings often argue that there is such a thing as a public service ethic, and it is this that makes public organisations distinctive from those in the private sector (Larson, 1997). Public service principles and public service ethics are given as reasons why public organisations are qualitatively different.

Principles such as fairness and integrity are used as reasons why public services should not be marketised or privatised for fear that such a change would compromise them (Lee Potter, 1998). Public service professionals often believe that they are motivated by higher goals than monetary gain, and that making them to participate in a marketplace vulgarises and compromises them. It also seems to be the case that many of those attracted to work in the public sector, including undergraduates on public sector management courses, have based their decision on a need to 'make a difference', and that they express this in contrast to those who may choose their jobs for more overt careerist reasons or for monetary gain (Boyne et al., 1999). This would suggest that public managers might claim to be different from their private counterparts in terms of the values they hold.

The argument that public managers have different values to their private counterparts is easily extended to claim that the ethics of public organisations are superior to those in the private sector. If public organisations pursue idealistic goals, then surely the way they operate and the values they hold are also more idealistic, and so worth preserving from the worst excesses of the marketplace that has led to corruption as was seen in the cases of Enron and Worldcom (McLean and Elkind, 2004)?

However, there is another school of thought that suggests that public organisations are far from the idealistic places described by their advocates. Instead of public management values being clear, Kernaghan (2000) suggests that there is a real need for a 'carefully crafted statement of values' (p. 102) upon which a 'comprehensive ethics regime can be built' (p. 102). If public values are different to those found in the private sector, there would seem to be a need for them to be more explicitly specified than has often been the case in the past.

Public organisations, rather than being principled and virtuous, can also be portrayed as inefficient and bureaucratic moribund organisations that serve not the public, but instead the people that work for them. The public choice view of organisation portrays public professionals not as altruists, selflessly acting to look after the interests of public, but instead as looking to maximise their own budgets and insulate their lives from the disciplines of market forces as much as possible (Jackson, 1990). According to this view, public professionals are not any more selfish than anyone else, they simply respond to the incentives available to them. Public organisations, often lacking competitive forces and giving considerable discretion to the professionals working within them, could be portrayed as providing little incentive to work hard and deliver a high-quality service. What is needed, according to this view, is for public managers to find incentives that reward good behaviour from public professionals and which penalises bad. As the incentives facing public managers and public professionals are what public choice theorists suggest to motivate people, they cannot be assumed to be working for the public's good (Le Grand, 2003, 2007), it depends on how public organisations motivate them.

As such, care needs to be taken in assessing claims that such a thing as a public service ethic exists, as this can be taken in two ways – one very positive, where public professionals are seen as selflessly working for the public good; and one very negative, that public organisations, because of their lack of market disciplines and lack of incentives to do good, are hotbeds of idleness and poor service. Given this lack of consensus as to whether public services and their values are distinctively good or bad, it makes sense to ask what current research has to say. Is there such a thing as a public service organisation, and how (if at all) do public organisations differ from their private counterparts?

The research on public and private management differences

There is a consensus in much of the research on public management that it has changed considerably in the developed world since the 1980s, moving from primarily an administrative function to one which looks far more to private management for its ideas and techniques (Dunleavy and Hood, 1994). As such, there should be something of a coming together of public and private management over time so that the two become more and more similar.

Research examining the differences between public and private management has attempted to investigate the notion of 'publicness' for 30 years, but has come up with surprisingly few clear answers. This might be because the research is predominantly based in the United States (Bozeman, 1988; Bozeman and Bretschneider, 1994; Rainey, 1989; Rainey and Bozeman, 2000; Rainey et al., 1976), where the public sector is smaller and perhaps less defined than in European or some Asian countries. This lack of answers may, however, also be because of a lack of systematic testing of ideas about 'publicness' that have tended to be rather taken-for-granted rather than being subjected to scrutiny.

Boyne (2002) presents a list of 13 hypotheses that have been advanced by researchers examining public and private management differences in factors such as their environment, their goals, their structures and their values, but finds convincing support for only three of them; that public organisations are more bureaucratic; that public managers are less materialistic and that organisational commitment is weaker in the public sector. He goes on to try and construct a causal argument for publicness in which the environment, goals and structures of public organisations combine to create a distinct set of values (p. 117). Boyne's 13 hypotheses are presented below in Exhibit 2.1.

Exhibit 2.1 Boyne's 13 hypotheses about the differences between public and private management

Environmental factors

Public managers work in a more complex environment (little evidence)

Public organisations are more open to environmental factors (little evidence)

The environment of public agencies is less stable (little evidence)

Public managers face less competitive pressures (little evidence)

However, there is a dearth of research in these areas (p. 103)

Goals

Distinctiveness of public management goals (little evidence)

Larger numbers of public management goals (little evidence)

Public management goals are more vague (evidence split)

Structures

Public management is more bureaucratic (strongest evidence of all in Boyne's paper (p. 116))

Public managers have to deal with more red tape (studies both for and against)

Public managers have lower managerial autonomy (studies both for and against)

Values

Public managers are more materialistic (some evidence)

Public managers have stronger public interest motives (some evidence)

Public managers have weaker organisational commitment (some evidence)

Boyne concludes that the 'available evidence does not provide clear support for the view that public and private management are fundamentally dissimilar in all important respects' (p. 118), suggesting that public management as an area of study or distinctive practice might be somewhat under threat. It would seem possible to challenge the notion that public and private management are different enough to justify being separate subjects. A qualifier to this argument might be that differences tend to be mostly in the areas of 'values', linking back to the discussion above on the public service ethic.

Besides most public/private difference research is being based on US studies, there are other problems as well. First, the data they utilise is now well over ten years old. If public management has changed dramatically in the last decade, and it is widely acknowledged it has (Pollitt, 2003), then this raises significant questions of the extent to which these studies accurately describe public management today. Has public management inexorably moved towards becoming more like private management, or have things changed?

In addition to this, further problems suggest themselves. As Boyne notes in relation to the absence of studies concerning the public management environment, researchers in the field tend to take for granted that the context in which public managers work is different from other sectors (Ross, 1988). They often assume that it is more complex, less stable and with weaker competition, but as there is little or no research demonstrating this to be the case, these hypotheses are categorised by Boyne as unproven, so they may or may not be true.

Equally, public management writers tend to suggest that the goals of the organisations they study are more complex and distinctive from those in private organisations, but again there is little research supporting these hypotheses. Boyne is making an important point – many of the differences public managers assume between public and private management are taken for granted and have not been assessed empirically. We should not assume that these differences are implicit to the nature of public management, and it is necessary to examine our assumptions and subject them to scrutiny. Equally, however, there are no grounds for automatically dismissing claims of difference between public and private management in the areas of context and goals if there are logical reasons for supposing that they might exist, but they do require further (or even some) research to make sure that these claims are valid.

If the evidence of whether there are differences between public and private management is inconclusive and very incomplete, an alternative is to try and suggest a model of what the key factors in public organisational life might be, and to suggest how they might play themselves out in different kinds of organisation. The next section attempts this, exploring a range of features characteristic of public-type organisations, and explaining how they might differ and vary according to the specific organisation being examined. For the moment, the terms 'public' and 'private' will be used, even though they are problematic, with the section after this attempting to shed light on what 'publicness' might mean.

Public management dynamics

Rather than saying that public and private management are intrinsically different (or the same), it makes sense to identify a series of tensions or dynamics that seem to particularly affect public management, and then to explore each in turn to see if it has explanatory power in considering the differences between public and private management. That way there is the potential to find that 'in some cases policy objectives are much better served by the market, in others we may find that core government agencies do a better job, and in others still that "crypto-quasi-pseudo" entities have the advantage' (Bozeman, 1988:673). This also fits with Boyne's suggestion that research in public management should examine 'mediated relationships' (Boyne, 2002:117) to explore not only whether public management is different or distinctive, but also why and how.

The next section works through a series of dynamics (shown in Table 2.2) that writing on public management has suggested are characteristic of the field, and in each

Table 2.2 Dynamics in public management

Dynamic	Description
Managers versus professionals	Should managers run public organisations or should professionals?
Accountability versus results	Should public services be concerned primarily with accountability or results?
Public values versus market values	Are public values more important than market values?
Efficiency versus customer service	Should public services strive for greater efficiency or better customer service?
Election versus selection	Should public managers be elected or selected?

case considers the relevance and importance of that dynamic for understanding public management, as well as how it might affect private organisations to which it might apply as well.

Managers versus professionals

One aspect of public organisations that is discussed in a great deal in more policy-oriented research (Haug and Sussman, 1969; Wilding, 1982), but which appears less frequently in public management discussions, is of the impact of professionalism on management (for an exception, see Exworthy and Halford, 1998). Public organisations often (but by no means always) have strong, established professionals working within them. The two archetypal professional groups are those of law and medicine, with both groups working for the public sector to varying extents depending upon the particular country in question. In the United States, public defendants and prosecutors often work for salaries far lower than those they could achieve working for the private sector, whereas in the United Kingdom the medical profession have had considerable autonomy in how they run health services for much of the NHS's history (Klein, 1990).

Professionals represent a significant problem for management in that the key characteristics of professionalism, autonomy, self-regulation and extended periods of training tend to lead to those in professional groups expecting to be able to manage themselves to a considerable extent. Management has been a recognised professional class in the United States since the early 20th century, whereas in the United Kingdom the founding of Business Schools came rather later, and managers still hold less prestige and status than their US colleagues (Wilson and Thompson, 2006). Public management has also developed within a particular context, where until recently, relatively poor rewards (compared to private management) were available in many countries. In France, however, prestigious schools of public administration have existed during the post-war period, and public management is therefore afforded a far greater cache than that in most other countries. In South Korea this is also the case, with public managers reporting that they have far higher job prestige and recognition from wider society than their private sector counterparts (Cho and Lee, 2001). In a situation where public managers are holding esteemed and respected positions, as in France and Korea, they should have a greater capacity to challenge to professional groups.

Regardless of context, however, professional groupings also tend to have specific, expert knowledge that makes it difficult for managers not trained in their specialist area to challenge and question them (Gillespie, 1997; Wilding, 1982) (see also Chapter 9). As such, professionals may believe that public managers simply do not understand what they do, and that they have no legitimacy in challenging or questioning their activities. In addition, those in professional groupings often come from elevated social background from families with professionals within them, and having attended the best universities to acquire their professional credentials. They may regard themselves as being a part of society's elite. Managers coming from less socially elite backgrounds may find themselves undermined not based on their management competence, but instead because they are regarded by professionals as being socially or intellectually inferior.

Professional power matters in all kinds of organisations, but many of the most established and important professional groupings work within public settings. The presence of strong professional groups means that managers have to negotiate their way through the barriers professionals will place in their way. Professionals will expect autonomy, the ability to self-manage and to be able to exercise expert knowledge that managers may not be able to challenge. Even if managers are able to demonstrate their expertise to professionals, they may find that they are snubbed or scorned on the grounds of professionals' social or educational status.

The extent to which managers experience these problems depends upon the status of management in the societal context being examined, as well as the status, educational attainment and prestige of the managers the professionals are facing. These factors are picked up again at length in Chapters 9 and 10.

Accountability versus results

A second organisational dynamic that particularly affects public services is the tension between the need for probity on the one hand and for dynamism and responsiveness on the other (Sukel, 1978). Public organisations tend to highlight these differences because public money must be accounted for not only in terms of its effect, but also in terms of normative expectations about conduct in public life. Again, these constraints are apparent in both public and private organisations, but the dynamic is especially apparent in public services. It is not enough just to be a successful public official; public managers must also show that they have high standards of public conduct. In the private sector the behaviour of President Bill Clinton in relation to his interns may have been regarded as unethical, but the prospect of impeachment would never have occurred – he would have been judged on his results rather than upon how they were reached. Equally, London Mayor Ken Livingstone was shown, in an edition of the TV journalism programme *Dispatches* in January

2008, drinking what seemed to be an alcoholic drink at an evening meeting with the public, and was held up to criticism as such. Livingstone was not being judged on the basis of his efficacy as Mayor (in that particularly example at least), his character was being questioned and his fitness to hold public office. It is far less likely that the Chief Executive of a private company would be held up to such scrutiny for drinking alcohol in an evening meeting with shareholders.

Although public managers are increasingly being held accountable for the results they achieve, there remain strong concerns about their conduct in achieving outcomes. Of course, private managers, especially since the founding of the corporate governance movement, have also found themselves having to account for their behaviour as well as their results. The difference is that public managers have moved from a focus and concern with the processes of their jobs, particularly in relation to their conduct and their ability to follow rules and normative standards of behaviour, towards one concerned with results, whereas private managers have moved from a focus upon results towards one increasingly concerned with conduct. There is movement towards a meeting in the middle, but from different directions.

Public values versus market values

A dynamic related to the one between accountability and results (see above) is the one between public values and market values. Market values are associated with those of the private sector, where the standard approach to management is often portrayed as one which combines having the best product or service with good marketing and good customer service (Christy and Brown, 1996). There is a strong sense of the market being the ultimate arbitrator of what constitutes a good product or service, of deciding in an objective way who has the best marketing, and of what good customer service comprises. Managers, in the end, are judged by the ability to meet the needs of the market.

Organisations which exist outside of the market environment, however, have to find alternative sources of legitimacy. Public services can be judged in terms of their output, but it is often difficult to measure the performance of a school or hospital, so measures of process, with a focus on elements such as accountability, are often used. Public organisations often argue that they offer higher standards of probity and accountability than market-based organisations, and that they should be measured against these factors rather than against output measures.

The tension between public values and market values also surfaces when considering the respective organisations who believe themselves to be serving. Market-based organisations have to meet the needs of many customers, but usually one at a time. Customer service is about dealing with the needs of the individual customer, whether or not that individual customer represents a business in itself, and so potentially multiple sales. In public organisations, even those that have to compete in markets, the collective public have to be served. This means that there is an immediate tension between serving the public as a whole and looking after the particular individual requiring service today (Quirk, 1997). Public services have to be carried out within a set budget over a set period, and public managers have to show that they are treating all their service users fairly. Public managers are required to serve the public not only as individuals, but also collectively, and in an environment of scarce resources they have to decide in what order the public are served, or even if they can receive service at all. Whereas market-based organisations tend to underplay (although not completely remove) the problem of who receives the goods or service – the one both willing and able to pay – this may be a central function of public managers, who must be able to show not only that they are balancing the needs of the public as a whole with the needs of the particular individual, but also that they are making the decision in a transparent and fair way.

The need for fairness in public organisations is likely to lead to the generation of rules and standard procedures which will be used to make decisions about who gets served and in what order – the creation of a bureaucracy. In today's world, 'bureaucracy' has become a term of abuse, taken to suggest a sclerotic, slow-moving organisation that is rule-bound and lacking in market or customer-focus. However, if bureaucracies lead to greater fairness, probity and accountability, then they may have much to commend them in non-market settings (or even in some market-based organisations where these values are important) (Du Gay, 2000). Indeed, Kirkpatrick and Ackroyd (2003) question whether new managerial archetypes, particularly those that are driven by market mechanisms, are any more effective than pre-existing forms of professional bureaucracies. Table 2.3 summarises the differences between market and public values.

Efficiency versus customer service

The tension between market and public values leads, in turn, to another related problem. Because public services often require significant professional involvement, and professionals are a scarce resource, public services have tended to be organised around the amount of professional time available than for the convenience of the individual service user (Tallis, 2005). This may seem intrinsically wrong – it seems an axiom of good customer service to place the needs of customers ahead of employees, and one of the claims of the 'new public management' is that it has helped move public services

Table 2.3 Market values versus public values

Market values	Public values
Individual customers	Individual requiring service
	Public as a whole
Customer focus	Fairness
Market success as criteria for success	Accountability, probity and fairness as criteria for success

towards customer-orientation rather than producer-orientation. But a little thought shows that organising public services around professionals may actually be more efficient than customer-orientation. Because professionals are the scarce resource in the production of many public services, their time is the limiting factor in the production of the good or delivery of the service. It makes sense to organise services to get as much from the limiting factor as possible – and this implies public service users are working around the professional rather than vice versa.

An example of a public service often organised in this way is that of the hospital medicine. Here patients will usually be required to wait to see a doctor, and although they may have an appointment time, if previous patients have overrun, or if emergencies have come in, the doctor may be running very late, leaving patients with substantial waits. Doctors are the scarce resource – it would make no sense for hospitals to employ too many doctors (even if they were available), only for them to have many days when they were not needed. It does make sense, therefore, for appointments to be made in an efficient way, and so be organised primarily in terms of doctors' time rather than patients'. However, too often in the past this has been used to allow excessively poor service where receptionists do not accurately report waiting times so that patients can at least see how long they are likely to have to wait, or where doctors routinely book patients in for the same appointment, or with ridiculous intervals between appointments, as this is likely to lead to patients having the longest possible wait. Organising appointments efficiently does not have to mean that no care has to be taken over service users.

Election versus selection

A distinction of importance in considering public/private splits is between appointment to management positions via the democratic process, via election, compared to appointment to post via a selection process. In some countries, significant use is made of the election process for public officials. The United States is a good example, where after political elections, a significant number of public official posts are appointed by those publicly elected (Ross, 1988). An example makes the point. In August 2005, New Orleans was tragically struck by Hurricane Katrina, which resulted in one of the most significant disasters in American history, with over 1500 people dying as a result. It seemed that after the events of 9/11, disaster management in the United States had undergone a refocusing under the Bush government in which the leaders of the Federal Emergency Management Agency (FEMA) suggested that it was an 'oversize entitlement programme' and that disaster victims should rely upon 'faith-based organizations' rather than the government for help (Schneider, 2005:516). The Federal Response to Katrina was initially led by Michael D. Brown, Head of FEMA, which was located in the Division of Homeland Security. Brown was heavily criticised for his lack of expertise in the area of flood defences (he had no experience of disaster management before his appointment to FEMA), with the suggestion that his appointment had been based on political rather than merit considerations.

In the United States, upon a change of Governor or President, a whole range of public appointments change because they are in the gift to those who have been democratically elected rather than being appointed through a selection process. This 'spoils' system also manifests itself in countries such as Italy, where political appointments, often based on familial affiliations, are still very common (Kickert, 2005; Putnam, 1993).

The alternative to being elected to public positions is for managers to be appointed through a selection process. Here, the availability of a job will usually be advertised, and so potentially available to everyone who wishes to apply for it, with the aim of the selection process to pick the right person on the grounds of their expertise, experience and ability to the job. Intuitively, this seems an appropriate way for public officials to be selected. However, there are also problems with it.

Where public officials have to work closely with politically elected figures, they do need to be able to get on, and if neither party is able to make the relationship work, then the delivery of public services is likely to be significantly affected. The appointment of the Chief Executive of what was eventually known as the NHS Management Executive in England is a good example of these problems. Victor Paige, the first holder of the role, resigned from his job in June 1986 frustrated by political interference and the lack of profile for management in the NHS (Edwards and Fall, 2005:43). This, in turn, led to disruption and the need for the Management Executive to have to search for a new manager at a time when it was only just becoming established. Had government ministers appointed some-one to the role, rather than it's going through a national selection process, the problem might have been avoided.

Appointment via selection addresses the potential problem of political appointments being unfair, but, if those elected to public positions are unable to get on with managers selected to run public organisations, a problem of a different kind can emerge. Where the civil service of a government holds full-time permanent jobs irrespective of who is elected to government, politicians may feel frustrated or patronised by public officials who regard them as transitory and uninformed, and may attempt to change the way government works by appointing their own advisors or consultants and attempting to circumvent civil service procedures. These tensions were very apparent in the United Kingdom in both Thatcher and Blair governments (Barber, 2007; Hyman, 2005; Jenkins, 2006).

Disentangling the tensions

Exploring the dynamics highlighted above allows both public and private managers to have a better means of assessing the differences both between and within their types of organisation. Table 2.4 summarises these differences.

Arranging the differences around the tensions explored below gives a list of characteristics for archetypal public and private organisations. These are best thought of as spectrums rather than binary opposites. As organisations become more manager-dominated, or where professional groups are weaker, we would expect managerial goals, language and

Table 2.4 Archetypal 'public' and 'private' organisations

Archetypal public organisation	Archetypal private organisation
Professional-dominated	Manager-dominated
Accountability-focused	Results-focused
Public values	Market values
Efficiency-focused	Customer-focused
Public goods	Private goods
Elected managers	Selected managers

targets to dominate. This means organisations become more archetypally private, even if they are publicly funded and provided. As such, instead of focusing on the rather muddy and confusing categories explored earlier in the chapter, this list gives a means of exploring the dynamics of organisational life. It surely makes a good deal more sense to examine the specific characteristics of organisations rather than attempting to say in general whether one is more public or private than another.

Conclusion – public management?

The debate around what constitutes public management seems to be divided into approaches that provide a justification for public service provision, and those that consider how public services should be provided. This not only comprises discussions of whether some goods or services are intrinsically 'public', whether the approach taken by public managers or professionals embraces a specific public ethic, and if it is better to appoint public officials rather than to depend upon elections or political patronage, but also embraces debates about whether public services should be insulated from market logics or not.

The existing researches on public/private management differences are interesting. In that, it seems to suggest that few such differences have so far been found, but also frustrating in that many of the taken-for-granted differences, based on the organisational environment and goals, remain largely uninvestigated.

Alternatively, examining a range of dynamics typically associated with public organisations allows us to consider a range of more interesting questions than attempting to assess the degree of publicness of a particular organisation or setting. If there is such a thing as public values, what does this mean in the way that public services are organised and delivered? Should efficiency be a more important criterion than customer service? Should fairness be more important than responsiveness to individual members of the public requiring the service?

Many of these questions will be addressed in subsequent chapters. For the moment, however, it seems fair to suggest that there is such a thing as a public service, even if it can be difficult to define exactly what it is in terms of its funding or provision. However, it seems more relevant and interesting to express publicness in terms of proximity to a range of factors that may also be found in the private sector. This suggests that there is considerable potential for many private managers to learn a great deal from discussion around public management, but equally that public managers could learn a great deal from some kinds of private organisations.

An awareness of the tensions of the kinds of problems that public organisations tend to experience allows managers to be aware of the challenges they are likely to experience. Exploring the mechanisms that underpin the differences between organisations more generally, even if they tend to be clustered in particular ways in public and private organisations predominantly, seems far more worthwhile.

The next chapter examines the role of the state in public management, exploring the assumption that one of the defining characteristics of public organisations is their link to the government of the day.

CASE STUDY

HRM in the public and private sectors

Boyne, Jenkins and Poole (1999) present a comparison of human resource management (HRM) in the public and private sectors that gives an account not only of how HRM has changed, but also of the differences in HR practice between the two sectors.

Their summary starts with an account of public sector HRM in the 1960s and 1970s presented by Farham and Horton (1996) that suggests it was dominated by a paternalistic style of management that purported to promote and protect the well-being of the workforce, particularly with regard to health, safety, and welfare. It was one with standardised employment practices that gave employees on the same grade the same pay and conditions, and which aspired to provide the same service regardless of the geographical location. It provided full-time employment, job security and life-long employment. White-collar staff had national pay structures and conditions of service, while manual workers had national grading systems and national job structures.

These practices occurred in an era of collectivised industrial relations with extensive scope for staff participation and consultation, and a strong role for Trades Unions in pay negotiation coming from higher levels of union density in public sector. The aspiration of HR professionals was to try and become a model employer, trying to set standards for private organisations to follow with regard to staff training and equality of opportunity. 'The softer norms and conventions of public management which differed from the more thrusting, market and sometimes anti-union values of the private sector' (Farnham and Horton, 1996:83).

Public sector HR traditions weakened since 1979 because of increased concern with economic constrains and the need to make public sector more 'business-like'.

Oswick and Grant suggest that they 'unconsciously mimicked aspects of behaviour exhibited by private sector counterparts ... adopted as a "knee-jerk" response to financial constraints experienced by the public sector which are due to the political and economic climate' (Oswick and Grant, 1996:15).

Four particular changes are suggested as having occurred since the 1980s:

1. Paternal management gave way to 'rational management' driven by demands for those leading public organisations to achieve effective job performance, high quality of output, customer service and value for money' rather than prioritising fairness, the welfare needs of employees and good relations with unions (Farnham and Horton, 1996:331). Power has devolved to line managers as a result rather than personnel specialists, reducing further the priority for equal opportunities and staff training.

2. Uniform and standardised employment practices were replaced by flexibility and differentiation. No jobs were to be guaranteed for life any more, with pay no longer determined by grade or the position in a managerial hierarchy, and promotion no longer based on seniority. Part-time and temporary jobs were offered, with salaries linked to perceptions of performance. The need for flexibility was illustrated by NHS organisations becoming responsible for pay and conditions of their own staff, and local councils opting out of national pay bargaining. Competitive tendering for ancillary and non-essential contracts led to the increased use of short-term employment contracts and an unwillingness to invest in staff training.

3. There has been a move from collectivism to individualism in industrial relations, particularly for managerial staff. Along with this, there has been a change from a concept of equity from pay at the 'going rate' or 'rate for the job' to being based on labour market and performance criteria. There were reduced roles for trade unions, and the introduction of Performance-Related Pay.

4. The public sector was no longer seen as a model employer, and was redefined as a laggard in its approach to HRM from the Thatcher and Reagan governments onwards. Traditional HRM was seen as a barrier to better organisational performance, and no longer a model for private sector to follow.

In sum 'public managers have been encouraged, exhorted, and in the last resort, forced to adopt a style of HRM which reflects private sector practices' (Boyne *et al.*, 1999:411). The rest of Boyne *et al.*'s paper assesses evidence for these changes, and suggests that practices in public and private remain different in many important respects:

i. Traditional paternal, standardised and collectivised HRM is more prevalent in public rather than in private organisations. Model employer practices (equal opportunities, staff training) are still more likely to be found in the public sector, despite claims that HR practices there are laggardly.

ii. It is possible that distinctions between public and private HR practice are becoming less pronounced over time – there may be convergence, or there could be a lag in adopting in which public and private management may remain different, even if both are moving in the same direction.

iii. The extent of convergence between public and private HR varies across agencies – commercialised agencies may be driven to emulate their private competitors (Poole *et al.*, 2006). Large public organisations may emulate private practices more closely especially if they have recruited staff from the private sector. Left of political centre councils may be more traditional in approach to HRM.

iv. Results may be consistent with persistence of public service ethos among public employees. Kessler and Purcell (1996:217) argue that 'the presence of professional groups, reinforced institutionally through their associations has not only affected the determination of terms and conditions but equally significantly helped preserve a set of values and principles potentially in tension with the newer management practices'.

Further reading

The most recent comprehensive review of public and private management differences appearing in an academic journal remains George Boyne's (2002), who has also examined the differences between HR practice between the two sectors (Boyne *et al.*, 1999). Boyne's work is heavily based on US studies carried out by, among others, Barry Bozeman (Bozeman, 1988; Bozeman and Bretschneider, 1994; Bozeman and Kingsley, 1998) and Hal Rainey (Rainey, 1989; Rainey and Bozeman, 2000; Rainey *et al.*, 1976, 1995). The first chapter in Christopher Pollitt's *Essential Public Manager* is also a very good summary of the discussion around differences between public and private management and whether they matter (Pollitt, 2003), and a personal favourite study was published in the prestigious Academy of Management Review in 1985, so is a bit dated, but well worth a look (Smith Ring and Perry, 1985).

The changing role of the state

Introduction

In the last chapter, it became clear that one of the assumptions made in a great deal of public management research, even though it is not often empirically verified, is that the external environment of public management is different from that found in the private sector (Sukel, 1978). One of the main reasons for this is the role played by the state in creating the rules and policies which public organisations are required to follow, and which public managers are responsible for implementing (Hood, 1998). Managers in both the public and the private sectors are clearly influenced by the activities of the state – it makes laws that apply equally to both pubic and private sectors. The difference, however, is that public managers are responsible not only for following the law, but will also find the state involved, to varying extents depending upon the particular public service and country being studied, much more directly in their organisations. If managers are working for organisations which are publicly funded, then the state will require them to be accountable for that expenditure. If managers are working for publicly provided organisations, they will find the state-setting policies and organisational forms that they must comply with. Even private organisations that work for the state will find that they are required to follow a range of additional rules in order to keep their state-funded contracts. In short, the more managers are engaged in activities that involve interaction with the state, the more they are likely to be held to greater account and have to follow state-set rules, policies and organisational structures that solely private organisations will not have to comply with.

The need for public managers to interact with the state means that public management is a complex area of academic study lying between the boundaries of several disciplines. On the one hand, it is clearly a branch of management theory, and so needs to be considered in terms of its relationship to private management, as the last chapter should have made clear. On the other, however, the greater role for the state in public management means it is directly able to influence the goals of their organisations through changing funding amounts or mechanisms or through reforms that might make public organisations more or less market-oriented, for example. Given this, this chapter asks the question

Table 3.1 Three types of state

Minimum liberal state	One-nation liberal state	Democratic socialist state
Smallest possible state	Small to medium state	Medium to large state
Belief in markets as preferred mode of governance	Belief in markets, but accepting the possibility that they might produce unfair results	Markets are tools, and can be used to increase fairness or drive up public service responsiveness
State seen as interference to functioning of markets	State seen as correcting market failure	State seen as responsible for producing better society
Public services best provided by the market	Public services provided by mixed economy of provision	Public services often publicly owned, supplemented by other provision where it increases fairness or responsiveness

how does the state work, and how changing ideas about the role of the state affect public management?

The role of the state is a very large topic in its own right (Jessop, 1990), and has vexed the minds of political scientists since the beginning of the subject. However, with the aid of modern scholarship it is possible to discern some long-term trends in state activity, and so gain a means of understanding how changes in the role of the state affect the view of what is required of public organisations and public management. A good way into this is to consider the types of state which seem to exist, and the implications of their forms for public organisation. Three types of state are summarised in Table 3.1, and described in greater depth below.

Types of state

The minimal liberal state

A good starting position perhaps is to try to imagine what the smallest possible state might look like. Advocates of minimal government such as two of the twentieth century's most famous economists, Milton Friedman and Friedrich von Hayek, tend toward the view that it is the state's responsibility not to be involved in the personal life of its citizens, and that individuals know far better than the government how best to spend their money (Friedman and Friedman, 1990; Hayek, 1944). The role of the state, in this view, is to secure the property rights of its citizens and to create a legal environment where free and fair exchange is facilitated by having, for example, a fair judiciary process and perhaps an independent police force. Advocates of the minimal state would argue that the vast majority of activities within an economy should be run by private rather than public organisations as the profit motive will drive those organisations to offer the best quality and most efficient service.

By having a minimal state, citizens within it will have to pay relatively little tax, and so it has an immediate popular appeal. But it also means that individuals will have to take responsibility for making sure that they have adequate insurance to cover them for periods of unemployment (as the state might pay only minimal social benefits, or perhaps not even pay benefits at all), as well as paying for private health insurance and access to good schools for their children. In return for paying very little tax, individuals have to take far greater responsibility for their lives, and the state intervenes only where market exchanges are shown to be unfair, or where private firms become so powerful that they achieve a monopoly, and so competitive forces can no longer assure that their services are both high quality and efficient.

This form of the state can be called the *minimal liberal state*, although the name given to it will depend upon the tradition of the particular political scientist advocating it. It is minimal in that it assumes that individuals will take the maximum amount of responsibility for their own welfare, and it is liberal (in the European rather than American sense) in that the allocation of goods in the economy is determined mostly by the market. In this form of state, there is not much in the way of public management. The state's responsibility is about overseeing a legal framework for the exchange of goods and to enforce property rights, requiring an independent judiciary and police force (although these may still be run by private organisations if they can be adequately incentivised) and so public management is about the administration of the legal system rather than the running of hospitals or schools. Any further involvement from the state is seen as interfering in people's lives, supported by a popular discourse of freedom from the government and complaints from vested interest groups where the government attempts to become involved in new areas.

The one-nation liberal approach

Where the state recognises that market solutions may not always work out best for those within the country, a *one-nation liberal* approach may appear. In this approach to the role of the state, the market is not seen as providing a solution in every area of economic and social life, as there is a recognition that in some instances it may underprovide particular services, or provide them on an unequal basis (Esping-Anderson, 1990). This leads to an acceptance of the 'public goods' argument in Chapter 2. Good or services such as street lighting, which may be under-supplied by competitive markets, or which may be non-excludable, present an argument which governments which favour social cohesion might regard as providing a compelling reason to extend their role to include these areas. Equally, in some areas of healthcare, such as vaccination programmes, another argument may surface. Where vaccination is provided on a market basis, individuals may opt out of paying and participating themselves in the belief that if everyone else vaccinates, then there is no need for them to. However, if vaccination levels fall below a certain level, then there is a danger of the outbreak of the particular disease, and so there may be a mis-alignment between individual and collective outcomes. On public health grounds (as well as national efficiency grounds), this creates space for an argument that the state should fund vaccination programmes through taxation to achieve the widest possible coverage, so that individuals are not deterred from being vaccinated because of having to pay the fee involved.

In the one-nation liberal view, that state still accepts the primacy of markets, but acknowledges that, in certain circumstances, such as those outlined above, they may under-provide a particular service, or not provide it at all, giving an argument for the state to get involved. Equally, there may be areas of provision where it might be more effi-cient for 'natural' monopoly to be granted. The example given in Chapter 2 of train travel makes sense in these terms as it would seem to make little sense to have several sets of railway lines going on the same journeys to allow competition to take place.

A one-nation liberal view is a pragmatic one, considering that in some circumstances government involvement is necessary to correct under-provision, and in others it is nec-essary because it might be more efficient (where competition might result in a perverse outcome). In addition to these, a third circumstance exists where one-nation liberals would advocate increased use of public provision – on the grounds of fairness. This is the 'one nation' part of the title. Advocates of one-nation liberalism are particularly concerned with education provision.

The way that children are educated has a strong impact upon their life chances, but children from richer parents might have an advantage in being able to send their children to schools with better educational records. This might be because of a peer effect, where high-performing children create expectations for other children to work hard, or it might be more class-based, where high-performing schools in expensive areas attract children from families who have more money and resources, or it may be down to the explanation that only the richest parents can afford to send their children to the best private schools. In any case, there is a danger of creating a situation where only children from families with high incomes can attend particular schools because they are the only ones that can afford their fees (in the case of private schools) or because they are the only ones within the areas from which the schools accept applications (for public schools). There is therefore a case for saying that good quality education should not be based on the ability of parents to pay fees, or to be able to afford a house in a particular area. If this argument is accepted, then there is a case for the state to be involved in schooling and for it to attempt to make sure that access to good quality public schools is achieved on as a fair basis as possible.

Achieving fair access to good public schools is an extremely difficult task – just because schools are owned by the state (or the private sector), it does not necessarily mean they achieve high standards of education, educating children well or offering fairer access. There is, however, an argument for offering children equal access to a good education which does not depend on the ability of their parents to pay for it on the grounds of fairness, and that excluding children from low-income families from achieving their full educational potential goes against the best interests of the economy as well, an argument based on efficiency.

The role of public management in a one-nation liberal approach is far more extensive than under a liberal minimal state. Public managers will have a wider scope of services to work in, with provision and education and healthcare (on the grounds of both fairness and efficiency) likely to appear in addition to the areas accepted as legitimate for state activity under the minimal liberal view of the state. Public managers will be involved strategically in overseeing the development of local areas to allow fair access to services such as education, becoming involved where it seems that richer parents are able to achieve an advantage for their children, perhaps through creating public schools to try and plug gaps in provision. Equally, they will have a significant role in running public services to make sure that they are of high standard and they meet the objectives set by the state. However, public provision and public management tend not be seen as automatic goods in themselves in this view. Rather they are a necessary evil to fill gaps where the private market is unable to meet the needs of the population as a whole.

The democratic socialist view

A further extension of the role of state comes in what might be termed the *democratic socialist* view of the state (Clarke *et al.*, 1992). Here the use of markets is not assumed to be automatically beneficial; instead they are a tool for organisation like any other. As such, the favouring of markets by both minimal liberal writers and one-nation liberal writers is not automatically shared by advocates of this view. The key goal of state activity for democratic socialists is a fairer, more equal society. Historically, the means of achieving this goal have been for the state to take over ownership of key services such as health and education, both providing and paying for them. In addition, democratic socialist governments have also gone further to extend the nationalisation (the taking of private and charitable organisations into public ownership) of industries that are regarded as being key to the economy.

This means that public ownership in a democratic socialist state tends to be more extensive than under the liberal one-nation view. Some democratic socialists have explicitly said that their aim is, through a gradual process of increasing fairness in the economy, to eventually try and achieve a socialist state, one in which the individualism of capitalism and the exploitation of the poor in marketplaces is forever done away with. However, this Fabian view of the state has become less popular in more recent years, with democratic socialism becoming associated with the view of those expounding 'progressive governance' (Giddens, 2003) or 'third way' (Birnbaum, 1999; Giddens, 1998; Westergaard, 1999) thinking. These versions of democratic socialism have increasingly looked to markets as an additional tool available to them, attempting to achieve fairness through citizens accessing public services through a marketplace of providers (Forbes, 1986). In education and healthcare, this has led to public providers in those areas (schools, hospitals, etc.) competing with one another for students and patients on the grounds that this might be the best way of achieving a fair result for everyone. A 'managed market' is put in place by democratic socialists to attempt to give all citizens an equal right of access, or at least a right of access based on meritocratic grounds such as educational qualifications. This is done in the name of attempting to achieve the dynamism of the market economy (as in liberal views of the state) combined with the fairness that can be achieved through public ownership.

Under democratic socialism, the role of public management is more extensive again than under liberal one-nationism. Public management is a means of levelling the playing field for all citizens to participate equally and fairly, as managers are likely to have to compete for public contracts, and so be responsive to user need, as well as often meeting centrally imposed targets for standards of service provision.

There are many other ways than these three archetypes of analysing the role of the state and its relationship with public management (see, e.g., George and Wilding, 1994), but these generic views can provide the basis for thinking about how the role of state has changed. To achieve this, examining key aspects of the state and how they have related to one another over the least century can be a considerable help.

The post-war economic settlement

In the period after the end of the Second World War, an extension of the role of government was apparent in most industrial nations. There are several drivers of this change, but two of the most important were based on the experience of the industrial economies pre-Second World War, and the implications of the war itself.

During the 1930s, the world went through a significant recession (Aldcroft, 2001). Stock market crashes in the United States led to big rises in unemployment across the world. At this time, most states offered only minimal unemployment insurance, and so where people lost their jobs on a large scale, it was largely up to them to find a way of coping. Governments, driven by a philosophy that was a mix of the minimal liberal state (in that they favoured markets and offered little welfare support) and one-nation liberalism (in that limited healthcare and some social benefits were sometimes offered), faced protests from their citizens demanding help and support in a time of financial hardship and deprivation. Governments, locked in a way of understanding the world that was based on balancing taxation receipts and government expenditure in any given year ('sound finance'), found themselves reducing their expenditures in recessions because of the smaller taxation takes from incomes and profits.

Governments expected, based on the tenets of classical economics, prices to fall to compensate for the lack of demand present in their economies, and eventually for markets to correct themselves as labour and other factors of production become 'cheap' (Blaug, 1997). Once this had happened, prices would fall to an extent that goods and services became affordable again. This is how the self-equilibriating economy is meant to work – that, given enough time, a fall in demand (a recession) will lead to a fall in prices, and the economy will automatically pick up again. This view of the world, advocated by those that believe free markets can resolve welfare as well as economic problems, led to a belief that government should be involved in the economy as little as possible to avoid distorting market signals and interfering with the free movement of demand and supply (Friedman and Friedman, 1990).

Keynes

The problem with the self-equilibriating economy was the time it took for price to fall, and the pain and hardship experienced by those out of work in that time. The great insight of the economist John Maynard Keynes was that prices might be 'sticky' (Keynes, 1997) – they might fall far more slowly than they rise. This is a huge problem for a free-market view of the world, as, if prices do not fall quickly, it may take a substantial period of time for the market to reach an equilibrium point of full employment. Instead of simply waiting for prices to fall, Keynes suggested that unemployment and falling output might require the government to intervene and 'pump-prime' demand by increasing its expenditures. This ran directly counter to the free-market-driven view of the economy; in a period of recession, tax receipts fall as there are less profits, and so the government, according to that view, should reduce its expenditures in order to balance its overall budget. Keynes suggested the opposite; that government should deliberately generate deficits in order to boost the economy as a whole and remove the deficiencies in demand. This was revolutionary stuff (Aitkenson and Olseon Jr, 1998).

The implications of Keynes' ideas were profound. He was suggesting that the government should increase its involvement in the economy on almost moral grounds; that sticky prices would mean that the population suffered the waste and indignity of unemployment when it was not necessary, and could be avoided. Keynes suggested that 'public works' programmes be instigated in periods of economic recession where the state invested in the country's infrastructure. Where the state could not find any worthwhile projects to invest in, he even went as far as saying that the unemployed should be employed to dig up disused mine shafts – anything that would give people a job, and which would in turn lead them to spend money that could be used to push the economy out of recession.

The flipside of this logic was that, when the economy was expanding, the government should reduce its role again, winding down public works programmes, as the lack of demand in the economy had been remedied and government intervention was no longer needed. Public expenditure was therefore viewed as a kind of automatic economic stabiliser, to be increased in periods of recession and decreased in periods of economic growth. The government had a legitimate reason to get involved in the running of the economy where there were economic problems (as there were in the 1930s, when Keynes' book was being written), but should withdraw again in better economic times. In practice, the former was relatively straightforward to achieve, but the latter rather more difficult, as the account below will make clear. However, the importance of Keynes' ideas in the extension of the role of the state in the post-war period cannot be understated.

The experience of war

The second factor affecting the role of the state in the economy was the experience of war itself. During the wartime, economic production is transformed from having large numbers of private enterprises organised around trade to being concentrated into government-funded or government-provided industries designed to wage war. This had profound implications for the role of the state, which extended its role dramatically into every area of life. States set rations on what food could be eaten, production schedules on what needed to be made, and organised the workforce to try and make sure that essential tasks were carried out from fighting to factor production through to scientific research. The state became involved in every aspect of the economy. Countries in Europe were especially affected by this phenomenon, developing wartime economies that were dramatically different from those they had in peace time. Countries where battles raged often had their private productive capacity effectively destroyed, and even in the United States the economy was substantially reoriented in order to meet the huge commitment of participating in the biggest war the world had ever seen (Aldcroft, 2001).

This huge expansion in the state's involvement into every aspect of their country's governance meant that there were a cohort of people in government who believed passionately that this role could be carried forward into peacetime. In countries where production had been substantially destroyed by the war, particularly Germany, it was a matter of life and death that governments intervened to rebuild infrastructure and production capacity. In the victorious nations, particularly the United Kingdom, huge debts incurred during wartime held the capacity to bankrupt the economy, and government-level action was perceived as being necessary to remedy the action rather than relying upon the private sector economy to solve the economic difficulties the country faced (Hennessy, 1994). Fuelled by the experience of 'total war' and the huge increase in government involvement this had led to, governments across the world increased the scope of their activities at its end. Politicians believed that wartime had not only shown how it was possible for the state to run the economy, but also that Keynesian economics suggested that the state had an ethical need and a strong legitimacy to be involved in the economy – the alternative was to rely upon market forces, and that had led to the recent memory of the Great Depression.

The post-war public settlement was therefore based on the experience of greater state involvement in wartime, and garnered legitimacy from Keynesian economic thought. Depending on how you view subsequent events, the greater international co-operation in trade coming from the post-war international economic settlement, combined with Keynesian economic planning and greater government involvement, led to either a sustained period of economic growth until the mid-to-late 1960s, or a period of lost opportunity where government over-expanded but was fortunate not to ruin the world economy because of the relatively calm economic waters of that time. What is apparent is that 20 years after the Second World War was a time of growing prosperity and year-on-year economic growth of a kind that has been seldom seen before or since.

The crisis of Keynesianism – fiscal crisis, crowding out and other crises

A number of problems served to undermine the post-war formation of the state.

Fiscal crisis

The first was the idea of the state undergoing a crisis of some kind. The fiscal crisis argument, originally based in the Marxist literature (O'Connor, 1973), suggested that state expenditure was dividable into two categories; social capital and social expenses. Social capital was state investment in the productive economy, raising levels of education, for example, to make the workforce more productive, or improving infrastructure so that trade could better flourish. Social expenses, however, were provided by the state to prevent the workforce from becoming so disaffected by capitalism that protest and rebellion undermined it. Healthcare expenditure on non-urgent or non-life-threatening conditions might be an example, unemployment insurance or benefit for non-productive workers might be another. Social expenses were often provided after a great national sacrifice, such as that of war, in order to make politicians appear as if they are looking after their country.

O'Connor's analysis has several elements in common with Keynesian economic planning, with the state investing in public works to make the economy more productive, and paying benefits to the unemployed not only prevent social crisis, but also on the grounds that it boosted demand in the economy in periods of recession. The problem, however, is that social expenses particularly have what is called a 'ratchet' effect – once they have been introduced it is very difficult politically to subsequently withdraw them. This is one of the problems of Keynesian thinking – in periods of economic prosperity, the government should be reducing its expenditures to help stabilise the economy, but withdrawing social expenses is difficult because the public are likely to experience it as a reduction in their rights, and it is a brave government that antagonises its electorate. The term 'ratchet effect' therefore refers to the problem that once a social benefit has been introduced, it is difficult for a government to subsequently withdraw. Social expenses therefore have a tendency to rise and rise.

O'Connor suggested that the tendency of social expenses to rise and rise creates a dynamic where the state is required to pay for a wider and wider range of public services until a point where 'fiscal crisis' is reached – where the government is unable to afford its planned expenditure, and is unwilling or unable to raise taxes any further to pay for them. The result is fiscal crisis – the government simply cannot afford to meet its commitments. O'Connor hoped fiscal crisis would eventually lead to the overthrow of capitalism, but the expenditure problems of governments, fuelled by rising oil prices in the 1970s, instead led to dramatic cut-backs in welfare expenditures in many developed nations. This created the space for alternative ideas about how the state might function to gain currency.

Crowding out

A related idea to that of fiscal crisis is that, if the public sector gets too big, it will result in investment expenditure in an economy going to fund public debt rather than being invested in private organisations. Private investment, it can be argued, will be 'crowded out' (Bacon and Eltis, 1978), and the productive, wealth-generating part of the economy allowed to stagnate as the state grows instead. This results in a different form of crisis to O'Connor's, in which the private economy is unable to support the large public sector as its taxation demands have grown too great, and the private economy stagnates because it is unable to generate sufficient investment to renew itself. The result is economic stagnation, with private firms, even if they have excellent ideas for new products or services, unable to attract the investment they need.

Other types of crisis

Along with fiscal crisis and 'crowding out', there was an associated form of crisis coming from the state losing faith in its ability to deal with the full range of problems for which it has taken responsibility (Pierson, 2006). One variation on this is the theory of government 'overload', where the government reaches a size where it can simply no longer discharge its responsibilities. This might be due to what economists call diseconomies of scale, where the size of an institution becomes so large that it is unable to co-ordinate its activities or control what it does, or it might be due to the state entering areas of activity it has no expertise to be able to manage.

Then there is what might be called 'ideational crisis', and which occurs where the policies the government has utilised in the past seem no longer to work. In the 1970s major industrial economies suffered from simultaneous rising unemployment and inflation (or 'stagflation'), which was not meant to happen according to Keynesian economic frameworks (Greener, 2001). As such, governments found themselves effectively caught in a situation where its espoused policies appeared to be failing, and an alternative source of economic ideas needed to be found (Hall, 1993; Oliver, 1997). There was a crisis of ideas, coming to a head in the 1970s when the international financial arrangements created after the Second World War (named after the place where they were decided, Bretton Woods) disintegrated and the world economy experienced inflation as a result of dramatic oil price rises. These factors caused a world-wide recession, the undermining of Keynesian economic thought, and the opportunity for advocates of different views of the state to gain a hearing from the governments of the world.

The state response to the crisis of Keynesianism

In response to the crises of the 1970s, the state has increasingly cast itself not as a paternalistic planner of the economy, as it became under Keynesianism (Pemberton, 2000), but instead occupying itself more of a managerial function (Clarke and Newman, 1997) in which it favours an entrepreneurial role instead of an interventionist one. In this view, the state attempts to intervene not in the demand-side of the economy, but instead in the supply-side to try and make its industries, both private and public, more competitive and productive.

The most recent manifestation of this idea is the 'social investment state' associated with Third Way thought (Giddens, 1998), where the state becomes a kind of super loss-adjustor on behalf of its citizens. In these circumstances, money is not described as being 'spent' by the state, it is instead 'invested'. The difference between the two is that, as well as the state granting welfare rights to the public, the public's responsibilities are also made clear – they no longer receive state benefits unconditionally, as something is expected in return. Social security benefits, for example, are paid on the grounds that individuals are actively trying to remove themselves from being dependent upon the state (public dependence on the state, in many respects, is the anathema to the Third Way project (Hoggett, 2000)), and unemployment benefit is paid only on condition that either work is being actively sought or that training is being actively undertaken. There is a move from a paternalistic, 'nanny state' to one where independence and autonomy are fostered. The state, in this view, should also be more selective about where it invests, being required to make a judgement about where the use of scarce resources should best be placed. It should spend money where the best returns for the economy as a whole can be generated, with none of the sentimentality of the past where failing industries were supported on the grounds of social cohesion.

Explaining changes in the state – the work of Bob Jessop

The work of Bob Jessop (Jessop, 1993, 1994, 1999, 2002) is of considerable help in explaining how and why the state has changed over the last 50 years or so and of reconsidering the role of public management within it. Jessop utilises four analytical spectrums through

Table 3.2 The changing formation in the state

Change in welfare state	Description
Keynesianism to Schumpeterianism	Move from paternalistic planning and focus on demand-side of economy to enterprising, entrepreneurial supply-side focus
Welfare to workfare	Move from social benefits being a right to having duties associated with them – the duty to earn benefits, for example
National to postnational	Move from national basis of economy and policy to use of both international and local bodies
State to regime	Move from centralised state provision to a plurality of providers often organised in a network form

which it is possible to explain and explore change. These analytical spectrums combine around certain points to form two 'ideal types', or forms of the state that attempt to capture the directions of state changes. They are meant to hold explanatory potential rather than provide a detailed empirical study of any particular case. They are summarised in Table 3.2 and described in greater depth below.

From Keynesianism to Schumpeterianism

First, Jessop suggests that the role of the state has moved from one predominantly concerned with Keynesianism to one oriented around Schumpeterianism. Keynes' work has been covered above, and was important for his view that economies, left to their own devices, may not always come into balance (equilibrium) at a point of full employment. Keynesianism (the approach of economists building on the work of Keynes, but not necessarily entirely representative of it) advocated greater state investment in public services in times when the economy may be below full employment, but can also be read as a means of attempting to stabilise economic cycles (periods of growth and recession) by increasing social benefits. Keynesianism advocated government intervention to stabilise the economy, with expert economists deciding how much the state should invest to keep the economy at the optimal level. It is therefore a paternalistic approach to running the economy, based on expert advice and opinion.

Schumpeterianism is closer to the liberal, minimal state view than Keynesianism. Schumpeterianism emphasises competition and enterprise in an economy, suggesting, in line with the changes discussed in the previous section, that the state should be concerned not with the demand-side of the economy (expenditure), but instead the supply-side (product and service provision). Schumpeterianism aims to create a more competitive economy through the reduction of state control and deregulation, the simplification or outright removal of rules felt to be hindering business.

The Schumpeterian view of the state is seen by its advocates as dealing with many of the problems that states attempting to pursue Keynesian approaches experienced. It attempts to address the increased growth in the public sector by suggesting government withdrawal from many areas on the grounds that citizens have become too dependent upon it rather than taking responsibility for themselves. This view of the state, as interfering too much in people's lives, tended to be associated with the political right (Murray, 1984), but has more recently been acknowledged by centre-left writers who are concerned about the dis-empowering effects on individuals of them becoming entirely reliant upon the state for their income, and the lack of life chances this might generate as a result (Le Grand, 2007).

Jessop suggests that states have tended to move from Keynesian approaches, which were more predominant in the immediate post-war period, to Schumpeterian approaches, which have become more predominant since the 1970s particularly, not least because of the economic difficulties many economies had in that decade and the reassessment of economic priorities this generated.

Under Keynesian thought public management is an expert-led, paternalistic affair, dominated by highly educated technocrats who are relied upon to demonstrate fairness through the creation of public systems for administering budgets and services for the benefit of the people. Services tend to be professional-dominated and supply-centred rather than being focused particularly on the needs of the individual receiving them (Stewart and Walsh, 1992). Schumpeterian public management, however, is more business-focussed, dominated by professional managers aiming for innovation and enterprise to deal with more competitive environments. It aims to create lean systems of control for the delivery of user-responsive services and tends to be suspicious of strong professional groups that may not be perceived to be acting in the interests of public service recipients.

From welfare state to workfare state

Jessop's second analytical spectrum runs from the idea of a welfare state to that of a work-fare state. Welfarism is associated with the view that services should be universal and given as a right to their recipients. This means that the state effectively guarantees the provision of a range of public services, which are granted not on the ability to pay, but instead on the basis of need. This clearly has strong overtones of attempting to achieve fairness, and so accords with both the liberal one-nation and the democratic socialist view. Workfarism, on the hand, emphasises both rights and duties. In return for receiving state benefits, certain behaviours are demanded in return. An example might help illustrate this. Under wel-farism, unemployment benefit might be given as a right to those out of work not only in the name of fairness, but also on efficiency grounds (see Keynesianism above). A workfare approach would be to grant unemployment benefit provided individuals could show they were actively seeking work, but require that those receiving the benefit work in the com-munity in return for the benefit, perhaps cleaning up graffiti or mending public facilities. As well as the right to receive benefit, there is a duty to earn it.

Jessop suggests that there has been a move from welfarism to workfarism as the twentieth century moved on, as the state becomes more aware of the dangers of individuals becoming dependent upon the state for their income. The change also came about as a response to criticisms that benefit 'scroungers' were being created, with the claim that many of the people receiving benefits were not actively trying to get new jobs, and were instead content to take state benefits instead. Workfare policies were pioneered in the United States in the 1980s, but perhaps summarised best by UK politician Norman Tebbit, who suggested that the unemployed should get 'on their bike' and seek work if they were unable to find it rather than become dependent upon the state.

In terms of public management, a move from welfarism to workfarism leads to public managers having to make decisions about benefit eligibility on far more complex criteria. The universal entitlement to benefit suggested by a welfare approach is straightforward to administer – the only problems might be paying the benefit twice, paying it to a foreign national or to someone who has died. As eligibility criteria becomes more complex under a more Schumpeterian system however, more information has to be gathered and processed about claimants in order to assess their cases, and to make sure that they have earned the right to receive any available benefits. This creates a more complex bureaucracy which will need to be managed to make sure decisions are made in a timely and fair way. When public bureaucracies break down, real financial hardship can be caused and so it is important that they are made to work well. In an era where the state routinely gathers more and more information about its citizens, data management and data security become increasingly more important, and public managers must develop an increased awareness not only of the potential of IT to assist in their decision-making, but also of how they can make information systems containing public information secure.

From the national state to the post-national state

Jessop's third analytical spectrum runs from the state being organised primarily on a national economy basis to instead a post-national form. Jessop suggests that, in the immediate post-war period, countries were organised on a national basis, with clear boundaries, and countries could regard themselves as largely masters of their own economic destinies. Post-national state organisation embraces three new tendencies. First, globalising tendencies have meant that economies are increasingly unable to act independently of one another; a financial crisis in the United States means economic problems for the rest of the world. As financial capital becomes more mobile, an economy not seen as performing well will experience an outflow of investment and with that a decline in its currency value as it is seen as less attractive by international investors. This economic form of globalisation means that countries have become more interlinked and more mutually dependent than before.

The second sense in which postnationalism is relevant in that state, where it has reached the point of 'overload' (see above), typically needs to get organisations and political bodies at more local levels to take greater responsibility and for the central govern- ment itself to occupy more a 'regulation' role in overseeing their activities rather than participating in them directly. The state becomes a regulator and oversees rather than necessarily a provider of services, and the organisation of the public sector becomes more fragmented and locally organised in the name of increased efficiency and local responsiveness.

Third, postnationalism, as well as suggesting the state needs to delegate more, also means it must take into account decisions by supra-national bodies such as the European Union (EU), or NATO, or the World Trade Organisation (WTO), into its decision-making. In the case of the EU, law can be passed that is legally binding upon member states. In the case of the WTO, agreements can be signed that determine the extent to which public services can be insulated (or not) from competitive forces.

Jessop suggests that the state has moved from being organised on a national basis towards a post-national basis since the breakdown of fixed exchange rates systems put in place in the post-war period, especially since the 1970s, which have then been exacerbated by the problems of overload becoming more apparent since that decade. If globalisation limits the behaviours available to national economies because of the fear of international capital flight, overload means that the state might seek to pass responsibilities down to more local levels because of the sheer complexity of trying to run public services for a whole economy.

For public managers, post-nationalism means a range of complex tensions have appeared. On the one hand, it should lead to a decentralisation of the provision of ser- vices as the central state passes provision to more local levels in an attempt to lessen the overload it is experiencing. This should mean a devolution of power as well as often the greater use of private and not-for-profit local service providers. On the other hand, it often also means that the state is able to claim that it is passing the responsibility for delivering services away from itself to other providers, who may find that the raft of rules and regu- lations imposed by the state means they have little discretion in how services are run, but take the blame where things do not work out well. Equally, because the state sets the rules by which services are run, it may change them at any point, or decide to reorganise fre- quently, making it extremely difficult for service managers to plan or organise effectively. These tensions will be returned to in later chapters as they represent significant concerns for today's public managers.

From state-based organisation to regime-based organisation

Jessop's final analytical spectrum runs from state-based organisation to regime-based organisation. State-based organisation is centralised, run from a definable centre, and with a bureaucracy and top-down implementation in place. The state is organised in a hierar- chy with central decisions passing down through organisational chains to the local level where they are implemented. This clearly has overlaps with the characterisation of the state as being nationally based, but adds analytical depth because it shows the possibility of national organisations having an unbroken line of command and a unified system of rules – the classic bureaucracy.

A regime-based organisation instead is one where networks of providers from the public, private and not-for-profit sectors combine to perform services for users at the local level. Instead of national organisation, attempts are made to achieve a more responsive local provision through provision that works across a patchwork of all types of providers. Service users then cross the boundaries between public, private and not-for-profit providers as they receive the service, with the aim that their experience appears seamless to them. If the state-based organisation emphasises universality and control, regime-based governance attempts to achieve instead responsiveness and flexibility.

Jessop suggests that as states have experienced overload and attempted to pass their responsibilities to more local levels, regime-based governance has become more prevalent. This shift has been fostered by new approaches to managerial thought emphasising 'N'-form (network form) governance (Kickert *et al.*, 1997).

In the situation where regime-based governance emerges as the dominant form, it is the role of public managers to try and link together the disparate range of service providers to form a coherent whole for the service. Public management is about managing networks of different providers, many of whom may not be public providers, into coherent services that meet the needs of the local population. This is an entrepreneurial role for public managers in the sense that services can be configured and reconfigured to closely match individual service user's needs, with different combinations of providers leading to a far greater range of service offerings being possible. Public managers must oversee the operations of these complex networks to make sure that they offer a high standard of service and responsiveness. They must ensure that new providers can enter networks of provision where they add value to it, and that providers who do not meet the challenge of working within the network are removed from it.

Two ideal types – the KWNS and the SWPR

The Keynesian, Welfare, National State (KWNS) is the first ideal-type form of the state and was the post-war form that aimed to create a stable environment for the economy to grow and give guaranteed rights for its citizens. It was organised on the basis of the national economy and public services tended to be provided by the state, rather than by the private or not-for-profit providers. The KWNS dovetailed neatly with both one-nation liberals and democratic socialists, albeit with different emphases on efficiency and fairness depending upon the particular political colour of the government in power. The KWNS formation had particular problematic tendencies built into it; the state tended to expand to take on new responsibilities but found them difficult to administer, and resentment grew of the amount of taxation the population had to pay to support government in its increased range of activities while at the same time, the public came to regard the service offered by public organisations as inflexible and unresponsive. Globalisation meant that the national level of the economy became difficult to administer as financial independence increased, with some decisions having to be made across whole economic areas (such as the EU) and some at a far more local level (at state or regional level) instead.

The Schumpeterian Workfare Postnational Regime (SWPR) is the second ideal-type state form and combines an emphasis on economic dynamism and enterprise with a requirement for citizens to take greater responsibility for themselves. It acknowledges the economic independence of states and the need to pass the delivery of services to more local levels. However, there are tensions here too. The emphasis on enterprise and personal responsibility can be seen as exclusionary, however, to those with economic and social problems and does not always acknowledge the difference that class-based differences can make to an individual's life chances (Sayer, 2005). Equally the SWPR can downplay the importance of state-based power by underestimating the importance of national governments and lead to a fragmentation of services through regime-based delivery. Service users can feel, where regime forms are organised poorly, that the resulting markets and networks of provision are confusing and unaccountable and that they are being passed from service to service without receiving what they need.

Jessop's aim in showing the flaws in each of the two 'ideal type' forms of the state is to demonstrate how each is potentially unstable or subject to 'crisis tendencies' that are a very part of the structure of each state form itself. These contradictions may remain dormant in particular economic and social environments, only becoming apparent or activated under particular conditions. For the KWNS, problems emerged in the 1970s particularly as economic globalisation became more prevalent and national states increasingly struggled to meet the financial and organisational challenges of running large public sectors. At the same time, increased consumerism and increased resistance to paying tax resulted in the public becoming disenchanted with the service offered to them by many public organisations.

These difficulties and contradictions were potentially present in the Keynesian form since its inception, but became activated in the difficult economic conditions of the 1970s and the increased focus on economic problems this brought to policymakers' attention. Equally, there are conditions under which the contradictions and problems of the SWPR might be brought more to the fore; were equality to become more of a focus of policy, or there to be a popular demand for the increased funding of public services, for example, this might lead back to Keynesianism or to a new approach to public services that combines different elements of Jessop's analytical devices.

It is important to make clear that neither of Jessop's ideal types are meant to represent any particular state, and that each state will have its own hybrids of each of the elements he suggests. As such, although the SWPR is the ideal type most redolent of recent state reform, there will be different emphases on each of the characteristics in any particular country. Stillman (1997), for example, asks why there might be differences between the contemporary forms of public administration present in the United States and Europe, and suggests, in essence. that Europeans 'deduce Public Administration from reason of state, whereas America's missing sense of state forces us to induct state from Public Administration.' (p. 337). The absence of a sense of what the state is for in the United States, and the way that freedom is often defined in terms of freedom from the state, leads to the need for American policymakers and academics to try and work it out from the way that public administration is conducted. In Europe, on the other hand, where a clearer sense of the role and purpose of the state is in place, Stillman suggests that public administration is derived from it instead. Stillman suggests that both of these approaches can learn from each other, but are a source of mutual misunderstanding because of their fundamental difference, with European having a deductive rather than an inductive way of thinking about the role of public administration. This leads to US scholars debating 'what is public administration' more than UK ones because of their inductive methodology, and to questions of democracy and bureaucracy to be more sharply defined and their relationship becoming more problematic – resulting in the extremes of state resistance at Oklahoma and Waco, despite the flexibility and adaptability the system often offers. There might be definable elements of the SWPR present in both countries, but substantial differences between the specific way the state operates in each as a result.

The SWPR and public management

If the SWPR is the ideal type closest to the contemporary state form, it is worth exploring what form of public management it encourages. Some of its aspects are shown in Table 3.3 and are discussed below.

Under the SWPR a stress on enterprise and competition is encouraged, with citizens expecting to have responsibilities to the state as well as the right to access services from it. Public organisations (where they exist) often have to compete with private and not-for-profit organisations for public funding in the name of increasing their dynamism and responsiveness. Public organisations will be encouraged to find other sources of funding in

Table 3.3 The SWPR and public management

Aspect of SWPR	Description
Schumpeterianism	Use of markets mean public managers must become more entrepreneurial, competitive and concerned with contracts
Workfare	Concern with assessing welfare claimants more closely to assess their eligibility
Postnational	Potential for more local delegation in management, but also for more
Regime	Need to 'boundary span' and collaborate to provide a seamless service, often at the same time as competitive relationships are formed

addition to those they can secure from the state, typically by looking to charge for 'value-added' services they can offer to the public (Moore, 1997).

Management in such an environment is about competing for contracts and finding new sources of income which might be charged for. In healthcare, this will mean competing in a market-type environment to secure government and insurance company funding, as well as seeking income generation opportunities for patients by charging for higher levels of service such as for private rooms or the use of computers or telephones. In education, universities are encouraged to try to attract lucrative international students alone with research grants and consultancy from national and international organisations to raise additional income from both state and non-state sources.

An emphasis on competition means that public organisations must develop expertise in marketing they may not previously have had, as they attempt to position themselves against other organisations they recognise as competitors and to find ways of attracting what they are encouraged to regard as 'business'. Users of public organisations become consumers in this view, with needs to be met and the right to be heard, that they are empowered through choice mechanisms in competitive markets, and they are encouraged to have expectations about the level of service they expect to see that lie well above those that the grateful recipients the KWNS state implied.

Public management is increasingly cast as a technical, objective managerial function under the SWPR, and this is deliberately contrasted with the more discretionary and judgement-driven public administration of the past (Barber, 2007). But of course, this is illusory. Decisions about what methods of public management are to be used and what methods will be used to measure their efficacy are inherently ideological (Spicer, 2001). The SWPR, in line with its more managerialist approach, attempts to stress objective and measurable knowledge, but this often comes at a cost of simplifying the task of public managers to one of attempting to meet centrally imposed targets that may not capture the complexity of the managerial challenge before them (Mannion et al., 2001).

Managers in public organisations under the SWPR face conflicting roles. Where they come from the background of the professional group that dominates their service (i.e. teachers in education, doctors in medicine), they may find that they have to change the established practices of their own peer groups as they call for greater user-responsiveness and competitiveness. Managers in such a situation are often faced with challenges to their own identities – are they to consider themselves professionals or managers, and when faced with dilemmas, whose side should they take? Should Headteachers demand their colleagues take greater account of student views, or side with the professional integrity of teachers where demands for greater responsiveness and exam focus are made, even if it places less emphasis on learning as a result, and more on the passing of exams?

Where managers come from non-professional backgrounds the situation is no easier. Managers may find themselves 'going native', becoming sympathetic to the view of the public professionals they come into contact with as they come to respect their expertise (Schofield, 2001). In such a situation, they may become defenders of the existing values of public organisations rather than implementing the reforms demanded by the state or the public. If they try and challenge public professionals, they may find their work frustrating and depressing, with public professionals apparently trying to block their progress at every turn, and providing numerous reasons why every change they propose cannot occur. Managers from outside of public organisations often regard their bureaucracies as suffocating, but many public officials may believe that the use of rules and regulations creates fairness and transparency, so that all users are treated the same. They may regard the price of less user-responsiveness being worth paying in order to achieve greater fairness. Bureaucracy is not automatically bad – in particular circumstances it may be a good thing or even necessary. Most of us would like to think that the drugs prescribed to us have been checked and rechecked rather than delivered to us at the lowest possible cost. If user-responsiveness and efficiency have their place, so do care, rules and bureaucracy.

As well as working within an increasingly competitive marketplace, public managers must also, paradoxically, find ways of creating increased collaboration. This is because as regime-form governance becomes more commonplace, they must find ways of creating services that span several providers. Managers in local government might have to find ways of contracting for services for refuse collection that cross several private and public firms. They must find ways of getting separate organisation to work together rather than against one another. Public managers must find ways of becoming 'boundary spanners' or, in social science terms, occupy 'structural holes' (Burt, 1993) that link together different providers and create additional value for separate services as a result. As suggested above, their role is that of the service entrepreneur, finding new configurations of existing and new services that add value to the public user experience. These new services can then be offered to the economy of provision available to users, and, if chosen, bring new income to those involved in the delivery of those services.

Conclusion

The state has changed considerably in the post-war period. Even though Jessop's ideal types do not reflect any particular state's experience, they are a useful guide in considering the tensions and difficulties that governments have experienced and the implications of changing ideas about the state for public management. The ideal-type formations reflect the movement from the KWNS formation to that of the SWPR, but in any specific state there will be a greater emphasis on some of the particular elements rather than others. The United States, for example, was a relative latecomer to large-scale state involvement in welfare, not putting in place its medicare and medicaid programmes until the late 1960s, whereas the United Kingdom established its National Health Service with a larger scale and scope over 20 years earlier. The United States, even at its peak of public welfare commitment, was arguably closer to the SWPR than the KWNS, whereas the United Kingdom was the opposite. The United States has therefore found it more straightforward to embrace SWPR ideas than the United Kingdom, and become the world-leader in the production of public management ideas (Moore, 1997; Osborne and Gaebler, 1993). This does not necessarily mean that it has better public services than everyone else, but its particular state formation has put it at the forefront of thinking about public service reform as it was already closer to the ideal type other states appear, to varying extents, to be moving towards.

Central to Jessop's analysis of the role of the state is the contradictions or 'crisis tendencies' that must be managed if reform is to be successful and a new 'spatio-temporal fix' found in which politicians, managers and other stakeholders can understand their respective roles. One such fix that has received widespread attention internationally, especially within Europe and the far East, is that of the Third Way. The Third Way, perhaps most clearly articulated by (Lord) Anthony Giddens (1994, 1998, 2002, 2007), is an attempt to create a pragmatic basis for the reform of the state and public services in order to 'renew' and 'modernise' them in line with the demands of the twenty-first century. Within the discourse, the idea of the social investment state is presented in which the state comes to act as a kind of super loss-adjustor for society at large, supporting people when they are unable to work, skilling them to meet the challenges of employment, but looking after those that are unable to do so for themselves.

Newman and McKee (2005), however, argue that the social investment state is problematic because it exhibits an instrumental form of the NPM (see the next chapter for a full description of this) and so its claim to be aiming towards longer-term goals of 'social investment' is likely to be compromised by a more mechanical approach to leadership. They suggest that wider political struggles around the role of women, children and social investment are co-opted and stripped of their legitimacy because the policies addressing these areas are pale shadows borne of the neo-liberal project rather than attempting to confront these issues in a systematic way. Their hope is that the idea of the social investment state can yet to be mobilised for a range of more progressive projects, even if it might still be constrained by the instrumentalism of the NPM.

There are strong links between ideas about the present and the future role of the state, and the way public management is conducted. Having given a broad overview of how public management has changed in the post-war period, the next chapter explores more specifically how the field of public management has developed in the post-war period, exploring in more details the specific ideas that have been advanced on how best to organise public services.

CASE STUDY

Public management in Europe

An excellent study of public management in Europe comparing France, Germany and Italy was published by one of Europe's leading academics in the field, Walter Kickert, in 2005 (Kickert, 2005).

Kickert presents what he terms a 'historical-institutional' study of the three countries that shows how 'the study of public management is ... influenced by the particular institutional context of state and administration in the respective country' (p. 539). In other words, the context inherited by politicians and public managers will strongly influence what happens within public management in any particular country. The three countries in Kickert's paper are influenced as follows.

In **France**, there is a 'highly qualified and esteemed ... administration' (p. 542) that has existed since the time of Napoleon, and which is run by an elite group of officials. There is also little difference between politics and administration, with senior politicians and official moving freely between the two. When near to retirement they are also able to retire to top positions in private and nationalised companies. National plans became commonplace since the Fifth Republic (1958), with the extensive use of economic forecasting, and there was an extension of nationalisation of industry during the 1980s, in contrast to the United Kingdom and the United States, where at that time privatisation was far more common.

Since the mid-1980s, however, reforms have taken place due to social and political pressures, and because of economic recessions and budgetary crises. Four periods of modernisation are suggested: between 1984 and 1986, when economic crises brought the ambitions of the Socialist government to an end; between 1986 and 1988, when a neo-liberal reform programme was brought in by a more political right government, but to which the civil service responded in a defensive way that blocked much of the planned reform; between 1988 and 1992, the Socialists returned to power and there were attempts at government modernisation using tools such as total quality management; and a fourth period of reform followed, which focused more at the state level and which commissioned substantial reports into the future of the state in France. This led, from 1997 on, to attempts at decentralising state activity, followed by attempts to improve human resource management (HRM) and to simplify regulations.

France is still dominated by the notion of 'service public', which is strongly associated with the legitimacy of the state carrying out its activities in terms of the interest of the general public, through an administrative function that has legal guarantees of security and equality – giving public management a basis in administrative law not found in the United Kingdom or the United States. Reform is made particularly difficult because the 'grand corps' of civil servants, especially given their close links to politicians, have been able to effectively block change (see also Flynn and Strehl, 1996). Cole and Jones (2005) suggest that the NPM in France has been 'domesticated' (p. 584) and that 'The ideological underpinnings of the NPM debate do not find a receptive terrain in French public administration' (p. 584). In Minvielle's (2006) words 'reforms are established incrementally, much more slowly than in the

English-speaking industrialized countries, because of the historical weight of the centralized state and institutional and political conservatism' (pp. 761–762).

In **Germany**, there have also been a tradition of legalism, but this has been gradually departed from since the Second World War, with a movement towards a neo-corporatist social market economy, and the German state got more involved in planning in the 1960s and 1970s, followed by a retrenchment due to economic problems in the 1980s.

The legalistic view dominated public administration in Germany up to the 1960s, when it became viewed as a barrier to state modernisation. Instead, administrative science was meant to form the backbone of the renewed civil service, with a core curriculum being established at University level, but much recruitment to the German civil service continued to be from graduates with a law background.

From 1989, debates have been dominated by reunification, leading to the establishment of new administrative curricula, and widespread municipal reform also led to a resurgence in interest in public management as a discipline. Reichard (2003) suggests that, comparatively speaking, Germany has retained its strong legalistic focus for administrative reform, being less pragmatic in terms of how policy is implemented than in other countries, with its reforms of public finance being most wide-ranging.

In **Italy**, there is a more generalised dislike of the state than in France and Germany, brought on not only by the experience of dictatorship, but also due to the strong family tradition in the country. There is popular dissatisfaction with the political system, not least due to actual and perceived government corruption, and frequent changes in government still appear common.

The civil service inherited by the government after the Second World War was perceived by the government as being 'old-fashioned, slow, legalistic, overstaffed' (p. 553), but instead of reform, the government sought instead to simply circumvent it. Political appointees became common, and a parallel administration was created, and an increasing number of jobs could be given to political supporters of those elected to power (a more extreme form of the 'spoils' system in the US).

The Italian civil service is large, and consists largely of those from the south of the country, where the public sector is a hugely important employer because of high unemployment rates. Examinations are meant to determine civil service entry, but the system seems to have largely broken down, and public workers are portrayed as giving poor quality and inefficient service and entering the service without the required qualifications. Politicians have little influence over the civil service and exercise control through political appointments and creating their own cabinets, leading to a deadlock where distrust and sabotage between the two groups are common.

Since the 1990s, and huge state problems with corruption, administrative reforms have become more common in Italy. Local and regional government have become strengthened through decentralising reforms, and top civil-servants became far more dependent upon their jobs to politicians, who could now appoint to the 55 highest official posts. However, it is unclear whether much has really changed, with the legalistic paradigm of senior civil servants still dominating.

In summary, France has a strong legalistic tradition, with high status and prestige administrators dominating, educated at national schools of public administration. Administrative reform has struggled to make inroads into this elite, but with some decentralising reforms occurring that attempt to achieve greater efficiency and effectiveness. Germany also has a strong legal tradition, and this has largely continued despite the best attempts of state officials to change it. No substantial reforms have taken place in the national bureaucracy, but public management reforms have been both more common and more successful at the levels of municipal and regional government, reforms that aimed at greater efficiency and effectiveness. Italy, in contrast, does not have a strong state tradition, with the civil service forming a separate bureaucracy by-passed by politicians, and leading to a parallel system of 'spoils' government. Corruption since the 1990s has resulted in some reforms to the system, but there remains a significant amount of resistance to them.

The legalism present in the three countries seems to have made reform difficult to achieve. In many respects the goal of efficiency, especially economic efficiency, runs directly against the idea of legal accountability that dominates these systems, and so achieving greater flexibility and managerial reform remains a significant difficulty.

Further reading

Bob Jessop's work on state changes has developed over a number of years and is most completely developed in his book 'The Future of the Capitalist State' (Jessop, 2002), but many articles present shorter versions of his ideas (Jessop, 1992, 1994, 1999). Jessop's ideas have been applied to case studies in Scandinavia by Jacob Torfing, and make for fascinating reading (Torfing, 1999a, 1999b, 2001). Kickert's work on comparing European approaches to public reform compared to those of the United States help provide a contrast between the two approaches (Kickert, 1997, 2005), and Christensen and Laegreid's work on how NPM has 'transformed' different states is also extremely valuable (Christensen and Laegreid, 2002).

4

Changing ideas about public management

Introduction

The previous chapter explained the changing role of the state and its impact on public management. This chapter revisits that material, viewed not from state theory, but instead from the perspective of public management. This change of viewpoint attempts to make clear how public management has changed not only in terms of its assumptions, its prescriptions, but also as an academic discipline. It asks the question, how have ideas about public management changed?

The chapter starts by outlining what will be called the 'public administration' model, the approach to the administration of public services that appeared to dominate its organisation until at least the 1970s. It then examines the reasons why academics, practitioners and policymakers came to question the usefulness of thinking about the role of those running public organisation in this way, and the shift to what has been widely called the NPM. It concludes by outlining strands of the dominant thinking on public management today, along with the difficulties and contradictions this seems to entail. It presents a case study to explore the 'reinventing government' movement that was linked to public reforms under the Clinton administration.

The public administration model

A good place to begin in considering the changes to both public management (the practice) and public management (the discipline) is a review article published by Andrew Dunsire in 1999 (Dunsire, 1999). Dunsire attempts to link the 'world of thought and the world of action' (p. 360) by moving between what public management academics (or to give the subject is more traditional name, public administration) have written about their subject, and what changes he detects as having occurred 'in the field'. Dunsire suggested that the situation immediately after the Second World War was one dominated by the principles of 'traditional public administration'. Stewart and Walsh (1992) suggest that:

1. Public provision of a function is more equitable, reliable and democratic than provision by a commercial or voluntary body;
2. Where a ministry or other public authority is responsible for a function, it normally carries out that function itself with its own staff;
3. Where a public body provides a service, it is provided uniformly to everyone within its jurisdiction;
4. Operations are controlled from the headquarters of the public body through a hierarchy of unbroken supervision;
5. Employment practices (including recruitment, promotions, grading, salary scales, retirement and pensions) are standardized throughout each of the public services (e.g., the civil service, the local government service, the armed services);
6. Accountability of public servants to the public is via elected representative bodies.

(Dunsire, 1999:361)

Traditional public administration, as an ideal type (perhaps most closely adhered to in the UK as well as in some other European countries), was therefore primarily concerned about the achievement of equity and fairness as goals, through public provision as well as public financing, attempting to provide a uniform provision of service through centralised control, utilising standardised employment practices, and legitimated through democratic accountability. This is a useful starting point because it is comprehensive in considering most of the relevant elements of public management and allows us to construct contrasts with other approaches to the practice and understanding of the subject.

The first principle of public administration was the view that public provision leads to services being more equitable and reliable than commercial or voluntary bodies. In previous chapters the one-nation liberal and democratic socialist views of the state were equated with a focus on fairness, and so there is a clear fit here between state ideology and public management practice. Public ownership should guarantee the provision of a particular service whereas relying upon both private and not-for-profit providers could carry greater risk. In the case of private provision, there is the danger of firms exiting where sufficient profits are no longer available, and charities or voluntary organisations may suffer from problem that a lack of available funding could lead to their closure. In both these situation, the state may have to underwrite provision by acting as a funder of last resort to avoid private or not-for-profit services being withdrawn, so there is a case for it simply providing them in the first place instead.

The idea that the state be responsible for public services leads directly to the second principle of public administration, that it should be responsible not only for planning and financing the service, but also for delivering it as well. Again, there are sensible reasons for this. The easiest way to ensure a service which is accountable to the government is for it to also run it, that way the service should have complete access to administrative records in order to fully scrutinise its activities. Of course, whether the state is capable of this level of scrutiny in practice is something of an open question, but theoretically at least there is a logic behind extending state responsibility for public services to state ownership and state delivery.

The third principle of public administration, uniformity, is again based on the idea of fairness. If the state provides a differentiated service, or as it is often termed today, a user-responsive service, then there is the danger that this might also be unfair, as it might mean some people receive a better service than others. In practice, it has been impossible to provide either an exactly uniform service or a fully differentiated one, but managers have increasingly been encouraged to be explicit about which end of the spectrum they are aiming at.

The fourth principle of public administration is that there should be a hierarchical chain of command from the public service headquarters through to the delivery end of the service. The most obvious organisational form of this approximates to a bureaucracy, and it has already been noted in Chapter 2 that a larger bureaucracy is one of the few aspects of public management where research suggests practice is distinctive when compared to private management. Bureaucracies put in place rules and define employee roles clearly with standardised employment practices (the fifth public administration principle) having a clear chain of command, and creating the opportunity for a link between policymakers, the heads of the public service and those responsible for delivering the service itself. A unified chain of command should therefore aim to minimise what has been called the 'implementation gap', the problem of getting the policy made by the state implemented 'on the ground' in public services that might be hundreds of miles away from where the original decisions were made. The state becomes, in the words of Oakeshott, a purposive association, one that is about implementing a unified chain of command to do the bidding of the central decision-making body, the state.

Finally, the accountability of public services is held to be via democratic means. The means by which this is meant to work varies from state to state and depends upon the balance of power between local government and central or federal government. Where a strong local democratic tradition exists, local officials may be held accountable for local services with which they are in frequent contact, and with the possibility of a considerable variation in services from one locality to the next, in contradiction to the principle of service uniformity. Equally, it is possible that senior public managers be elected, with the majors of major cities being held accountable via the ballot box for their ability to run local services. Alternatively, in a more centralised democracy, politicians who have little or no contact with the day-to-day activities of many public services may be held democratically accountable for them, prompting the need for considerable information-gathering bureaucracies to be put in place so the politicians can try and find out what is going on within them.

In any of these approaches to democratic accountability, if public officials are not adequately held to account through the democratic process then the system is in danger of breaking down. Fox and Miller (1995) write of the 'incredulity of representative democracy' (p. 25) in critiquing the idea that public administration is accountable to 'the people' through the democratic process, suggesting that the 'loop' model of democracy in which the public vote for credible candidates to run public services, and reward them if they do well, is mythical. Their claims are based on data from congress elections that shows the significant advantage that incumbents have in any election process, and that typically Americans have next to no idea of who their local politicians are or what they stand for. This is clearly a significant problem for the traditional model of public administration; if it is not legitimated through democracy, then how should it be accountable? This problem will be returned to again in a moment, as well as in Chapter 7.

The problems with the public administration model

Even in trying to present a straightforward description of the ideal type of traditional public administration a number of anomalies and difficulties have already been noted. Those running public services can never completely eradicate such difficulties, they have to learn instead how well they can be contained or smoothed over. Dunsire suggests that one problem of the six principles listed above is that they are remarkably atheoretical (that is, they are not underpinned by a coherent set of ideas, but were instead based more upon 'muddling through' (Hennessy, 1997) or an 'incremental' political process (Lindblom and Woodhouse, 1993) rather than being based on anything more rational). This problem appeared to be particularly present in the United Kingdom, where, in contrast to the United States, public administrators regarded the learning of management techniques as being largely irrelevant to their activities (Thomas, 1978). The lack of business schools and the lack of a national school of administration, as was present in France, meant that public administration could appear rather atheoretical and the province of generalist civil servants.

A criticism Dunsire makes of the traditional public administration model is that it was unable to deal with demands, especially from the 1970s onwards, to bring the three 'E's of economy, efficiency and effectiveness. Many public officials saw the three 'E's as contradicting the principles of fairness and equity with which they worked. One reason for this was the lack of training of many public officials to deal with new management ideas, especially in countries such as the United Kingdom. In France, the post-war period saw the establishment of elite training colleges for public officials, but this carried with its own risks of the danger of establishing a rather singular view of what public administration was about that could become quickly outdated if societal or economic conditions changed.

In practical terms, the attempt to introduce the three 'E's into public administration resulted in attempts at reforms that tried to rationalise the delivery of services in order to control costs, and which often attempted to increase the control of central and local policymakers over the provision of services. This was necessary because policymakers became increasingly frustrated with the 'implementation gap', or the problem of getting the bureaucracies they (or their predecessors) had created to get on and meet the policy goals they had put in place. Policymakers found out that the theoretical existence of a hierarchy did not mean that central policymakers or managers actually held a great deal of power in deciding how public services were delivered on the ground. Entrenched professional groupings often held considerable autonomy at the local level, with the ability to be able to ignore the demands of central administrations to reform services. This ability to 'veto' policy often carried with it the ability to opt-out of accountability mechanisms as well, leading to public services having the kinds of legitimacy problems Fox and Miller suggested in the previous section. If public services were accountable to neither the state nor local citizens, in whose name did they operate? What were local people to do if public services were found to be lacking, and how could improvements be made?

The lack of responsiveness of public bureaucracies to either citizen or consumer demands led to two particular criticisms. The first was the democratic problem suggested above. If the democratic loop that was meant to lead to public service improvement was flawed, then public services might also be less accountable than their designers suggested, but this meant that there was little scope for the public improving them. However, there was also a second criticism.

The users of services, having received an extension of their welfare rights in the post-war period, now appeared to begin to take the right to use public services increasingly for granted and began to demand that services be improved. Public services users began to become increasingly aware that they were not receiving services for free, but were in fact paying for them through increased taxation, and as economies got richer and citizens paid more tax, they began to ask more question about how 'their' money was being spent (Haug and Sussman, 1969). In liberal economies, such as the United States, this discourse was especially widespread, with popular movements against the increasing role of the state being supported by lobby groups seeking to preserve the pre-eminence of private enterprise. Even in economies such as the United Kingdom, where citizens were used to higher taxes, complaints appeared about very high marginal tax rates, and were encapsulated by the Beatles song 'taxman' in the 1960s, which suggested rather bitterly that the British people were in fact working only to raise funds for the Inland Revenue (the tax collection body) rather than for their own ends.

This service user-based critique of public services was extended by US theorists who criticised the self-serving nature of bureaucracies by claiming that they were often not run primarily for the benefit of those working within public institutions rather than those they were meant to serve (the public choice model, discussed in Chapter 2). This approach, based on the utility theory of economics, suggested that the incentives public officials worked within (lack of competitive structures, prestige based on department size and budget) meant that they were more likely to try and maximise their share of their organisations' resources than to try and improve the quality of the services they were meant to be delivering to the public. If public managers were not accountable to their citizens via democratic means, there were logical reasons why they might be pursuing their own interests rather than those they were meant to be serving, These elements combined to present a damning critique of the traditional public administration view, suggesting that public managers were neither accountable nor controllable.

One possible response to claims such as these was for public organisations to improve their democratic mechanisms and to make sure that they were accountable to the public. Equally, they could have tried to demonstrate long records of public service rather than self-serving behaviour. However, it is difficult for an organisation to demonstrate that it has been doing things right in the face of concerted criticisms that fit with increasingly popular prejudices that public bureaucracies are inefficient and self-serving. As societies became more individualised, the collective goals of public organisations and the administrators that attempted to achieve them began to look increasingly anachronistic and dated. New modes of organisation for public services seemed to be needed.

Towards a public management

From the end of the 1970s, both the UK and US governments went about turning the principles of traditional public administration on their heads. The Reagan and Thatcher governments shared a suspicion of large government and began to articulate new ideas (or at least the restatement of old ideas) for the way public services should be run. Thinkers of what became known as the 'New Right' (Flynn, 1989) advocated services being transferred into the private sector as liberal, minimal state ideas gained credence and politicians preached the virtues of individuals providing for themselves rather than depending upon the state. In such an environment the market was reified as the ultimate arbiter of what held value and what did not, and the planners of the 1950s and 1960s were recast as meddlers and 'do-gooders' who interfered with the laws of supply and demand.

Services that were formerly both financed and provided by the public sector were privatised where politically possible, and where full privatisation was not possible, ways of subjecting public services to market disciplines were sought. Markets for public services (often referred to as 'quasi' markets in the academic literature) were created where private and not-for-profit providers were encouraged to enter and compete with public organisations in order to try and drive up standards. Managers were required to contract with one another for services that attempted to specify their quantity, but putting in place quality standards often proved far more problematic because of the intrinsic problems of measuring the activities of public organisations.

Instead of the state directing public organisations to deliver services in relationships based largely on trust (because of the difficulty of measuring the activity of public organisations and the presence of substantial professional groups), contracts were introduced that moved relationships instead onto a more legalistic footing and potentially put in place penalties for non-compliance (Walsh, 1996). These changes often associated with the idea of creating a 'hollow state' that no longer provides services but simply oversees contractual arrangements for them. Brinton Milward and Provan (Brinton Milward and Provan, 2003) argue that the central task in the hollow state is the use of tools like 'contracting and collaboration to manage networks of organizations from all sectors – public, private and nonprofit effectively' (p. 15). They suggest, in line with public choice theory, that this creates the need to establish clear principal – agent relationships to do this, along with the need to establish network with 'enough stability to maintain its ability to manage a set of jointly produced services' (p. 15).

The move towards a market-driven role with clearly defined contracts is a little ironic. At exactly the time that sociologists and management writers chose to emphasise the importance of businesses generating trust and exploring informal relationships (Burt, 1993, 2000; Granovetter, 1985, 1973), public organisations seemed to be going in the opposite direction. The view of public organisation being based around market relationships often had the tendency, perversely given the goal of making them more business-like and lean, to increase bureaucracy as it was necessary to bill, pay and monitor large numbers of new contracts that had previously not existed. Equally, the evidence that market-based models have supplanted bureaucracies is limited, with Boyne suggesting that even though other forms are 'preached or practised' (Boyne, 1999:4) the main challenge in relation to bureaucracy is 'not to replace it, but to make it work better' (p. 4). Bradley and Parker (2006) share this view, suggesting that even though public managers might want their organisations to move away from resembling bureaucracies, they tend to persist despite their best efforts. Bearing these concerns in mind, certain tendencies towards change, however, can be seen.

Fragmentation and flexibility

The entry of private and not-for-profit providers into public provision meant that public services were no longer offered in a hierarchical chain of command, but have instead become more fragmented, or to use the contemporary management term, 'N-form', or networked. Following fashionable management theory, public organisations found themselves not just subject to external competition for contracts, but also required to put ancillary work such as cleaning services for tender, meaning that public employees in these areas had to organise themselves to compete with private sub-contractors to retain their jobs or face losing them. Contracts being offered to an even greater range of provider organisations meant that managers were required to find ways of working across service and organisational boundaries to attempt to 'join-up' provision to meet the needs of their users.

Standardised employment contracts became the target of reformers who wanted to encourage greater work flexibility, challenging standard terms and conditions and precise job specifications that they perceived to be interfering with the right to manage. Public service workers who belonged to trades unions also found themselves under greater suspicion as unions were identified by governments as barriers to the functioning of free labour markets. Reforming union legislation made it more difficult for the bastions of union activism, those in public organisations, to engage in strike action. The 'corporatist' approach of one-nation and democratic socialist governments, in which unions were often included in discussions of national policy, gave way to them being excluded from policy and regarded as dinosaurs that blocked economic growth. Public managers were expected to lead their organisations rather than acting as mediators between professionals and trades unions, carrying forward government agendas and making sure that the implementation gap of the past was narrowed. If bureaucracy could not deliver the reliable delivery of policy, then perhaps the state could depend on managers to act as 'corporate rationalisers' (Alford, 1972), to challenge formerly entrenched professionals and drive forward real change.

Consumers and charging

Instead of delivering universal services to the collective public, public managers were encouraged to treat public service users as informed consumers with needs to be met. Viewing the public as individuals rather than part of a general public meant that different conceptions of the management role could be voiced. Managers sought to increase their revenues by finding ways of charging for levels of service above those that were offered as standard. Hospitals offered superior facilities such as private rooms and access to telephone and televisions in return for additional payments, and school managers tried to find ways of offering before- and after-school clubs for the children of working parents where they might allow additional funds to be raised. Public organisations were encouraged to offer their services to those in the private market that might be willing to pay for them; occupational health functions in public organisations could be marketed to the private sector, and children's libraries might offer busy parents crèche facilities and child activities where they could safely leave their children.

IT and performance management

At the same time as the changes above, advances in information technology meant that public organisations could be placed under far greater central scrutiny than ever before. Computers made possible the recording and measurement of far more of the activities of public organisation than had ever been the case before, and to the publication of comparative league tables provided the opportunities for citizens to see how good their local services were (or at least how good they were at meeting the centrally imposed measures) compared to those in other areas (Bloomfield and Coombs, 1992).

The public 'naming and shaming' of poorly graded public organisations attempted to address the problems of democratic legitimacy discussed above in new ways. Instead of public services being theoretically accountable to the elected public officials or to the electing population at large, but without clear mechanisms for exactly how this was to occur, they became increasing performance managed by central government, which acted as an evaluator on behalf of the public (Flynn, 2000). This change in accountability mechanism was made in the name of increasing user responsiveness through increasing accountability upwards (despite the claims that bureaucracies were being abolished), attempting to create new forms of democratic legitimacy in which the central state acted on behalf of citizens, and the citizens, in turn, decided who should run the state. As such, the state, in systems where top-down accountability where stressed, claimed to be speaking 'for the people', supplanting professionals, who had claimed the same legitimacy in the past, form this role.

The growth in performance measurement also meant that public organisations could be scrutinised for their resource usage more acutely, leading to parsimony becoming a goal of management in the name of demonstrating that services were becoming more efficient (Hood, 1991).

It is relatively straightforward to create a second ideal type of public management by simply taking the list of 'traditional' public administration principles and working out their logical opposites. This results in the following:

Instead of equity and fairness, the new form of public management stresses user responsiveness and a differentiated service in the name of consumerism and achieving greater responsiveness (Walsh, 1991). Service differentiation comes with the possibility of some users getting a service that more closely meets their needs than others, and so has the potential to work against the perceived fairness and equity of the past. Instead of public provision, providers from the public, private and not-for-profit sectors are encouraged to compete for public contracts on the grounds that it will drive up standards. Instead of uniformity, as noted above, public services attempt to offer a differentiated service rather than assuming that 'one size fits all' under the old public administration. Instead of hierarchical provision, flat responsive organisations are encouraged in which local managers take responsibility for making decisions. Instead of standardised terms of employment, managers are given the discretion to reward their staff as they see fit as a means of offering locally differentiated services. Finally, instead of democratic accountability, accountability is meant to be achieved by services becoming more user-responsive, moving the service from one organised around a citizen model (democratic accountability) to one instead that treats users more as consumers with needs to be satisfied. Alternatively, a different form of accountability can come through the increased use of performance management systems where the central government attempts to scrutinise local services on behalf of the electorate as a whole.

Table 4.1 therefore summarises the two ideal types of public administration and NPM. However, most countries have struggled to find coherent ways of dealing with the difficulties that the NPM has introduced. They have particularly struggled to reduce bureaucracy, with attempts at introducing public markets often leading to an increase in rules, regulations and administrators collecting data. There also seems to be a difficulty in increasing user-responsiveness because of the increased use of top-down forms of accountability that have often appeared as the state becomes increasingly assertive in its use of performance management techniques that make it difficult for services to diverge too much from centrally imposed norms.

Table 4.1 Public administration and its opposites

Traditional public administration	Opposite
Equity and fairness	Differentiated service
Public provision	Mixed provision (public, private, not-for-profit)
Uniformity	Differentiation and diversity
Hierarchical provision	Flat organisations
Standardised terms of employment	Differential, local terms of employment
Democratic accountability	User accountability
	Central state accountability

A new form of public management

A new ideal type of public management much more in line with a more liberal view of public provision has become the form of running public organisations increasingly favoured by states. In that model, service is differentiated according to user need, managers encouraged to run their services to be more response to individual service users and to treat them as consumers. A diversity of provision is encouraged rather than uniformity. Services are not necessarily provided by the public sector, but could be provided from a range of providers from either public, private or not-for-profit sectors, probably positioned against one another in a competitive relationship. The movement from public administration (the traditional public administration approach outlined above) to public management (the second ideal type) has been widely written about, with authors creating competing typologies of the types of the NPM that they have found in the institutions they research (Newman, 2000).

Whether the NPM represents a new paradigm, an entirely new approach to the management of public organisations, remains a moot point. Gray and Jenkins (1995), for example, suggest that the NPM is based on public choice economics, as well as on 'strands of corporate management thinking' (p. 93), but does not form a new paradigm because there is no new unified theory of public management within it. They suggest instead that it is necessary to adequate theorise what a non-public choice models of public management might look like, to add a constitutional dimension to public management that addresses the lack of democracy present in the NPM, and to test new frameworks empirically to bring together public administration and public management approaches, exploring both the practical and the political implications of policies.

Public management as an academic discipline

Public management as an academic discipline, in line with the fragmentation of public administration into more 'regime-form' type organisation, appears also to have broken up into more diverse forms than before. Some writers, especially those from policy backgrounds, have tried to show how coalitions might be built to achieve better implementation (Sabatier, 1988). Other academics have constructed detailed case studies examining both the successes and failures of particular public programmes in line with the approach often found in the private sector of examining businesses that exemplified particular practices to see how they achieved success or failure.

In the United States and the United Kingdom as well as across New Zealand and Australia, however, the most significant stand of new thinking came through the shift to examining what has become known as the NPM movement. Hood's inaugural lecture at the London School of Economics (Hood, 1991) coalesced thinking and defined the public management shift that had taken place as one moved the discipline away from studies of policy to studies of management. The new approach emphasised quantitative methods of appraisal and performance management above qualitative, judgement and experience-based approaches. Organisations were characterised as breaking up hierarchies into semi-autonomous units of provision, contracting and moving provision 'out of house' rather than attempting to achieve a unified production of services. This came along with a focusing on outputs rather than processes or inputs for public services, creating the potential for incentivising public managers through performance-related pay rather than paying them fixed salaries. Hood suggested that the NPM emphasised the freedom to manage rather than the need to follow rules, that it moved organisations towards a marketing approach rather than a producer-dominated one, and stressed public organisations becoming more self-regulating than central regulating (although, as we have already seen, performance management systems developed in the 1990s appear to have swung the balance back to more central regulation again). In Hood's view, these changes were a mix of responses to the criticisms of public choice writers in the 1960s and 1970s and an updated 'scientific management' where control could be exerted through the rational application of measurable management programmes.

The biggest problem with the NPM movement is that its advocates often define the term in many different ways. As such, just about any organisational form that does not represent the public administration archetype can be argued to be a part of it. Hood's work is useful in synthesising an early ideal type of what the new form public management might look like against which particular examples of public management might be compared to.

Another problem comes with the conceptualisation of the network form of organisation as having a central part to play in the NPM. The difficulty is that term 'network' is in itself rather meaningless, and a host of contradictory definitions exist that attempt to capture what might be meant in its use. In some cases networks are defined in terms of what they are not – they are neither markets nor hierarchies, but a third form of organisation (Exworthy et al., 1999). Elsewhere networks are used as an all-embracing structural concept with hierarchies and markets representing simply particular configurations of networks. Networks are also characterised in influential literature as being a form of organisation having no individual single, dominant central organising agent and where organisation is achieved through a 'differentiated polity' of links between government and the increasingly diverse range of providers it depends upon for the delivery of public services (Rhodes, 1997). Finally, networks are sometimes characterised as representing a form of governance where the state is no longer able to manage and organise by itself (having something in common with the government overload thesis of Chapter 3) and where managers must find strategies for managing within this new environment through consensus-building approaches (Kickert *et al.*, 1997). The absence of a coherent understanding of exactly what networks are is a significant problem if the NPM is defined in terms of an increased use of them.

Postmodernism

A further development in the public management literature has come through its increasing interest in post-modernism. This approach often has a different understanding of the crisis in public administration of the 1970s, suggesting that its problems were not because of any particular events, but instead because it never really could work. Fox and Miller (1995) present a wide-ranging critique of running public organisations through bureaucracies and particularly the attempt by public administration to legitimise its activities on democratic grounds. In much the same way, Majone (1989) produces a critique of public administration's focus on rational decision-making. Fox and Miller share much of this analysis, and show how taken-for-granted approaches to policy and management depend inextricably upon the organising concepts and ideas dominant in a particular time, inevitably favouring the already-strong through the reproduction of existing power relations, and leaving out the disempowered and dispossessed time and time again.

In the post-modern view, traditional public administration failed because of its dependence on the meta-narratives of rationalistic decision-making and democratic accountability, both of which might be interesting theoretically, but cannot be supported by their practice in reality. Public administration is portrayed as a modernistic project that is no longer sustainable.

Whereas Majone recommends that it is necessary to regard policymaking and public management in a rhetorical way, Fox and Miller suggest it is necessary to take a more discursive approach to understanding policy and administration. In doing this, they want public management to become part of a process of deliberative democracy, with far greater efforts being necessary to achieve public involvement in policy formulation and implementation. Fox and Miller therefore want public administration to reconnect to the people in order to resecure its legitimacy. They therefore seek to replace assumptions about rational decision-making with greater public deliberation and involvement in public services.

There are two considerable problems with Fox and Miller's prescriptions; first, with political participation rates declining it is a lot to ask for people to get involved in the time-consuming and energy-taking process of scrutinising and deliberating public organisations. As Stoker (2006) advocates, what may be required to resurrect public involvement in public services is a 'politics for amateurs' in which the public are able to engage with service change and direction on more straightforward terms than the very high level of involvement that Fox and Miller suggest. Second, it is not entirely clear how Fox and Miller imagine public administration delivering the goods once policy has been formulated. Does their rejection of bureaucracy extend to the implementation of policy as well as its formulation, and if it does, how do they envisage public services being organised? How should the public interact with public managers, and what would their roles be in doing so?

Criticality

The turn of the public management discipline to post-modernism is a part of its general tendency to become more critical in orientation. This move to becoming more critical does not mean that academics have criticised public managers or public policymakers (although a lot of this does go on), but instead suggests that public management needs to take a more critical stance (Learmonth, 1999; Marston, 2000). Advocates of this view suggest that it needs to become more questioning and find ways of challenging taken-for-granted assumptions about the way public management works. This has led to the increased use of the analysis of public management practices through sociological approaches including deconstruction (where take-for-granted assumptions about practice are exposed and those practices reconstructed to be more inclusive), discourse analysis (unpackaging the ideas and practices underpinning reforms typically through an exploration of their language), and, as a result, the analysis of power and power relationships has become far more significant in the public management discipline than was previously the case. It has become as common to ask 'who gains' from reform programmes as 'what happened' as a result of their introduction.

Problems

This fragmentation of the public management discipline has led to a far wider use of theory than was present under the old public administration view. This has led to scholarship becoming both more complex and more nuanced, as well as being more academically grounded than before. However, this increasingly complex and theoretical approach has led to practising public managers who are not initiated in the ideas and language of the many public management sub-disciplines perhaps finding themselves feeling isolated from the academic study of their own discipline, and with the feeling that they have little to learn from it. This is clearly a shame – academics and managers have a great deal to learn from one another, and closer links between the two might reduce the tendency of public managers to rely upon consultancy organisations that sometimes appear more interested in selling new management ideas than engaging with the very complex problems public organisations face (Greener, 2005a). Academics, in turn, have a great deal to gain by engaging in the problems of public management not only in terms of generating new empirical (case) material, but also in attempting to test out some of their ideas in practice.

Conclusion

By a way of conclusion, this chapter will assess the influence of ideas upon public manage-ment, and go on to explore whether it is possible to say that there is a dominant form of public management present in the world today.

Ideas and public management

What is apparent in looking back over the history of the disciplines of public adminis-tration and public management is that they both have been very influenced by the world of ideas. The post-war settlement in place in the developed economies saw most of their governments picking up at least some of the ideas of Keynes (see Chapter 3) to justify an expansion in government, and this clearly linked to an understanding of the world leading to the dominance of the public administration approach that, in various forms, seemed to have appeared in most developed states in the post-war period. The 'counter-revolution' against Keynesian ideas from the 1970s onwards came about through the active lobbying of prominent 'new right' academics who found governments increasingly sympa-thetic to their market-based view (Cockett, 1995). The increased prominence of business schools from the 1960s onwards has led to a new generation of public managers becoming increasingly immersed in the language of the MBA (Masters of Business Administration) and more aware of finance, business modelling and performance management than would ever have been the case before.

The source of many of the big ideas that have circulated in public management since the 1980s have come from the United States (Osborne and Gaebler, 1993), with their advocates often seeming to act as 'entrepreneurs' of ideas, touring the world to achieve greater awareness of their work, and carrying great influence in areas such as healthcare (Enthoven, 1985). In more recent times, the work of theorists who have attempted to chal-lenge the ideas of the NPM have found influence through 'progressive governance' and 'third way' networks where pragmatic approaches to policymaking and public manage-ment are advocated that suggest that markets, used as tools rather than as their own ends, can be harnessed to achieve greater fairness and increase the productivity and efficiency of the public sector at the same time (Giddens, 2003, 2007). At the same time as this, space has been created for writers to attempt to reassert some of the traditional values of public administration, but in a more modern context through the notion of 'public value', in which those in charge of public services are regarded as attempting to satisfy the needs of their users collectively in the same way as private organisations meet the needs of their shareholders (Moore, 1997). In this view, public managers are charged with free-ing their employees to propose new ways that public value can be increased, and this has shifted the debate away (a little) from the satisfaction of individual service users as con-sumers towards thinking more about how collective improvements to public services can be achieved. This moves the emphasis away from individualism back towards collective citizen accountability, but with a strong advocacy of public manager entrepeneurship attached in order to attempt to overcome the bureaucratic tendencies of public organisations in the past. Given this plurality of ideas it has become difficult to identify a single, dominant form of public management, but certain trends can be seen.

A dominant form of public management?

The dominant form of public management, in terms of the academic discipline if not entirely the practice of the discipline, has become one where the tenets of the NPM, in all its flavours and inconsistencies, have come to the fore. Public management has become more regime-oriented, but its disciplinary emphasis on network form governance has often led to a lack of clarity about the exact form of the changes that are taking place.

It is difficult to claim that there is one specific form of public management emerging, but it is possible to say that there is a general trend towards the sort of tendencies described earlier in the chapter, including many of those identified by Hood. Public management has become more inclined to use private management techniques, has become more output-oriented and target-focused, and it has been increasingly organised onto a more user-focused basis.

This emergent form of public management has a particular direction, but is far from being a homogeneous form. The institutional and cultural inheritances of the state where they are being introduced will strongly influence the version of public management that appears there. Countries with strong localist tendencies will tend to try and find the ways of continuing in that tradition (Kickert, 1997), those with strong central governments and electoral systems that allow for majority governments to rule strongly will tend to produce the most radical reforms (Wilsford, 1995), and countries with separations between local and federal government will have to form compromises that other states may not find necessary (Johnston, 2000). Christensen and Laegreid (2001) find that in Norway (where there was no perceived economic crisis and little incentive for change), a soft version of the NPM was put in place, whereas in New Zealand, which faced strong external pressures, weak countervailing cultural forces and a parliamentary form they call 'electoral dictatorship', a far more radical version of the NPM was implemented.

Changes are also apparent in particular geographic spaces. Lynn (1999) shows that, across North America, the nature of change in public management reflects the national politics and administrative histories of Canada, Mexico and the United States. Canada has been searching for fiscal retrenchment at both national and provincial levels, Mexico influenced by the transition from oligarchy to democracy at federal, state and local levels, and the United States preoccupied at the federal level by the initiatives from the 'Reinventing Government' movement.

If different versions of the NPM appear to have been implemented in different countries, then does it even make sense to talk about a single NPM? Pollitt (2000) suggests that the emperor is not quite naked, but rather in his underwear. He suggests that the NPM is not just 'windy rhetoric' (p. 195) as downsizing has occurred in many countries, measured efficiency has increased, and some services have become more user-centric and flexible. However, unmeasurable aspects may have taken a turn for the worse, and many staff and citizens may have suffered 'degenerating conditions as a consequence' (p. 195). He does, however, suggest that the NPM has never really extended beyond Australasia, North America and the United Kingdom, with methods being applied more selectively in other countries.

There is therefore a need to take a pragmatic approach to understanding public management on a world-wide basis, accepting that reforms will work out very differently from state to state (Pollitt and Bouchaert, 2000). This is exciting as it generates a range of different findings and attempts at dealing with the problems experienced by the public administration approach, but it can also be frustrating as there really is no single best answer as to how public services might be best managerially reformed.

It is also possible that the NPM has already had its day. Denhardt and Denhardt (2000) have long suggested that the opposition between the NPM and the old public administration are less relevant to the twenty-first century than they were to the twentieth. Instead, they suggest 'new public service' should be based on democratic citizenship, community and civil society. They suggest seven principles by which the new public service should be run: they should serve, not steer, establishing shared interests between groups rather than attempting to control the public; they should put the public interest as their aim, not as a by-product of their reforms; that public managers should think strategically and act democratically, suggesting the need for collective efforts and collaboration; that public managers should serve citizens not customers, placing an emphasis on dialogue rather than the aggregation of individual self-interests; make clear that accountability is not simple and must meet multiple aims and stakeholders; that public managers should value people, not productivity, leading to collaboration and shared leadership and based on respect; and that public managers should value citizenship and public service above entrepreneurship, leading to the goal of making a contribution to society becoming important than achieving an environment favouring entrepreneurship. Denhardt and Denhardt offer a view of public services that, in common with Fox and Miller, stresses the importance of public accountability rather than either the consumer-driven model of some versions of the NPM, or the flawed democratic notions of the old public administration. Whether states are prepared to implement their ideas, however, remains to be seen.

Newman (2000, 2002), Newman and McKee (2005) have also argued that a movement beyond the NPM is now discernable. In relation to her analysis of the situation in the United Kingdom, she suggests modernisation goes beyond the NPM in three respects. First, in that the negative consequences of market fragmentation were acknowledged in an attempt, especially apparent in the early years of the Labour administration, to move towards 'joined up' governance. This leads to the second change, as collaboration replaced competition in line with contemporary business thought, moving to less adversarial and longer-term models of contracting. Third, Newman argues, there was the introduction of new discourses of citizen and user participation. User participation was extended to include not only choice (in addition to market research and complaints mechanisms) but also user voice through more active participation in service design and planning. These changes, however, have led to some significant changes and tensions; managerial flexibility works against central performance management; 'joined up' government requires new styles of leadership and management that do not fit well with the NPM as presently in place; managers have to find ways of delivering success for their own organisation while working in collaborations and dealing with 'cross-cutting' issues; and there is the problem of trading long-term goals against short-term efficiencies. Newman suggests that these contradictions must be managed and reconciled, but whether this can occur within the dominant discourse of NPM managerialism is questionable.

CASE STUDY

Reinventing government

Michael Spicer is a US Professor of Public Administration who writes a great deal about the role of ideas in public management. His wonderful book on the relationship between the state and public administration (Spicer, 2001) illustrates how US and European public administration grew out of dominant ideas in those countries, and so has links to the case study of Kickert's work in the previous chapter.

Spicer's work is also important because of his study of the reinventing government movement that became important in public management, especially in the United States, during the 1990s (Spicer, 2004). The central doctrines of reinventing government (expressed most clearly in (Osborne and Gaebler, 1993)) are the 'elimination of red tape; holding administrators to account for measurable results; emphasising customer satisfaction in agency dealings with the public; empowering front-line managers to make their own decisions; contracting out whenever possible with the private sector for public-service delivery' (Spicer, 2004:357). The reinventing government movement sought to present itself as an objective restatement of the separation between politics and administration, and therefore as an ideologically neutral series of ideas for the better running of government that could be applied universally. In the words of one of the inventors of the approach, 'reinvention applies to all types of organizations' (Osborne and Plastrick, 1997:47).

Vice-president Al Gore echoed the sentiments of the reinventing government movement and in arguing in the US National Performance Review that entrepreneurial government was about casting aside red tape, and giving public managers a sense of mission. President Kennedy was held up as an example of creating a mission by giving NASA the goal of landing a man on the moon by the end of the 1960s, giving the organisation a remarkable goal to work towards. This clarity of purpose was contrasted with the situation in many public organisations that had to meet multiple, and even competing goals, and with government itself seen as creating much of this confusion by giving public managers unclear objectives. Rationalising government was about depoliticising the process of governing public organisations to make it 'more rational and teleocratic' (p. 358).

Spicer makes the argument that far from being an ideologically neutral series of tools, reinventing government is an example of reform based, following Oakeshott, on the principles of purposive association, which run counter to the constitutional form of governance found in the United States, that of the civil association. Purposive associations are formed when individuals recognise themselves as bound together for the 'joint pursuit of some coherent set of substantive purposes or ends. Individuals within such a state acknowledge themselves and their actions as instrumental to the attainment of the purposes of the state' (p. 355). Human activities are seen as being directed towards the cooperative achievement of something substantive, with individuals conforming in both their own actions and their own ends to the achievement of a common, shared set of ends. A civil association, in comparison, is based upon the protection of diverse interests and ends, and of celebrating diversity instead. This can be linked back to constitutional idea of individuals being made free from the state wherever possible.

Spicer suggests that the US principles of civil association are in opposition to the purposive governance reforms of the 1990s encapsulated in reinventing government, and that it is necessary to find administrative reforms that go with the grain of this form of governance rather than against it, to work with traditions rather than against them. He suggests that there may be dangers of imposing a teleocratic approach to governance in a political culture that is fragmented and divided. Spicer suggests that the reinventing government reforms have not worked out as their formulators suggested, or as politicians imagined, because of the lack of fit between their proposals and the civil traditions of the United States.

Further reading

Stewart and Walsh's work provides an excellent account of the public administration approach (Stewart and Walsh, 1992), and Dunsire's paper a neat summary of how the discipline has changed (Dunsire, 1999). Readers interested in debates around the Public Administration should have a look at a wonderful collection published as the approach began to come under fire in 1971(Chapman and Dunsire, 1971). The reinventing government movement is expressed most clearly in its original manifesto (Osborne and Gaebler,

Part 2

Organisational ideas in public management under challenge

5

Paying for public services

Introduction

Public finance has already been mentioned several times in the first few chapters in this book. Intuitively it seems fairly obvious that one of the distinctive elements of public organisations is that they are paid for by public money – this is what makes them public in the first place. This is still largely the case – public services are usually paid for, at least to some extent, from public funds. However, private finance is playing a more significant role in the financing of public services as public organisations are increasingly trying to attract funds from the private sector through a number of means including user charging. Public financing has become a more complex area than has historically been the case, and so has become an important topic for exploration in its own right.

This chapter presents some facts and figures on public financing before moving on to considering the case for the public financing of public services, the problems it has caused and the alternatives that have been suggested. It then presents some models of the way that public services are financed, before giving a conclusion. It asks how should public services be paid for?

First though, it is useful to get some idea of the differences in public funding between countries.

Some facts and figures

The size of the public sector varies considerably from country to country in terms of its size as well as whether it is growing, contracting or staying about the same. Table 5.1 gives a sense of this.

In terms of general trends, few countries show a growth in the overall size of government spending as a proportion of GDP between 1990–2008 and 2009 (both of which are estimates). Most appear to have seen a growth in government expenditure between 1990 and 1995, brought on by difficult world economic conditions that led to growth in public

Table 5.1 General government outlays by country (% of nominal GDP)

	1990	1995	2000	2005	2008	2009
Australia	35.7	38.2	35.2	34.8	34.0	34.2
Canada	48.8	48.5	41.1	39.2	38.5	38.5
France	49.4	54.4	51.6	53.7	52.7	52.3
Germany	43.6	48.3	45.1	47.0	43.7	43.2
Italy	52.9	52.5	46.1	48.3	48.1	47.5
Japan	31.8	36.5	39.1	38.2	36.5	36.5
New Zealand	53.2	42.0	39.6	40.5	42.4	43.0
Norway	53.3	50.9	42.3	42.3	39.5	39.5
Spain	42.8	44.4	39.1	38.5	38.8	38.7
United Kingdom	41.9	44.5	37.1	44.6	44.8	44.6
United States	37.1	37.0	34.2	36.7	37.6	37.7
Euro area	50.4	50.6	46.2	47.5	46.1	45.7
Total OECD	40.9	42.2	39.1	40.8	40.6	40.4

Source: OECD Economic Outlook 82 database, Annex Table 25.

sector expenditures to compensate. Since then, however, most country's public sectors have seen a contraction (except for Japan, which started from a low base).

The size of public sectors vary considerably. In Japan, which is an exemplar of what has been called the 'Confucian welfare state' (Dean, 2002), social protection depends to a large extent on family support and the private sector employing staff not strictly necessary for their function (Ormerod, 1995). The recession in Japan has seen these surplus staff hit hard as employees are laid off due to economic stagnation. The United States also sticks out as being at the lower end of public expenditure, showing its strong tradition of depending upon civil association to solve welfare problems, with a weak central government that only introduced national health insurance as recently as the late 1960s, and then not in a comprehensive form.

At the top end of public spending in terms of the overall size of the economy is Sweden, which has nearly double the level of public expenditure as a proportion of GDP to Japan. The period 1990–2008/09 shows a dramatic fall, however, with expenditure coming into line with that of France, one of the major European economies, albeit one with a long-established public tradition. Germany saw a rapid rise in public expenditures at the beginning of the 1990s, not least because of reunification, but has attempted to reduce the size of the public sector amidst rising unemployment and fear of economic stagnation.

The United Kingdom saw a rise in public expenditure at the beginning of the 1990s, despite the presence of a Conservative government that had promised to reduce the size of the welfare state, and then a fall in the first years of the Labour government as it kept to tight public expenditure proposals it had inherited upon coming to power. In the 2000s the main growth of government expenditure has come through increased investment in the National Health Service, where it has introduced radical reform to try and improve what it perceives to be a poor quality of service.

Table 5.2 Government final expenditure by function (% of total)

	United States (%)	Sweden (%)	UK (%)
General public services	12.8	13.8	10.5
Defence	11.6	3.4	5.8
Public order and safety	5.7	2.4	5.8
Economic affairs	10.3	8.5	6.8
Environment protection	0.0	0.6	1.6
Housing and community amenities	1.7	1.5	2.1
Health	20.4	12.3	15.7
Recreation; culture and religion	0.9	1.8	2.1
Education	17.3	12.7	13.2
Social protection	19.4	42.9	36.5

Source: OECS Stat Extracts Dataset 11, Government Expenditure by Function 2004 data for US, 2003 data for UK and Sweden.

Across the OECD nations as a whole public expenditure has remained remarkably constant at around 40 per cent, which has become a kind of benchmark for many states of the size required of their public services. The Euro area, however, has seen a decline from well above that figure, over 50 per cent, with increased fiscal discipline between 1995 and 2000 particularly resulting in a fall in size of the public sectors as they prepared for the launch of the Euro currency.

Table 5.2, in contrast, shows the proportion of government expenditure of some of the countries below arranged by government function or service.

The above table shows some remarkable differences. The United States spends double the amount of the United Kingdom, and nearly four times as much as Sweden, on defence, and despite having a healthcare system where around 40 million Americans are uninsured spends a huge amount of public money on healthcare. Sweden spends over double the amount of the United States on social protection (generally speaking, social benefits), with the United Kingdom not far behind.

Different countries then have very different priorities for how they spend public funds. The United States proportionately places a premium on defence, public order, healthcare and education, but spends little on social protection. Sweden has a small defence budget as well as spending less proportionately than the United Kingdom or the United States on health and education, but has a larger public sector than the other two countries and so this is a small proportion of a larger expenditure as a proportion of GDP. The United Kingdom spends a great deal on public order and safety proportionally, as well as on social protection, despite over 20 years of governments attempting to find ways of reducing state benefit payments.

Given these huge differences, we are left wondering why some public services are funded by the state and some not. What is the case for funding public services?

The case for the public funding of public services

The classic form of public financing is where the state collects money through taxation, and uses the available funds, along with payments for items such as benefits and repayments of government debt, to pay for public services. The case for the public financing of public services was made in an earlier chapter, but is worth revisiting.

The public financing of services might be necessary because some services are regarded as being intrinsically public in nature either because competition cannot be made to work for them or because charging for them is non-excludable. Both of these arguments provide a justification for the public financing of public services.

The argument for public financing in relation to the difficulties of making competition work is based on the possibility that 'natural' monopolies might exist. This view suggests that might be most efficient if they are allowed to have a monopoly, or be the only provider of a good or service in a given area. There are few situations where it makes economic sense to have roads or railway lines running parallel to one another, so these provide an example. There might be some logic in having toll roads running next to public roads to attempt to divert those that are willing to pay away from public provision and to experience a less-congested road experience as a result. In areas where competition is impractical allowing a private monopoly carries the danger that the market might be exploited through higher than necessary prices. If the public sector runs the monopoly instead, however, and it can be held accountable for the running of the service (although this might be a big 'if', as Chapter 4 makes clear) it may make economic sense for the public sector to provide a particular facility or service as a monopoly, funded through general taxation.

Non-excludabilty is perhaps an even stronger argument for public funding. Non-excludable goods are those that are needed by many people, but which are difficult to charge for per item of use. Street lighting is the example used earlier – the people in a local area are taxed with that money then being put into a fund to pay for it on the grounds that everyone will benefit, whereas attempting to charge for lighting as it is used would be expensive and complex. Equally, asking people for voluntary contributions towards the cost of street lighting is unlikely to work because some people, even though they may be extensive night-time travellers and so substantial beneficiaries of street lighting, might attempt to 'free-ride' by assuming someone else will pay. If everyone takes the 'free rider' view, no funds will be available for lighting, and so a collective outcome is reached which is in few people's individual interest. The use of taxation provides a means for overcoming this problem.

There are other arguments in favour of the public financing of public services as well. First, there is the case where charging for a service which is generally used by the population will discriminate against those on lower incomes as they will have to pay proportionately (in terms of their income) more for that service than those on higher incomes. The use of taxation, which is collected at least partially proportionally to income through income tax, suggests that it might create a fairer way of paying for services used by large numbers of people. Where the service in question is regarded as being a basic human right, as having access to healthcare often is, then this would suggest that the service should be paid for by the state. In publicly funded healthcare systems everyone has the same access to the same services, but people pay different contributions to the cost of the service, based upon their individual tax contributions, which in turn are related to their incomes.

Finally there is also an argument that paying for some services via taxation might be the most efficient way of paying for them. Where a service is provided to a large number of people, and collecting charges on an individual basis might be expensive and time consuming, it might be more efficient instead to collect extra taxation to pay for it and to fund the services through the state instead. This often provides an argument for the preservation of public services than for new services becoming public. In situations where there is a political consensus that the charging of services should be attempted, but the costs of collecting the proposed charges would exceed the revenues of imposing them, they represent a poor policy decision. For many years there have been proposals for imposing 'hotel' charges in hospital beds in the UK National Health Service (that is, charging patients for hospital accommodation), but the cost of collecting those charges, especially where many patients would probably gain exemptions from them on low-income grounds, would probably exceed the revenues they would generate. As a result, they have never been implemented. The efficiency of much public financing therefore seems to present an argument for not changing existing public funding arrangements.

The problems of public funding

Paying for public services with public funds has several arguments in favour of it. However, there are also a number of problems. One of these is directly related to the taxation collection system as a whole.

General taxation funding

General taxation is the fund available to the government and is made up of direct taxation (typically income tax and corporation tax on profits) and indirect taxation (typically sales tax or value-added tax).

Paying for public services from general taxation requires the government to tax its population. An increase in funding for a particular public service will mean an increase in taxation unless savings can be found from cutting government services in another service (which may be unpopular – see below), unless the economy is growing, thereby giving the government an increased taxation take, or the government is prepared to run an increased financial deficit (which will certainly, in the modern world economy, make it a less attractive place to invest on international financial markets).

Increasing taxation is unlikely to make a government popular unless it is able to demonstrate that the increase is necessary and the area where it is being spent is regarded sympathetically by the public. An increased spending on child welfare may be popular, but the public may not be quite as sympathetic on giving increased benefits to single mothers, even though the two may come to much the same thing. Keeping taxation constant may even prove to be unpopular in a situation where the public believe that they are already paying too much tax, and it is a standard electoral strategy for right-of-centre political parties to campaign at election times to decrease the tax burden on the population. This means that there are strong tendencies for politicians to want to keep public expenditure within limits, and to keep taxation as low as possible.

Funding public services through general taxation does not guarantee any public service a set budget, rather it makes available a general fund which is used to pay for them. Each individual service must then usually make its case to the government department in charge of finance, or to the body responsible for running the government, for the amount of funding it requires. Typically the amount allocated to a government department will be strongly related to the amount it received in the previous year, so finance has a strong incremental element (Wildavsky, 1997), and that budgetary allocations have a strongly historical dimension. If a particular service has done well in public financing in the past compared to others, this does not mean that the less well-funded services will be better funded in the future, even where there is a strong case for funds being reallocated. Future budgetary allocations will tend to bear a strong resemblance to present and past ones with typically only marginal changes in funding either up or down.

The reasons for future budgets being strongly tied to present and past allocations are primarily political. If a particular service receives a considerable reduction in funding compared to past budget allocation, this will certainly lead to a reduction in the provision of that service. However, services, once the state has started to provide them, can be politically very difficult to remove from public provision. Once the public become used to receiving a service funded publicly, they may resent having to pay for it themselves again, or if it is expensive, simply be unable to afford it.

Equally the public might resent a reduction in the level of public service provided compared to that previously received – there might be less schools to choose from or rubbish collection occur less frequently. This phenomenon, where the public experience a reduction in the services provided to them adversely, tends to lead to a 'ratchet' effect – once services have been paid for by the state, it can be politically difficult for it to stop (this is an argument strongly related to the 'social expenses' argument by O'Connor – see Chapter 3). Where services are no longer publicly funded, or where public managers have to ask for contributions towards their running, this can lead to both the government and public managers becoming politically unpopular, and so they are often reluctant to make such a move.

The ratchet or social expenses problem means that the pattern of public funding for a particular service can become disconnected to its value or to its need. If a particular state has always spent a considerable amount of funds on, for example, healthcare, it can be very difficult for it to reduce these sums, even if it believes that the money would be better spent elsewhere. Cutting back on health service spending might be badly received by the public, and the government in question have to pay the electoral price for their decision, even if it was the right one to make.

A second problem is that because public services tend to have a significant proportion of wages and salaries in their total cost (as services tend to generally), an increase in funding for public services may reward better those working in them, but not necessarily increase the measurable output of the service. In the United Kingdom, the increased settlements given to the National Health Service since 2000 have been labelled by many sections of the media as a waste of money because they have not always meant that more people are treated, with the funds contributing especially towards an improvement in pay for doctors within the service. As such they have been portrayed in the media as a missed opportunity or a waste of public funds, when it may be that doctors were simply deserving of increased pay.

The problem of measuring whether increasing funding for public services actually improves their performance is exacerbated by the intrinsic difficulties in assessing the quality, and even quantity, of their output more generally. It is difficult to measure improvements in the performance of a school or a hospital because of the nature of the service it provides. If a school's exam results improve, does this mean it is educating its children better, or simply that it has become better at coaching them for exams? If one hospital has a lower death rate for a particular treatment than another, does this mean it is curing more people, or that it is treating more healthy people?

Increasing the funding of public services may not necessarily lead to an increase in the outputs which politicians are using to measure standards, even if they have improved. If politicians cannot demonstrate a definable improvement in performance, they may be reluctant to increase funding, even if it is justifiable on the grounds of staff simply deserving pay awards or historic under-funding. The issue of performance management in the public sector is picked up again more fully in Chapter 8.

Hypothecated funding

An alternative to the general taxation method of funding services is to 'hypothecate' funding for particular services. This means that the public will be told that a particular percentage of their taxation contribution is being used to pay for a specific service, with the idea being that this increases the accountability of the funding system. Services that are popular, such as healthcare and education, might be suitable for this kind of funding. Hypothecating funding in this situation might allow politicians to argue for increases in taxation to fund a particular service, so launch a campaign for extra sums to educate young children or to pay for improved healthcare.

The danger with hypothecated funding is that increasing the funding of services may not show demonstratable or quick improvements in their output (as noted above), and so runs the risk of politicians not being able to demonstrate improvement for the sums they have invested. Equally, it is fine for the public to have their taxation linked to services they are happy to pay for, but what if finance is hypothecated for areas they do not agree with? Defence expenditure might be necessary for the security of the state, but is unlikely to be popular amongst all sections of the community, who may wish, if expenditure is hypothecated, to want to withhold that part of their taxation payment. Hypothecation makes clear the links between taxation and expenditure, but where that public expenditure is in areas that particular sections of the public do not agree with, marking it out so visibly may incur resentment from them.

The problems of financing public services from public funds – summary

The difficulties of funding public organisations from public finance are concerned primarily with the taxation burden that they create, and which is increasingly unpopular with the public in most nations because of the tendency for public services to grow, and so to require increased levels of taxation.

However, there is a built-in financial tendency for public services, once they have reached a certain size, to remain at that level. Reductions in the sizes of public services are likely to be politically unpopular, even if they come with tax cuts, and increases in public provision require funding, and where the economy is not growing, and so able to pay for them from increased receipts from the same rates of tax, will require taxes to go up. Increasing the rates of funding for individual public services may also be difficult as it may not lead to quantifiable service improvements or require cuts in the budgets of other public services. There are considerable pressures in place to keep the budgets of public services about the same level from year to year.

The alternatives to the public financing of public services

If using public finance to pay for public services comes with significant problems, what are the alternatives?

Using private financing to pay for public services

Private financing can entirely replace public funding, or be in addition to it. Parents might send their children to a public school, but their children receive extra school trips, more tuition and a wider range of learning materials if their parents are prepared to pay additionally for them. Public hospitals may offer a basic level of service to the entire public, but be able to provide private rooms, a choice of food, bedside telephones, televisions and private rooms to those who are prepared to pay extra. Public organisations have increasingly had to find ways of charging for these extras services because of the reluctance of politicians to provide increased finance for them, and because of the need to demonstrate that they are being more efficient – providing higher levels of service for the same level of public funding. Providing extra services at an extra cost provides a necessary, but possibly divisive answer to these problems, as not everyone will be able to afford the 'premium' level of service.

Where private charging is introduced into public provision then this also tends to mean that services are at least partially provided by the private sector as well. Although the financing and provision of services is at least theoretically a separate issue, with there being good reasons why privately financed services might be publicly provided (to guarantee provision and minimum standards of service, for example), private financing will often lead to private provision.

It is important to be clear about what balance is expected between public and private financing for a service. A range of possible options are summarised in Table 5.3.

At one end of a spectrum private financing might be used to provide an additional service that most of the population do not regularly require. For example, in refuse collection, the state may not routinely take away particular kinds of rubbish, especially those that are particularly bulky or potentially dangerous. In these circumstances, it might be legitimate to expect the individuals that require such refuse services to pay additionally for them. Public managers will need to arrange for such 'additional' services to be managed as efficiently as possible and to try and make sure that the costs of providing such a service do not exceed the costs of running them, but this is a relatively straightforward role compared to the difficulties that come from a more widespread use of charging.

Next along the spectrum of public and private financing we might imagine public providers extending their range of offerings to those that lie a little outside of their usual services with the aim of extending their revenue base. Local authorities or local governments might have a range of in-house experts in a range of areas, despite the move to sub-contract services as much as possible from the 1980s onwards, and there may be opportunities to charge for the provision of these services on the open market. Estate services such as gardening and maintenance, for example, might be offered to the private sector through the market. Engineers are employed in civil maintenance departments and occupational health employees can advertise their services to the private sector in addition to their public employers. Public employees in these areas still work the majority of the

Table 5.3 The range of possibilities for public and private funding

Public funding with no private charging
Public funding with charging for non-standard services
Public funding with charging encouraged, and public provision offered to the private
   market
Public funding given income targets for private income generation
Public–private partnerships
Private funding

time for their own public service, but in addition to look for opportunities to try and raise additional income from the private market as well, particularly in times where they may not be at full capacity workloads in their public work.

If public workers can advertise their services to the private sector, it is a relatively short leap to giving them income targets to raise in addition to meeting their public duties. From being a desirable extra, income generation becomes an important part of their work. In UK universities, for example, it is becoming increasingly common for academics to be given income generation targets. These targets might be met by taking on additional teaching or consultancy or by successfully applying for research grants. Income targets might be made up from raising private sources of finance (through consultancy or teaching private sector students on short courses) or from public funds (through additional public teaching, or raising public research grants). Perversely, however, Newman, Raine and Skelcher (2001) suggest that targets can lead to a stifling of innovation, especially where they are accompanied by an attempt for a central or federal government to exert greater control. They found that inflexible targets created barriers to innovation, especially with regards to the proliferation of performance indicators, and sometimes even to local authority managers having to take the risk of not meeting a centrally imposed target in the short term in order to deliver long-term benefits locally.

Where public employees are expected to find additional sources of funds, public managers will be expected to find ways of incentivising and policing reward systems so that income generation targets are fair, and that the targets are set over appropriate timescales. To continue with the example of higher education academics, bonuses or promotions might be awarded to those whose work is judged to have been successful, but finding an appropriate timescale to make a judgement might be difficult. Annual timescales might be too short to consider successful research grant applications, and it may be several years before it is clear where a particular research programme was successful or not. If academic papers are cited by lots of other writers this may be an indication they have been influential, but it can also be an indication that they are widely recognised as being of poor quality. Academic managers will also have to give serious thought to what they will do in circumstances where staff are either overly successful or appear to be struggling. Either case brings with it its own problems.

If academics are very successful in raising external funds, they might find themselves in a situation where they become over-loaded, perhaps as a result of taking on too much consultancy, or being unexpectedly successful in grant applications. In this situation, managers will have to find ways of supporting academics to make sure that they are able to honour all of their commitments, or perhaps encouraging them to involve colleagues more often in their activities to reduce their individual workload. At the other extreme, where academics are not able to attract external funding, perhaps by not succeeding in grant applications, or being unable to provide consultancy, this will result in them appearing, by these criteria, to be unsuccessful in meeting their goals. However, this may not always be the case; some academic disciplines will, at any point in time, tend to have more funding opportunities available to them than others, and it seems odd to demand staff apply for grants that may not be actually available. The careless imposition of targets in a system where extra income is expected to be raised year-on-year will act as a disincentive as well as potentially leading to high-quality staff leaving, and so must be handled with some care.

Public–private partnerships

Where the system of public service financing goes beyond putting in place external income targets for public services, more regular collaboration with the private sector might be sought. The form of financing that might be encouraged in such a system is the use of public–private partnerships (PPP). The PPP is a relatively recent idea in implementation, but has existed theoretically for several decades. In this situation, public organisations, as the name implies, work with the private sector in some form or another to combine expertise or funding through the formation of an organisational partnership of one form or another.

The term 'PPP' conceals a great deal as the exact structure of the arrangements between public and private organisations might vary considerably from country to country (Grimshaw *et al.*, 2002). One model, favoured in the United Kingdom, is to get the private sector to provide construction expertise to the public and to get it to invest in infrastructure, with the public sector then paying for the capital project involved over an extended period, perhaps as long as 30 years. In this circumstance the public sector often gets much-needed capital infrastructure investment without having to pay for it up-front (as such, it is a lot like a hire-purchase arrangement), with the private sector partner benefiting from a guaranteed income source for several years, often at a considerable profit.

The private finance initiative (PFI) has been an example of a PPP that has gained momentum over the last ten years and resulted in a large number of hospitals and schools being built that would simply not have otherwise appeared, but the long-term costs of this building programme remain hugely contentious (Public Finance, 2007). Perhaps the best way of thinking about the PFI version of PPP is as a risk transfer. The public sector transfers to the private sector the risk involved in putting together a significant capital project, but the private sector transfers to the public sector the risk of making sure the contract is drawn up on terms that are of good value to the public purse. It seems, on balance, that the private sector has got the best out of this risk transfer so far, utilising its expertise in contracting to make considerable profits against local public managers lacking expertise in negotiating and contracting (Asenova and Beck, 2003). In both the United Kingdom and Australia, significant concerns have been expressed over the value for money of the scheme in prominent capital building projects.

In Europe, the idea of the PPP has been extended to try and include more social goals, and in Germany and Switzerland particularly, the notion of 'Public Social Private Partnerships' has become more prevalent. These attempt to combine long-term financing within an explicit social agenda that encourages co-operation between a larger number of partners (they must have at least three) and which attempt to combine both financing (the main area of focus of PFI) with a framework for dealing with the practical delivery of services. Unlike many PFI agreements, which have limited disclosure agreements for fear of breaching commercial confidentiality, openness and transparency are amongst the key principles that partnership must sign up to, and, for the private partners involved can be a way of displaying greater corporate social responsibility. These European innovations are important because they demonstrate a different stress on PPP compared to those often found in the United Kingdom and Australia, moving away from the simply raising of public finance towards more genuinely collaborative arrangements. However, only time will see if these new approaches create genuinely better value for money than has often been seen on previous projects.

Private provision

At the final end of the spectrum between public and private financing would be a model where private financing dominates in both public and private provision. Even advocates of a free-market approach would probably suggest that some public employees remain funded by the public sector – particularly the police – especially where their responsibility is to protect property rights. However, it is possible to imagine a model where the state is dramatically reduced in size and the private sector expected to finance most of the things we presently regard as public services. The logic behind this is an appealing one – if we all pay a lot less tax, then we would be richer, and so be able to afford to pay school fees for our children, healthcare insurance for our families, and we could subscribe to pay for access to roads we needed to travel on. The argument behind this view is that individuals, rather than the state, are best placed to decide how their money should be spent. Receiving a pay-slip and seeing exactly how much money has been deducted in terms of taxation, or having to meet a very large annual payment to the state to discharge taxation responsibility, can be a demoralising one, and even the most strongest supporter of public services can sometimes wonder what on earth it is we are getting back for all the money we pay to the government.

This individualistic view of society is appealing in that we would all have a lot more cash if we paid a lot less tax. However, we would all have to take a great deal more personal responsibility as well. Being unable to afford schooling for children would lead to a choice between not providing schooling at all (which would have significant implications for the future of the economy), of relying upon charitable schools for education (which were commonplace until not so long ago), or self-educating children at home (which families might struggle with where parents have to work full-time), or of simply not having children until such a time that schooling can be afforded. The decision to bring children into the world would be based, even more explicitly than it presently is, on the ability of parents to afford them. The ability to drive a car would depend not only on the ability of individuals to afford to buy a car, petrol and insurance, but also on being able to pay charges to drive on roads. If the public sector did not provide them, all roads would be toll-roads.

In a private market, public managers would not really exist. If provision was private, then either banks or shareholders would have to be satisfied, and so profits are made. There might be opportunities to work in charitable institutions with not-for-profit goals, but the constant concern in such enterprises would be ensuring continuity of funding to allow services to continue to be provided. Charitable funding means that services depend upon contributions, and sometimes substantial benefactions from the better-off, in order to be able to continue to operate. In times when giving declines, difficult choices might have to be made about the future of services. In these situations, the role of managers in the third sector (in charities and other not-for-profit organisations) becomes an outward-facing one, attempting to raise money from potential givers, as well as trying to make the best possible use of the money raised. To some extent, all organisations need to do this, but the pressure grows considerably where funding is solely from either market transactions or charitable giving, and there may be a tendency for time horizons of planning and work to become considerably shortened in an environment where money is continually being sought to allow services to be offered in the next period (Hutton, 1996).

Funding and the nature of public services

Utilising private markets in public provision questions about the nature of public services; do services commonly regarded as being public cease to become public when they are offered by the private sector instead? This can be usefully reviewed looking at the situation in US hospitals based on private, and to some extent, not-for-profit provision. Hospitals that have to satisfy the needs of shareholders as well as those of their patients may have a need to deny access to medical care for those that are unable to pay for it through insurance, or where the hospital to be able to offer it on the grounds of need (pro bono work). Assuming that in the United States, as elsewhere, doctors and nurses are motivated by doing public good, this may cause a considerable clash between their private values and the ability of their organisation to fund them. Michael Moore's film *Sicko* presents a damning indictment of such as system where he shows insurance companies attempting to find ways of preventing patients from receiving care, and hospital managers becoming a little too concerned on their need to make money rather than look after patients.

The tension between budgetary responsibilities and patient care is not exclusively limited to non-public providers, but is certainly amplified when organisations have to work outside of the public setting. Managers providing public services in a privately financed environment have difficult choices to make; they must find a way of making sure that their organisations are viable and that patients/customers who can afford to pay their bills do so, but that the organisation meets its goal of doing good for the general public to the maximum possible extent.

Funding public services through private means does not change the nature of the service intrinsically, it does lead to managers having to deal with some difficult questions.

An open-minded view of this dilemma is that it simply means that managers have to incorporate the wishes of shareholders or other financial partners into decision-making processes in the organisation alongside the range of other stakeholders with whom they must deal on an everyday basis. The concern is not that managers in these organisations are having to make themselves more financially accountable – this is a fact of life for all employees in public organisations more generally. It is that the financial imperative of making sure that services break even or generate a surplus becomes the overriding emphasis of all management in such organisations to the extent that they lose their public mission. Different funding mechanisms do not automatically change the nature of public organisations, but they do have a tendency to make more explicit the underlying logics of their operation.

Conclusion

In all, the values of a particular society will play a strong role in terms of the choice made about how public services should be funded. Societal values produce institutional inheritances that strongly influence the choices made over service financing. In a country where individual freedoms are valued highly, and where a strong private market presence has been the case, as in the hospital sector in the United States, it will be extremely difficult to make an argument for greater public provision. Attempts to reform healthcare in the first Clinton administration failed so publicly that subsequent governments have been reluctant to try and face up to the problem of around 40 million Americans having to get by without health insurance. Strong interest groups from insurance companies and powerful hospitals will lobby fiercely to prevent change to the healthcare funding system, which is the most expensive in the world, but still fails to provide healthcare for the entire population. This is entirely understandable – if the free market is the preferred mode of governance, then inequalities will tend to exist as they provide the dynamism through which markets incentivise improvements. In working in a private sector-dominated environment, public managers face the dilemma of providing a service for their individual, fee-paying customers and meeting their obligations to the public as whole, including those that may be unable to afford their services.

At the opposite end of the funding spectrum a different dilemma is in place. Funding services entirely from the public purse may create a dynamic where there is little incentive for managers and public professionals to behave in a responsible way towards resources. As well as this, there may be a little incentive to provide a high-quality service as, with the profit motive lacking, public organisations may continue to operate whether they are making a substantial surplus or a substantial deficit. The challenge facing public managers in publicly funding settings is finding ways to incentivise high levels of performance whilst at the same time respecting professional autonomy. They must also find ways of getting those delivering services to treat budgets seriously where they lack the legitimacy and imperative that the marketplace confers on them. A publicly funded and provided service may mean that the collective good overrides the importance of the individual to whom a particular service is being provided, and that budgetary goals are seen as being unimportant.

CASE STUDY

Public and private schooling

Services which are paid for publicly in one economy might be charged for in another. In the United Kingdom, most children are educated in schools paid for publicly, but in the United States public schools are sometimes regarded as being where only the children of the poorest families are taught. Even this, however, is subject to considerable variation, as there are cities in the United Kingdom, where many middle-class families choose to pay for their children to attend private secondary education providers because of concerns about the standard of public provision. This contributes towards a self-fulfilling prophecy of poor public education as only those parents that cannot afford a private education send their children to public schools, and high-income parents, who are also likely to be more highly educated and more likely to demand improvements from local schools, send their children to private schools instead. This has the danger of generating a failure of 'voice' (Hirschman, 1970) where the most articulate groups in society are no longer engaged with public services.

In private school education in the United Kingdom, other problems emerge. The United Kingdom has some of the most famous private schools in the world, such as Eton, and such schools have charitable status, implying that they do good not only for the pupils who enter them, often with their parents paying substantial annual fees, but also for the general community.

The charitable status of private schools has come under increased criticism in recent years, with some schools struggling to demonstrate that they are providing much good for the public at large. The present UK Labour government has suggested that private schools may need to do more to demonstrate this general good to the public than at present and so retain their charitable status. Private schools typically offer bursaries to students whose parents might struggle to afford their fees, but is this enough? Should managers in private schools be required to demonstrate that they are contributing in a far wider sense to local communities in order to be able to claim the tax advantages of being a charity? Private schools have to balance their commitments to their fee-paying parents by providing the best possible education to the children in their case, with a charitable duty to do good more generally. This is a significant challenge for managers within them.

In the United States, there is a strong concern with getting public schools to work better. The prestigious *Academy of Management Journal* recently published a forum discussing the work of Professor William Ouchi (Ouchi *et al.*, 2005). Ouchi's book *Making Schools Work* (Ouchi, 2003) suggested that the biggest obstacle to public schools improving was the large, centralised bureaucracies that often came with them. The solution, in Ouchi's view, is to 'decentralize decision making down to the operating subunits . . .. It applies to every industry in the country' (Ouchi, 2003:930).

Ouchi compares New York City public schools with local Catholic schools, and found that 'the New York City public schools had 10 times as many students as the Catholic schools, about 1.2 million and 120,000, respectively. The Catholic schools had 22 central office staff; if the city had a proportionate number, it should have about 220. Actually it had 25,500' (p. 931). He argues that the creation of this bureaucracy takes the control of the individual schools away from their Principals. Ouchi compares the situation in Edmonton, where decentralisation has occurred and nearly 92% of the budget is controlled by Principals, with New York, where around 7% of funds are under their control, and suggests that in Edmonton that 'the public schools have become so popular that there are no private schools left' (p. 931).

Ouchi suggests that one of the main difference between public and private schools is that in private schools everyone teaches through from the headmaster to the librarian, allowing them to have smaller assignment loads to mark and comment upon than public schools with large bureaucracies, and this motivates students to improve by offering them the chance for one-to-one tuition.

In all, Ouchi's prescription boils down to 'local solutions and autonomy' (p. 933) for the improvement of local schools – in many respects bearing a similar argument to the reinventing government movement (see Chapter 4). In terms of funding, however, his argument is arguably more radical in allowing individual school Principals the maximum amount of autonomy in how they spend their funds. Can devolving budgets and allowing autonomy really be the driver for improving public education? Ouchi seems to believe so.

Further reading

The OECD website is a little difficult to navigate and find particular series of data, but is overall an excellent source of facts and figures concerned with public financing. A good place to start is at www.oecd.org/statsportal, but you may find that some of the data series require a subscription to that. If you are in Higher Education, your library may be able to provide access.

Ouchi's work on public schooling in the United States is frank about the need for a greater decentralisation of funding, and is worth reading as it tends to provoke extreme reactions from public managers (Ouchi, 2003). Charging is advocated by writers concerned with the public value movement (Moore, 1997) and an interesting discussion of the variation in public funding is provided by Jackson (2003).

The use of markets in the
public sector

Introduction

The vast majority of the services now associated with the public sector were once delivered via the private market in some form or another before the creation of welfare states. Healthcare systems, for example, developed through doctors being able to charge patients for care, and those patients that could afford to pay navigated themselves through a market of competing services.

Recent public reforms have tended to try and reintroduce the dynamism of the market into public services on the grounds that it will make them more responsive and user-focused. The questions this chapter seeks to answer is not only how markets change public management, but also asking what conditions need to be in place for a market to work for public delivery? When do markets work and when do they not? Before these questions can be explored, however, it makes sense perhaps to begin by trying to be clearer as to what is meant by the term 'market' in the first place.

What is a market?

For a concept that is so widely used in economics, business and management, it is surprisingly difficult to define exactly what a market is. Economics textbooks present enticing frameworks showing how supply and demand interact to deliver equilibrium prices and quantities available for purchase in a cut-throat world where firms enter and exit at a moment's notice and consumers are ruthless and supremely well informed in their purchasing decisions. Economists have always claimed that they are describing the way markets work, but in more recent years criticism from sociologists have suggested that instead they are providing elaborate theories that prescribe how markets should work rather than reflecting any empirical reality (Callon, 1998, 1999). Sociologists examining buying and selling in settings such as stock and commodity markets have suggested that, even where conditions exist that are close to the preconditions specified by economists for their efficient operation, the economic theory of the market bears little resemblance to what is actually happening. Instead, they suggest, it takes a huge amount of regulatory effort and organisation to get buyers and sellers to behave anything like the way economists say they should be, and that the term 'market' is therefore both a reified, theoretical idea advocated by economists and a series of very different exchange processes experienced by individuals (Aldridge, 2005). It is therefore important to separate the idea of the market from the practice of it, and to be careful not to mix up the two. The influence of economics-based ideas on public markets has been huge (Ferlie, 1992), but that does not mean that they actually resemble the theory much in practice (Ferlie *et al.*, 1996).

The preconditions for a market to work

Given the ambiguity over what a market actually is, it seems important to define what features need to be in place to claim that a market exists. One way of doing this is to think about the configurations of buyers and sellers that markets require. Markets are often contrasted with monopolies, with the latter form being where there is only one provider, or only one dominant provider. As monopolies are not well regarded because of their potential to exploit their unique seller position, it makes sense to suggest that one pre-condition for the functioning of a marketplace is that there need to be several providers in place, and that they are in a competitive relationship with one another. There need to be enough providers to prevent them colluding and so forming an effective monopoly. On the supply side, a market needs a minimal number (five seems a good starting point) of providers in a competitive relationship with one another. On the demand side, a situation where there is one dominant purchaser (a monopsony) needs to be avoided as this will skew relationships too much in favour of those purchasing goods or services. A dominant purchaser will leave providers in a position where they are weak because losing favour with the major purchaser in the marketplace will mean they go out of business. To achieve some kind of balance there must therefore be a reasonable number of purchasers.

In addition to the relationship between buyers and sellers, purchasers also need information about the goods and services offered by the suppliers, and to be able to understand it. There is little point in having a competitive market for a service that no one understands as any selection made will be arbitrary. Equally, providers need information about the potential customers in a marketplace so that they can inform them of the goods or services they are offering. Markets cannot function without good information circulating and both buyers and sellers being able to understand it.

Equally, markets need at least a little renewal from entry and exit into them. Where providers have been in a market for a number of years, their form of competition may have settled down into a form where each has found a comfortable place with little threat or drive for improvement any more. There needs to be some means of preventing this

Table 6.1 The basic preconditions for a market to be able to work successfully

Minimum numbers of supplier in a competitive relationship with one another	Without a competitive relationship not clear what the purpose of a market is
Minimum number of purchasers who understand providers' offerings	Without understanding of providers' offerings, purchasing will be ineffective, and contacts will have significant transactions costs. Minimum number needed to prevent purchasers from having too much power
Some means of entry and exit	Without entry and exit, danger of market stagnating and becoming uncompetitive

from happening, but without providers in markets changing so frequently that there is no continuity of supply, and purchasers being unable to understand how the market works any more.

A market therefore exists where there are a minimum number of suppliers of a good or service organised in a competitive relationship on the supply side, and a minimum number of purchasers who understand the offerings of the suppliers, on the demand side (Le Grand, 1991). These elements are summarised in Table 6.1. Without these basic pre-requisites, it is hard to see how a market can work. Being careful in what is necessary for a market to exist is not simply a definitional issue. Defining the pre-requisites of a market allows an analysis of how markets that have been constructed to deliver public goods will work, whether they will favour the supply or demand side, and what challenges public managers face in the particular market environment in which they find themselves.

Different kinds of public markets

It is important to be aware that there are several kinds of markets, and that significant differences might exist from one setting to another. A generic model exists where the conditions for a market are most closely met; there are a reasonable number of purchasers and providers, and they understand each other's offerings as information about the market is clear and understandable. Then there are simple variations on this; where there are relatively few providers compared to purchasers; where providers are organised in more of a collaborative than competitive relationship; where there are relatively few purchasers compared to providers; and where purchasers have little understanding of the market when they are working within. By working through these variations it is possible to see how the role of public managers varies in each situation. A good starting point is to examine the generic model of the market and how it might apply in a public service setting.

Table 6.2 Sources of competitive advantage

Source of competitive advantage	Benefits	Problems
Quality	Allows users to choose best providers and drive up standards	Quality can be difficult to measure and assess, and selection on arbitrary measures instead
Cost	Drives up efficiency	May creating skimping on service quality and to public-funded services having to provide expensive services where new entrants will not enter markets
Niche	Allows focus on a single core service	May need public-funded services to provide cover for gaps in provision

The generic or 'balanced' market

In a balanced market there are a minimum number of suppliers organised competitively, and a minimum number of purchasers with an understanding of the suppliers' offerings. There are likely to be public managers on both the supply and the demand side, so it is necessary to examine both perspectives on the market.

Managers on the supply side

On the supply side, a competitive relationship means that managers have to be aware of what others are offering within the market, and to try and improve upon it. In line with business theory more generally, there are several possible sources of advantage they might seek. Managers might seek to gain an advantage over their competitors based on the quality of the services they offer, the cost of those services, or by providing a niche product that is presently not being provided by the market (Porter, 2004). These sources are summarised in Table 6.2, and discussed in detail below.

Competing on the quality of public services

Measuring the quality of public services comes with particular problems. In education, exam results might be seen to be a good index of quality as the most measurable outcome for students, and these can be used in national or international rankings of schools and universities. As rankings and ratings have become more significant, it has become an important part of public managers' jobs to attempt to drive up the elements of their provision measured by rating systems. This can create difficult tensions where rankings fail to capture (as they almost invariably do, because of the difficulty of measuring the output of public services) the nature of the service. Exam results do not really capture fully whether schools are doing a good job or not, even if they are clearly a very important factor.

Rating systems can have perverse effects upon public institutions. In higher education, for example, rating systems might measure student opinion and the proportion of students receiving 'good' degrees from a particular institution. This seems sensible on the surface of it, but can create problems where managers encourage lecturers to simplify teaching and not challenge students in order to try and achieve better student feedback. Pressure can also be brought to bear at exam boards, where student marks are approved, for lecturers to give higher marks than they strictly believe should be awarded in order to achieve particular proportions of degree classification awards.

Any performance measure or rating system risks creating perverse incentives for providers of services, getting them to focus not on the service as they believe it should be delivered, but on whatever variables are currently being used to rank organisations in those areas. The problems of performance measurement are explored in greater depth in Chapter 8 and are clearly a significant part of being a public management in a market environment.

Where there are very strong central performance management systems in place for public organisations they will not only have to try and compete with other providers based on the measures they use, but may also be required to conform to a whole range of measures imposed by the state as well. In this situation, managers may have to choose which targets are most important, or even whether they believe that the targets and measures are so unreflective of the goals of their organisations that they will focus their energies on other areas of their organisations instead that may be less easily measurable.

Those designing performance management systems for central government have sometimes expressed incredulity that managers are unable to both conform to central targets and provide what they believe is a good service to the public (Barber, 2007), but there is a real possibility that managers might be so disillusioned with targets and measures from outside rating bodies or from the central state that they begin to work on an entirely different basis, meeting only the targets that might lose them their jobs, and judging for themselves whether their organisations are a success or not (Greener, 2005). Where this happens, the market environment is in danger of breaking down as it no longer carries the support of those working within it, and the state perhaps needs to think again about its use of markets and measures.

Competition on cost grounds

Depending on how markets have been set up, competition may also be possible within them on cost ground. In some cases the state may have explicitly removed this option, trying to force competition to be on quality grounds only, by setting a standard price to be paid for a specified service. In other cases, however, competition on cost may be a central part of public contract competition.

The choice of provider when contracting out of public services is often decided largely on cost grounds. In this situation, services are put out to tender and the provider who is able to offer the level of service specified in the contract at lowest cost will often secure the contract. This offers the chance for public services to be offered at the lowest possible cost, and so to drive up efficiency.

The problem is that there may be some areas of public provision which are simply so complex and subject to variation that providers may not be interesting in entering a market for them. Some medical treatments, for example, are so difficult to perform and have such a wide variety of outcomes that it may be difficult to standardise a contract and the cost of the service might not be specifiable in advance. Equally, social care services that are provided for long periods of time may require an almost open-ended commitment to supporting particular people with special needs, and may make it extremely difficult for private or not-for-profit providers to guarantee service into the future. In these kinds of case, public provision may have to be offered to guarantee that the service takes place not irrespective of cost, but without it being a focal point for concern.

A related problem is that, where complex contracts are necessary between suppliers and providers, or where significant infrastructure is needed in order for contracts to occur, transactions costs rise significantly and may mean that any efficiency gains from markets are reduced or driven out. Where neither purchasers nor providers understand the market being put in place, and are required to make use of complex technologies to make it work, then significant transactions costs will be incurred in terms of both their time and the opportunity cost the new systems might create by distracting them from serving the public. Competing on cost will therefore become extremely difficult for smaller providers who may find the transactions costs of being involved in the market make their entry into it unworkable.

Competing through niche advantage

Finally, niche advantage can be sought where provision focuses on a clearly defined product or service where the market is not meeting the needs of a particular group very well at present. Because most public provision is in the area of services, there is huge potential for them to become more individual and tailored to meet the public's needs. Niche providers entering the market may mean that the group that they service have their needs particularly closely met, so providing a very high level of service that publicly funded providers may not be able to achieve.

The problem with providers seeking niche advantage is that, by definition, they are not interested in serving the market at large, and so other providers will have to be meeting the gaps in the market that they leave. If this does not occur, public provision may still be necessary to make sure that the public's needs as a whole are met, and this may have to occur through monopoly provision if no competing suppliers can be found. A second concern is that niche providers, because of the narrowness of their provision, may have an unfair advantage over other providers as they will typically be smaller than large providers, and so have a cost and resource base that allows them to operate more flexibly.

Promoting organisations in public markets

In a balanced market environment, public managers on the supply side must try and make sure not only that their organisations are performing well according to the measures currently in place to assess them, but also that the purchasers of services know about their performance and understand what is distinctive about their organisations. This is an often overlooked aspect of public service management. It is one thing for public managers to know that their organisations are performing well, but quite another to be able to demonstrate it to the users and purchasers of their services. What this entails is for public managers on the provider side to try and construct a 'frame' for explaining the performance of their organisation, which has a straightforward message, and which shows their organisation in a good light. This is extremely hard – the frame chosen must be straightforward enough for non-specialists to understand, but complex enough to capture the performance of their organisation and be representative of it. This is the role of promotional marketing in the public sector – not to miss-sell or confuse potential purchasers, but to portray their organisation in such a way that both represents it and explains its strengths. The role of marketing in public management is clearly far more significant in a market environment, and is explored in greater depth in the next chapter.

On the supply side then, public managers are responsible for ensuring not only that their organisation is performing well (as they will always be), but also that they can demonstrate that it is performing well when compared to its competitors in a form that the purchasers of services can understand – the two are not the same thing.

Managers on the demand or purchaser side

A balanced market environment means that purchasers cannot exert a greater influence than suppliers. The purchasers in a public market might be individual users for whom the state purchases a service (by paying for it directly) or by the state giving individuals budgets by either paying funds to them directly or by giving them the ability to spend state funds to a particular level, through a system such as using vouchers. Equally, in many systems of public organisation the state may also purchase services from either public or private providers on behalf of users, who then have little or no say in the choice of the services purchased.

Assessing contracts

Where public organisations are acting as purchasers, one of the key roles of public managers is attempting to assess the needs of their particular public, and to make sure that the services that are purchased meet them. This is the case whether the managers themselves are purchasing the services on behalf of the public, or whether the public are purchasing them through some kind of voucher or devolved budget system. It is incumbent on public managers on the demand side to make sure that providers are held to account for the quality of the services they provide. A market-based system means public services are accountable through contracts, and so it is vital that those contracts are monitored and assessed in terms of both their value for money and quality. Where a particular provider is not meeting the required standard, managers need to make sure that corrective action is taken. Because of the difficulty in measuring public service outputs, it is possible that purchasing managers may even need to override the opinion of service users in their decisions about the level of quality of service the providers are offering. An example will illustrate this.

Where a university is allowing (or even encouraging) staff to teach material that is not challenging, and then over-marking student papers, the students themselves, if they are primarily focused on exam results only, may be delighted with this. However, managers on the supply side of the marketplace are plainly failing in their duty to provide an education by focusing on elements of their service that are easily measured rather than dealing with the underlying idea of education – to get students to learn. As such, it may be left to managers on the purchasing side to intervene, acting against students' wishes if necessary, to drive standards back up either by sending their students to other institutions or by demanding that educational standards improve at the university that is under-teaching and over-marking.

In some circumstances the user view might be entirely appropriate in assessing service performance. In an age often taken to be one in which the consumer voice should always come first, it can be regarded as patronising and old-fashioned for public managers to be assessing whether the public should have the final say in judging standards of public organisation performance, but it is necessary because of the tensions between individual and collective service provision, and because serving the needs of users may not necessarily be in the collective public interest – as in the example of the university above.

There may be other means by which both purchasing and providing institutions may be held to account, with democratic accountability being the most obvious. Political representatives might attempt to hold public organisations to account, or they may even be elected to run public organisations, particularly at city level. The existence of markets, however, clearly gives public managers the responsibility of ensuring both that contracts are monitored to give the public a good standard of service and that the measures of success in those contracts are not so crude as to fail to capture, or at least acknowledge, the complexities of measuring public outputs.

Again, as noted in Chapter 5, arranging PPPs have become an increasingly important part of public managers' roles. The problem appears to have been that the relative lack of experience of public managers in writing and negotiating contracts, compared to their private partners, has led to the private partners often getting the upper hand and putting in place terms that have given them substantial advantages over the course of the contracts (Asenova and Beck, 2003). It has not helped that public partners in PPP agreements have often effectively been told that they are the only route to securing much-needed capital funding, and so they have been given little or no choice in entering into such agreements. Public managers have had to acquire a great deal of contracting expertise very quickly, and the often absence of national templates or standard forms of contracts has not helped them.

Making contracts

Before contracts can be assessed they must be brokered, and so public managers will be responsible for the decision of which services will be purchased, how much of them, at what standard, and from whom. In Chapter 5, research suggested that budgetary allocations tend to be largely a function of decisions made in the previous year. In many cases, purchasing decision tend to be subjected to these pressures. Once particular providers have received public contracts to provide services, it can be politically difficult to withdraw them. Where public organisations lose public funding, their future may be jeopardised, and the state must make a conscious decision because the removal of public provision in a given area might mean it loses direct control over all provision in that area. This is public services act as a provider of last resort, guaranteeing that services will continue even if all private and not-for-profit providers decide to exit from the market, and the state retaining its provider of last resort function means that there are political limitations on the extent to which the market mechanism might be allowed to operate.

Equally, however, the state might deliberately favour private providers by giving subsidies and better rates of funding than those available to public providers in order to attract new entrants into public markets. Attracting new entrants might be justified on the grounds of dissatisfaction with existing providers, or on the grounds that in the long-term, a larger number of providers will drive the price of services down and the quality up, and so paying a subsidy for new entrants might be cost-efficient in the short term. These kinds of arguments were made in the UK National Health Service in the 2000s to attempt to achieve a more 'mixed' economy of providers in the new internal market for care introduced then, by getting private and not-for-profit providers to compete with existing public hospitals and clinics.

Costs and benefits

Decisions about which public services should be contracted for have led to the development of a range of increasingly complex techniques since the 1980s, with economists particularly prominent. Complex models of the benefits and costs of services have been compiled that then attempt to list services into rank order of which achieve the greatest benefits at least cost. Health economics has become an industry with both academics and consultants constructing indexes of possible treatments and advising governments how their money can be best spent to achieve maximum returns on their investment in healthcare. Quality adjusted life year tables, for example, attempt to examine the cost of treatments in terms of the health benefits they give, adjusted in turn for the quality of life they might deliver.

In the United States, experimental attempts at local democracy have been made where those responsible for purchasing health services have consulted with citizens to attempt to draw up a list of which services should be funded using public money and which should not. The difficulty this raises is that the services economists advocate worthy of funding may be very different from those that professionals in the service believe are important, which may be different again from those that the public would like to see receiving funding. In these circumstances, it is difficult to see how public managers are meant to make purchasing decisions. They have a duty not only to purchase services according to what represents best value for public funds (which is likely to follow the advice of the economists), but also to take into account the views of the professionals that often have to deliver public services (which would favour that group), as well as serving the needs of their local population (who may have views which are extremely hard to either collect or summarise in any coherent fashion in themselves). Where these different groups produce very different priorities, making final decisions is a very political exercise as it attempts to incorporate the wishes of these possibly competing voices, but decisions also need to be justifiable. Given these tensions, public managers responsible for purchasing decisions appear to be in a near impossible situation.

Lotteries

One response to the dilemma of what the state should do where there is a shortfall of public funds to provide a particular service is to fund them through the use of a lottery. In the Untied States, the states have conducted experiments in allocating government funding that first works out how many people meet the eligibility criteria for potential funding (such as severity of illness, for example), and then allocates funds according to a lottery system with only a limited number of those meeting eligibility criteria subsequently receiving state funding.

In the United Kingdom, school places have been allocated by lottery to try and avoid parents of children from more wealthy backgrounds taking up all of the places at schools rated highly. In this case, every child who requires a public school place in a given year is given a place within a local area randomly, with the hope that this will mix up ability levels and social classes to the extent that no school will have a built-in advantage because of where parents live, or because of previous school results. The upside of this is it should be possible to judge schools entirely free from 'input' considerations such as the educational abilities of their intakes and the wealth of their parents. The problem is that many parents, fearful of their children being allocated a place at a school they do no like, have taken their children out of the public schooling sector and have chosen a private school instead, leading to the potential for the area as a whole to suffer from a lack of 'voice' (see Chapter 5). Lotteries highlight the tension between trying to work out a fair system between the public as a whole and the individual members of it. They may work well in providing a fair chance for everyone, but that may not be consolation for the individual member of the public that feels he or she has lost out as a result.

Intermediaries

A further complication (if one is needed) is that intermediary bodies often appear where markets are created in public services. Intermediaries appear where markets have reached a level of complexity that some kind of brokerage, or information-based role, is required. Healthcare again represents a vivid example of this. Insurance companies might be licensed by the state to oversee funding arrangements for the provision of healthcare, often receiving funding from the state to supplement payments made by individuals and their employers. These insurance companies then might purchase case, using a mix of public and private funds, from both public and private providers, or even from their own organisation if they provide as well as purchase care, but may themselves not be public organisations.

Where non-public intermediaries are an important part of the process of delivering services, this creates an additional level of complexity as public managers may be responsible for overseeing the performance of the service in question, but depend upon intermediate organisations to deliver and purchase care on their behalf. In these circumstances, their responsibility is to attempt to hold these intermediate organisations to account on behalf of the public they are serving. Issues of accountability and blame come to the fore, as it is crucial that public managers do not simply blame these intermediate organisations where problems occur, but that they do scrutinise their performance. Policymakers need to make sure that there are clearly defined roles and responsibilities so that where a public service failure occurs, which at the worst could be disaster such as a train crash, it is important that the response of every organisation involved in the network of provision is to not to try and blame someone else. Sadly, this appears to have been the case in the period since rail privatisation in the United Kingdom, with track companies attempting to blame sub-contracted maintenance operators, no one being prepared to take responsibility for the lives lost. The creation of intermediaries must not take responsibility out of the system.

A similar range of problems can also occur where public managers purchase services from private providers. The danger in these circumstances is that problems are not learned from, as they instead degenerate into cycles of mutual blame with no organisation prepared to take responsibility. The contract environment can make this worse as admitting to error can mean a threat of withdrawal of the contract in the future for providers, or for allegations of incompetence in purchasing for managers involved in errors on that side. In either case, a contractual environment always carries with it the threat of legal action where errors are made. This can provide a strong disincentive for collaborative working between purchasers and providers which public managers have to work hard to overcome, as they will have to find ways of resolving disputes in a way where learning can take place, but accountability is still in place.

In practice, balanced markets, those not dominated by providers, purchasers (or intermediaries), presents a model of distributing resources based upon a 'governance' approach. Here, a regime of organisations is established in which no organisation is able to dominate any other, and so must form relationships with other organisations based on either trust or contract for the system as a whole to work. The extent to which this is the case varies considerably from service to service and from nation to nation. In centralised Parliamentary systems the state will tend to retain a stronger role in the policy process and the management of public systems because of the strong sense of central accountability and the continuing temptation to get more involved in the everyday running of public organisations. One of the defining features of the United Kingdom is its centralised political system and its first past the post electoral system, leading to whichever political party, so long as it is able to retain a Parliamentary majority, being able to pursue policy change more or less as it wishes for its time in power. As such, the United Kingdom has tended to see radical public reform under both Thatcher and Blair governments, and underwent a programme of nationalisation and public service expansion in the 1940s under the first post-war Labour government under Attlee. In the United States, however, because of the more fragmented state system, radical public reform has been more difficult to achieve with Presidents attempting radical reform, especially in contentious areas such as healthcare, finding their reform plans blocked in Congress, where a different political party may hold a majority, and far more power is passed to state-level government away from the federal centre. In the latter instance, where power is already far more diffused, the governance model seems more explanatory than in systems where central dominance persists.

Provider dominance

Having explored a 'balanced' view of the state as an analytical ideal type, it is now possible to explore the implications of variations of it in terms of provider and purchaser power. The first of these might be where there are relatively few providers compared to purchasers.

In this situations public management purchasers face a problem; each provider has several purchasers where they can secure contracts from, but each purchaser has only a limited choice of providers. Public managers on the purchasing side therefore face an even more difficult situation in the balanced market, as the threat of removing a contract from a provider because of poor performance is less credible where there are fewer providers to contract with, and the scope of competition reduced. Purchasing public managers therefore approach a situation where they may be trying to achieve a contestable rather than a competitive market – one where the threat of competition is used to attempt to drive improvements from providers rather than competition itself. Purchasing public managers have the threat of moving contracts to other providers, but may avoid using markets competitively because moving that would lead to all the available providers being exhausted relatively quickly and purchasing credibility reduced as a result.

Where there are relatively few providers and several purchasers, this will tend to lead to purchasers being smaller in size than providers, creating asymmetric power relationships. In these circumstances, purchasers have an incentive in establishing long-term relationships with providers, but providers may be more interested in contracting with several purchasers because of the increased flexibility this offers them. A public manager on the provider side will therefore want to spread the risk of the high volume of the contracts they hold by working with several purchasers, and although this does not mitigate against long-term relationships, it has the potential for managers on opposite sides of the purchaser/provider divide to want different things from the market relationship. This therefore creates the potential for conflict.

The main danger where providers have potential to dominate a marketplace is the phenomenon economists refer to as 'cream skimming' (Le Grand, 2007). In this situation, providers are able to exert their dominance by giving services only to members of the public that they believe will be the cheapest or easiest for them. In education cream skimming means picking the students most likely to score highest in exams and be the easiest to teach, and in healthcare it means providing insurance or health services only to those that suffer the least illness. If some providers are able, through their dominance of the market, to achieve this position, it has the potential to undermine the system of provision as those less educationally able may find it difficult to get into a school, and those who are really ill find it difficult to be treated. Cream skimming is a serious problem in public markets, and great care must be taken in organising markets to make sure that it is minimised.

Cream skimming is especially problematic for public managers as it creates additional dilemmas for them; they clearly have strong incentives to get their organisations into a strong financial position in order for them to be able to keep providing services, but if they take this too far through cream skimming they might undermine the whole basis of public services.

In all, where providers are relatively few, this will tend to guarantee them at least some contracts from purchasers, giving public managers on that side of the market greater power, but also the temptation to engage in cream skimming. Public managers must try not to do this and remember their duty to the wider public, and policymakers that are responsible for overseeing and creating public markets must try and take away the potential to gain from it as much as possible.

Purchaser dominance

The opposite case to producer dominance is where there are relatively few purchasers compared to providers. In this situation purchasing public managers are likely to be larger in size than providers, but may want to spread their purchasing across several providers in order not only to give themselves or service users the widest possible choice of providers,

Table 6.3 The market in conditions of provider and purchaser dominance

Provider dominance	Purchaser dominance
Contestable market because of lack of competition	Competitive market because several providers available
Purchasers have strong incentive to form long-term contracts	Providers have strong incentive to form long-term contracts
Danger of cream skimming	Danger of purchasing not being representative of public it serves

but also to reduce the risk of depending entirely upon one. Providers, on the other hand, will have to negotiate with purchasing managers who have considerable power in the contracting process than they have, and so will be keen to foster long-term relationships to try and reduce the risk of losing contracts. However, this carries the risk of providers becoming over-dependent upon a particular purchaser, putting them in a vulnerable position should they lose that contract.

If the smaller-scale providers break up their activity across several purchasers, that may result in them asking for contracts of a relatively low volume, increasing transaction costs for them, but making their future more secure as the loss of one contract will not automatically lead to failure. Purchasing organisations will decide, however, how the market is structured, as they hold not only the funds to drive it, but also those funds that are concentrated in a relatively small number of organisations.

The problem most likely to occur where there are relatively few, dominant purchasers is that they are likely to lose contact with the purchasing wishes of their public. The more people a purchasing public managers must represent, the less representative of that public their decisions are likely to be, and the more difficult it will become to consult with them.

Table 6.3 summarises the market situation in conditions of provider and purchaser dominance.

Additional difficulties in getting markets to work

There are additional difficulties in getting market mechanisms to work in public settings. The first is where providers organise themselves not competitively, but instead into collaborative relationships. One of the confusing tendencies of public policy is its tendency to revert between requiring providers to compete with one another to create cost saving and drive up quality and requiring providers to collaborate with one another to provide new service pathways and to provide a seamless 'joined-up' service for users (Newman, 2002). Where collaboration becomes the norm, so that providers find themselves offering more and more services in concert with one another, this increases the chances for service users to move between interlinked contracts as they may be more likely to co-operate and they are not positioned against one another in a competitive relationship. Equally providers may take the opportunity in collaborative situations to specialise in particular services, making themselves indispensable and to occupy points in the networks of provision where, for a particular service to be delivered efficiently, the contract must be negotiated through them. In this situation, there is a danger of the provider creating an effective monopoly for itself.

Contracting can present problems because it can result in public managers becoming less democratically accountable as a greater stress is placed on contractual performance instead, and it may also lead to a reduction in the opportunities for democratic involvement for citizens or consumers in the administration of public services as organisations become more concerned with commercial confidentiality and meeting the thresholds specified in their contracts than on meeting the needs of the public more generally (Kirkpatrick and Martinez Lucio, 1996).

Practical examples of specialising in collaborative relationships might occur where a particular organisation owns much of the local infrastructure, for example, in waste disposal. Although they may not provide services in relation to it directly, all the providers of waste disposal services in the local area have to make contracts with the infrastructure provider in order to be able to provide a service to end users. In this case, the infrastructure provider insulates itself from the local economy and effectively becomes a monopoly. Where public markets have been constructed in areas considered 'natural' monopolies (see Chapter 2) this phenomenon is more likely to occur. Where railways are privatised, for example, the problem of who should own the track remains a difficult one as all the providers of trains will have to contract with the body, which therefore has little competitive incentive to improve the service it offers to the train companies. This problem has the potential to undermine the entire basis of the competitive market, but might work well if providers are positioned collaboratively with one another.

A second problem occurs where purchasers have little understanding of the offerings of providers within the market. This might occur where the offerings of public organisations are complex and not easily reducible to simple league tables or performance measures. Healthcare can often be a good example of this. Organising hospitals to compete with one another to improve standards and reduce costs appears to make sense, but only if the performance of the hospitals can be compared and purchases be able to tell which would be the best to purchase on behalf of the end users, local patients (and the public more generally). If the job of choosing between providers is difficult for health managers, this may be doubly the case for the users of services. In this case it will be the job of health managers to attempt to produce information that will allow users to make informed choices, but this, because of the complexity and specificity of health services, will be very difficult.

Health decisions are complex because they can involve professional judgements about not only how patients should be treated, but also what is wrong with them in the first place. It is no accident that doctors take so long to train. Expecting patients to be able to acquire detailed medical knowledge and decide which treatment is right for them is plainly unrealistic. The nearest patients may come to this state of knowledge is where they have long-term, chronic diseases and so acquire considerable experiential and theoretical knowledge about their own condition, and so possibly exceed medically trained staff in their knowledge of their own specific situation. This is because of the second characteristic of health knowledge – its specificity. The job of the doctor is to translate the available medical evidence and knowledge into a form that allows them to diagnose the patient before them, and to work out the best treatment for them. Medical knowledge is not just about abstract knowledge, but the ability to make this specific to the particular patient. Providing patients with information to allow them to make their own decision is extremely difficult. At present websites and patient information leaflets exist to attempt to provide patients with what they need to know when making healthcare decisions, but necessarily have to simplify the complexity of the decision process. Should the choice of healthcare provider be made on the basis of who has the shortest waiting list, or the longest? The former might indicate that no one else wants to go to that particular provider, and the latter that everyone else agrees that this is the best provider but will mean a longer wait. Should patients choose the provider with the lowest death rate or the highest? A low death rate would appear a good choice, but could simply be driven by the doctors at that particular hospital only admitting patients who do not really need treating. A high death rate might be excusable where the doctors treat only the most difficult cases, and may indicate that those doctors, because of their experiences at dealing with difficult cases, are likely to be extremely proficient at simpler ones. If health managers and even other healthcare professionals struggle to interpret health data it seems unrealistic to ask patients to attempt to try to.

In other public services, however, the decision may be easier to make. Where the decision is less complex and less specific, users or managers might be better able to examine the relative performance of providers. In secondary education (high-school education) the results of exams taken at the end of schooling give at least some indication of the success of schools. Of course, they are not the only indicator worth considering, but the average experience of a student in a school is far more likely to be representative of the average patient in a hospital. Students are expected to attend similar classes and take similar exams at the end of their time at school, but patients may be at hospitals for a range of different conditions at very different times of their lives. As well as this, in contrast to at least 'one-off' medical services, students can move to other schools if they find that the one they are going to does not meet their needs.

The decision of which school to attend is less specific to the individual than the choice of hospital – the experience the school providers is more concerned with classes and other groups rather than individuals. Equally, the choice of school is probably less complex as parents are able to visit schools before choosing them, speak to parents of children in the local area to find out their experiences of their children attending the school, look at independent inspection reports of the school, and also examine school exam results. The decision of which school to send a child is not an easy one, but parents can generally understand the choice before them and are able to combine the available information into a form that allows them to choose.

Whether the purchasers or end users can understand how they are meant to be making choices is an overlooked but extremely significant part of a public market. Just because it is possible to combine providers in a competitive relationship and put in place a number of possible purchasers it does not mean a market will work well. The simple provision of information by providers is not enough – it must also be understandable by potential purchasers and enable them to make informed decisions. Without this, there is a danger of purchasing decisions in the market becoming arbitrary or incoherent.

Equally, positioning public service users as individual consumers through the use of markets runs the risk of creating problems that require collectivist responses; public managers have to find answers to serve whole communities whereas the answer that is more convenient or best for any individual member of that community might be rather different. Aberbach and Christensen suggest (2005) several tensions that can emerge between the individualism of markets and the collectivism of the political aspects of public management, and which are shown in Table 6.4.:

Table 6.4 Consumer and citizen roles of users in public services

Consumer role	Citizen role
Individuals have preferences acted upon through market mechanisms	Communities have preferences acted upon through collective voting and political action
Consumer sovereignty and authority	Authority and accountability of political leaders
Consumers satisfied individually	Citizen needs met collectively
Profit incentive	Equitable provision goal

The tensions above lead to a significant problem in that, Aberbach and Christensen suggest, it is often extremely difficult to identify exactly who the consumer or customer is in public services, and even if they are identifiable, should public managers be focusing on meeting individual users needs or the needs of their communities as a whole?

Problems with intermediaries

There are other cases where markets may run into problems. Where market intermediaries become dominant, this creates clear problems for public markets. Insurance companies in healthcare are an obvious example. In many countries the administration of health insurance is not carried out by the state, but instead by intermediate institutions. These insurance organisations are funded from a varying mix of public and private money, depending upon the particular country. The key point is that, in order for the health-care system to work, insurance companies take over the job of managing finance, allowing the state to concentrate its energies on other tasks before it. These intermediaries can be a good idea because they can depoliticise difficult decisions about which treatments should be funded and which not, and which providers should receive contracts and which not.

At the same time, however, intermediaries may have agendas of their own over which the state does not have direct control, and if they are poor at their job, it destabilises the provision of healthcare through inappropriate contracting. In this situation public managers may be required to work around the deficiencies of the insurance company to attempt to ensure that provision is not so badly disrupted as to remove confidence in the healthcare system. Equally, state officials may find they need to financially bail out insurance intermediaries where there is a danger of their bankruptcy because of the problems their failure would cause across the whole network of public provision. This can lead to a situation where the state must effectively underwrite private intermediaries, and private intermediaries facing 'moral hazard', where they have little incentive to behave in a financially responsible way because they know the state will bail them out if problems occur, and so feel free to engage in high-risk behaviours.

Another example involving intermediaries comes where the private sector tries to reduce the risk of providing public services and sub-contracts provision to another private company. In such circumstances it can become unclear exactly who is responsible for the final delivery of the service, and who should be held accountable where service falls below the required quality standards. Instead a nest of intermediaries might appear where contracts have been sold on and resold with no one wishing to take the final responsibility for service provision. Public provision contracts have sometimes come to resemble speculative contracts for the financial services industry, as assets to be purchased and then sold on for a profit where possible. It is hard to see how this is in the interest of the service being delivered, or exactly how those employed to deliver the services are to be efficiently managed in these circumstances.

Conclusion

This chapter has shown that the notion of a market is problematic. This is an important point as it is a term that often claimed it is obvious what markets are, and how they should work, when in practice markets can mean a number of different arrangements and present a range of difficult problems. For markets to work in the public sector a number of pre-conditions need to be in place; there needs to be real competition in place with sufficient purchasers and providers to make this happen; choice must be informed in that it must be based on criteria relevant to the market which is understandable by both purchasers and providers; and market imperfections such as cream skimming must be avoidable (Le Grand, 2007). These pre-conditions are outside the control of public managers, but if any of them are breached, then it will have significant implications for them.

If competition is not real, then providers can form cartels or partnerships and a more collaborative system of provision might occur. This may not be a bad thing, as it might be easier for managers to arrange a seamless service provision where providers are not in direct competition with one another, but does take the dynamic of relationships present away from those expected of a market. Equally, where purchasers dominate the marketplace a whole range of different problems occur because of the different asymmetry of power this causes, and because purchasers are likely to have become so large that they have lost touch with the needs of their local publics. A common way of dealing with the problem of markets becoming overly complex is the use of intermediaries such as insurance companies, but these bring new problems as the interests of the intermediaries may not reflect those of the state or of the public managers required to work with them, and because of the difficulties of accountability their use can cause.

If the choice is not informed, then there is a real danger of markets producing perverse outcomes. Purchasing decisions, be they made by individuals or by public managers, need to be based on good information, and for that information is to be understandable. Neither of these factors has been especially easy to achieve. Good information depends upon good information systems, and the record of investment in public sector management information systems, especially where they involve complex information technology, is not happy one, with huge amounts sometimes being spent and very little tangible benefit generated. Even if good information can be captured it then must be communicated, and it cannot be assumed that it is always straightforward to show what good public sector performance looks like, and what this means in terms of the use of league tables or other performance data.

Finally, cream skimming is a problem that can potentially undermine any attempt to set up a public market. If providers become dominant in the market they may attempt to narrow the range of public they provide their services to in order to minimise cost or disruption to themselves, and this goes against the principle of public service, as not all the public will be served. In practice, because public organisations tend to have professionals in place who have at least some autonomy in their decision-making, public managers will struggle to cream skim unless they are able to put in place incentives for professionals to deliberately act against their own codes of conduct. Doctors might be told to treat only particular groups of patients, and not to attempt to help all their potential patients. Schools might deliberately put in place exclusionary admissions policies to make sure that they get the best students only. Undoubtedly this either explicitly or implicitly goes on in a number of public organisations. The job of public managers wishing to serve the public as a whole is to try and minimise it while at the same time accepting that they work within considerable resource constraints that mean they often cannot provide a service to everyone.

Bozeman (2002) provides an excellent checklist of the situations where markets in the public sector might fail (what he terms 'public value' failure). Bozeman suggests that markets tend to fail when (1) mechanisms for value articulation and aggregation have broken down; (2) where imperfect monopolies occur (particularly where government monopolies would be in the public interest); (3) where benefit hoarding occurs (where public commodities and services have been captured by particular providers or interest groups); (4) there is a scarcity of providers; (5) a short-term horizon threatens public value (particularly where longer-term horizons give very different behaviours to short-term horizons); (6) where the conservation of public resources is threatened; and (7) where market transactions threaten fundamental human subsistence (perhaps leading to man-made famine, political imprisonment) (Bozeman, 2002:151 especially). Bozeman's list provides a good way of ending this chapter; where his conditions have been breached, then the thoughtless imposition of a market could lead to very significant problems.

CASE STUDY

The creation of markets in the NHS and UK public schools

The National Health Service in the United Kingdom is often presented as being the archetypal public service organisation in that, for the majority of its history, it has been almost entirely publicly funded and publicly provided and insulated from the pressures and disciplines of market competition. Public schools (taken in this case to be schools funded and provided by the government) have been in much the same position. However, since the 1980s, there have been repeated attempts by the government to introduce competition into both healthcare and education – there have been an attempt to create markets in each.

The drive for market-based competition in schools has come from two reforms. The first is giving parents the right to choose (or more accurately, to express a preference of choice) which school their child should go to. Prior to the reforms, Local Education Authorities were effectively responsible for deciding which child attended which local school, with it usually being a simple matter of where a child lived deciding which school they attended. The introduction of choice meant that parents could choose a school that was not the nearest to their home. Parents were usually asked to rank schools in order of preference, with the Local Education Authority or schools then trying to find a place at the school at the top of the list, and working their way through parental preferences where places at their first choice school were not available.

The first problem of school choice is that popular schools are often over-subscribed, and it is difficult to expand them as this will mean having to add to infrastructure and increasing teaching staff, which may not mean standards can be preserved (even if there is space for expansion). Equally, it is politically difficult to allow those schools graded as poorly performing to close as it may mean some children have long journeys to school, especially where the school is in a rural area, and even that some communities might lose their local schools completely.

Allowing funding to follow the choices of parents of where to send their children allows good schools to receive more funding, but only if they can expand to meet need, and often only after they have expanded will they receive additional funding, leaving a financial gap until then. Whereas parents might feel qualified to judge which school to send their children to, being able to visit schools, look at their exam results, and remove their children from them if things do not work out, they may have little choice in practice if the most popular schools in a local area are already over-subscribed.

Where popular schools are over-subscribed, some of the children who choose them must be disappointed, leaving the problem of how to decide who should get in, and who should not. This can be settled by allowing children nearest to the school first call on places, but this tends to result in good schools becoming hot spots for rising house prices as parents who want their children to go to a good school move into the area. This can act against children from less-well-off parents, who may also have less understanding of how to make sure that their children attend the best school in a choice system (Ball *et al.*, 1995).

Alternatively, places could be allocated on a lottery basis, which means that the process for the system as a whole is fair, and that schools can be judged on their ability to teach children from right across the ability range. However, children who are assigned schools believed to be poor will believe the system is working against them, and their parents, where they can afford it, will want to remove their children and put them into private schools instead. Again, this has the potential to act against the children of less-well-off parents.

In schooling then, there seems to be a theoretical ability for many parents to be able choose the school for their children, as they understand how such a choice might be made, but there may be problems in making the school infrastructure follow the incentives of the market, and it may work against children from less-well-off parents.

In healthcare the problem may be the other way around. In most urban areas there are likely to be many places where most patients can be treated for health problems. Specialist care aside, there are likely to be several hospitals or primary care doctors who can treat a particular problem, and, as long as an information system can track who is treating which patient and funding can be made to follow the patient, there seems to be the infrastructure to make possible the development of a market for care.

The problem is how patients are meant to make informed decisions. Medical knowledge is specialist, and may take several years to acquire. Despite claims that it is now possible to research most conditions on the Internet (Nettleton and Burrows, 2003), an awful lot of inaccurate of biased information exists, and it is sometimes difficult to separate quackery from fact (Tallis, 2005). Many medical interventions are also likely to be one-offs, so unlike schooling, where children can be moved if things do not work out, choices may not necessarily allow the chance for learning. Equally, as many medical treatments are invasive and even dangerous, the penalties for choosing the wrong place to be treated might be considerable.

Given the difficulties of patients making informed choices, their choices might instead be based upon non-clinical factors such as the proximity of the treatment centre to home, the availability of car parking or public transport or the attractiveness of its buildings. These are important in the decision, but surely not as important as the level of care offered, which is often very difficult to measure or assess. In healthcare markets, the opposite problem to schooling may well be in place. There may be the infrastructure for a market to take place, but patients may not be able to make informed decisions about where they should be treated.

This analysis has significant implications for public managers in the two areas. In education, managers face less of an infrastructural problem from competition as they are less likely to lose all applicants for their schools. Risks must be taken to expand schools as funding will not follow until additional students can be admitted, and it may involve considerable expense to put up new buildings and employ new teachers if the school is already at capacity. If schools are not attracting students, the challenge will be finding ways to avoid laying off staff who may be needed if applications rise again, and trying to keep infrastructure fully deployed through the use of community programmes or child care, for example.

In healthcare public managers face greater risks from competition, but patients may find it very difficult to choose between providers. This means that public managers must actively use promotion strategies to make sure that their provision is well regarded. This may involve advertising to reassure potential patients, as well as investment in non-clinical aspects of provision such as car parking or building appearance, both inside and out. This clearly clashes with the logic of public service, as it could mean taking funds away from patient care. The consolation is that patients should get better more quickly in a well-maintained and presented environment.

This analysis carries significant implications for the use of market in the public sector. It implies that, instead of, as often appears to be the case in the United States and the United Kingdom, markets are the automatically preferred way of organising public services, it is a false premise that the relationship of state to citizen is the same as that between the private enterprise and its client (Larson, 1997). The use of widespread marketisation would make state bodies more responsive, but strip them of their public legitimacy. Both public managers and public policymakers must instead find ways of safeguarding their role as guardian of the public interest. There is a need for a 'portfolio' approach to management of public services in which some services might be suitable for marketisation, but for others this may not be appropriate at all (Greener, 2008).

Further reading

My own work has tried to explore the implications of markets generally (Greener, 2008) and in the contexts of healthcare and education specifically (Greener, 2003, 2003a, 2005b). The work of John Clarke and Janet Newman has examined UK public reforms introducing markets from critical perspectives that make for fascinating reading (Clarke and Newman, 1997; Clarke *et al.*, 2007, 2006). Equally important is the work of US psychologist Barry Schwarz, who suggests that giving the public choices in areas where they do not feel able to make them can be hugely disempowering (Schwartz, 2004).

Julian Le Grand has been examining the potential for markets to be used in the public sector for several years, and his recent work uses economics-derived frameworks for exploring their benefits and drawbacks (Le Grand, 1997, 2003, 2007), although Le Grand clearly believes they should be more widely used. To some extent this is mirrored in the work of Britain's most famous sociologist, Anthony Giddens, who in recent years has been a prominent policy advisor to the Labour government in the United Kingdom (Giddens, 2007). The UK government, in turn, have shown a strong preference for the use of markets in the public sector (Minister of State for Department of Health *et al.*, 2005).

7

The role of users in public services

Introduction

Chapter 6 examined the role of markets in the public sector. This chapter considers what role the public should play in public services. It proceeds by first presenting the approach that has perhaps most influenced the NPM – that public organisations should become more marketing-oriented, and by doing so, achieve accountability to individual service users in the same way that goods and service providers in the private sector are accountable to their customers. It deals with what exactly marketing is because, as with the use of 'markets' in Chapter 6, there is some confusion as to its meaning, and what its implications might be for public service accountability. The chapter then goes on to explore the implications of taking a marketing-based approach in the public sector, before looking at the difficulties that might arise, and what might be done to overcome them. The chapter then moves on to public participation, a more collective approach to public participation than the individualised, marketing approach, considering the various means by which this is often attempted in public organisations. It suggests that the best ways for service users to participate in the running of public services might be through co-production or through 'collectivised individualism', where user voice is collected and acted upon rather more routinely than is often achieved at present. It concludes by considering the implications of the analysis for both marketing and public participation for public services.

What is marketing?

It is useful to separate the ideas of markets from the idea of marketing. Marketing does not necessarily require a market – organisations do not have to be in competitive relationships for marketing to be used. There are a number of possible definitions of what marketing is, but the one used here, and which probably captures the approach as well as any other definition, is the approach to organisation (sometimes framed in terms of a philosophy or belief of organising) that places the customer at the centre of the organisation. For public organisations this is a radical step indeed. Many public organisations have been organised around the highly qualified professionals that are central to their delivery rather than the users they are meant to be serving.

There may be good reasons for having a professional-focus rather than a user-focus; doctors are a scarce resource as they take so long to train and their time is often in short supply when they have qualified. From an efficiency perspective, it may be better to organise patients around the doctor rather than vice versa, as this will allow more patients to be seen, creating a benefit for the system as a whole, as well as getting patients seen more quickly. Where the service professional represents the bottleneck or scarce resource in a system, there is certainly a case for the service to be organised around him or her rather than the service users.

However, organising services around professionals may require service users to have to wait for long periods, to find themselves turning up for appointments which they share with several other users because this allows the professional to see more people. This can lead to service users feeling that their time is being wasted and that they are receiving disinterested, almost rude service from the professional when their turn eventually comes. What professionals may regard as giving objective, efficient service may be interpreted by users as disinterested and rude. There seems to be at least something of a clash between an objective, efficient service, and an engaged, user-centred service (Newman, 2002:87). These can be made more apparent by considering the implications of the marketing approach for public services more generally.

The implications of the marketing approach for public services

A marketing approach to public services leads to their delivery being turned on its head. Instead of starting with the question 'how best can services be delivered to secure maximum possible efficiency from the professional', the guiding principle is 'how can services be organised to place the needs of the customer first'.

Table 7.1 shows the tension between services organised around professionals and those organised around end user (the marketing approach). Public services are often associated, as earlier chapters have made clear, with the attempt to provide a service that it is objective and fair service, requiring some level of space between the user and the professional, under considerable time pressure, and with standards of service being assessed by the professional's peers. A marketing-organised service, however, is geared towards the needs of service users instead, where professionals are expected to engage with them in a friendly and personal way, taking place a clearly defined time chosen by the user, and with users setting the criteria for whether the service was delivered successfully or not. In many respects it is a complete inversion of the public administration approach described in Chapter 3.

Amongst the tensions in Table 7.1 perhaps the most contentious is the last, whether professionals should have their work peer-reviewed, that is assessed by other professionals, or whether the users of their services should be the arbiter of what counts as good service.

Table 7.1 Professional-organised services versus marketing-organised services

Professional-organised service	Marketing-organised service
Need of the professional (to be efficient within a scarce time resource)	Needs of the user (to receive high-quality service)
Objective service	Engaged service
Impersonal service	Personal service
Time pressure (because of the need to move on to next case)	Clearly defined appointment time (to allow full discussion of issues)
Peer-review	User feedback

This debate is particularly important as it can lead to services being performance managed in entirely different ways. A professional who is acting in line with the codes of conduct and standards drawn up by his or her peers may behave towards users in an entirely different way than one who is attempting to achieve the best possible feedback from end users. Teachers in the first instance, for example, might want to demonstrate depth of knowledge, evidence-based pedagogy and class control, but if attempting to secure higher feedback might find themselves attempting to gear classes towards exam performance rather than learning, reducing complex ideas to bullet points, giving lots of handouts, and allowing students to disrupt lessons for fear of reprisals that might come from criticising them. Of course, many good teachers are student-centred as well as excellent professionals, but there can be very definite conflicts that can come from the competing demands of trying to be both peer- and student-centred. Taking a marketing approach involves the considerable redesign of public services. Two examples will hopefully demonstrate, around a hospital and the home visit for an elderly patient from social care.

An x-ray appointment

A patient visiting a hospital for an X-ray is a useful case study. If this is designed from the professional's point of view something along the following lines would tend to occur. First, the patient would be given an appointment time that fitted with the needs of the radiographers, and which would be regarded as offering only a generalised, one-way commitment from the hospital. The commitment would be for the patient to turn up at the time suggested, or risk not being X-rayed. However, this would not be a commitment from the hospital to X-ray the patient at that time – patients would be expected to wait if services were running behind schedule where emergencies had arrived or if professionals felt that more urgent cases required earlier treatment. Next, patients would be required to wait in a shared area so that they could be called when their time came, and probably would have to change into hospital gowns upon arrival so that the radiographer did not have to wait for patients to change their clothes once the time came for them to be seen.

Changing areas would typically be very basic, as funding high-quality areas would be seen as an unnecessary waste of money that took away funds from the most important part of the service – the X-ray itself. When they were eventually seen, patients would be treated quickly and efficiently, but often without much courtesy, and patients that required reassurance and patience might find it in short supply. Where children required X-rays they would expect to receive much the same service as adults, with it being up to parents to provide appropriate distractions both before and during the X-ray process to make sure that children did not disrupt the waiting facility or take up the radiographer's time by crying or refusing to have their X-ray taken.

After the X-ray was taken, the patient in either adult or child case would be told to get changed, and not given any feedback on the result, even if it was obvious to the radiographer, because this would take up more of the radiographer's time. Results would be communicated formally through a letter or by the patient seeing a doctor later on, often after having to arrange another appointment with another wait attached to it.

In contrast, a marketing approach would reverse most of the logic described above. Patients, upon needing an X-ray, would be able to ring the radiography department, expect to be seen at their convenience rather than the radiographer's, and to be able to turn up at the appointed time and be seen immediately. Appointment times would be adjusted to suit patients and extended or reduced, leading to the need for a far more flexible system of the time booking within the department. Patients would expect to wait in a high-quality area with distractions for children if necessary (perhaps video games or at least non-broken toys and children's magazines).

Patients would be given high-quality, private changing areas as it would be acknowledged that their dignity is important to the overall provision of the service. The X-ray itself, although the most important part of the service, would be seen as one component amongst many that leads to offering patients an excellent service. Patients might be preseen by a nurse to assess their needs, to explain what their X-ray comprised of and to provide reassurance and any other additional information as required. Children would probably be seen in a separate room, decorated to appeal to younger people, perhaps with a video playing something appropriate in a corner to distract the child from the X-ray itself.

After the X-ray was taken, a nurse would escort the patient back to the changing area and be on hand to answer any questions. The radiographer would then make himself or herself available to give preliminary results and refer the patient on to whichever healthcare professional was appropriate for further care. Where patients required hospital support to get home, this would also be organised as soon as the patient's appointment finished (or perhaps even earlier, in order to make sure that the patient was taken home without a delay).

The contrast between the two approaches is extraordinary. Individual readers will be able to consider which is closest to their own experience. The key point, however, is that it is the responsibility of the public manager to work out which model their service is currently providing, and to work out what its problems and drawbacks might be. There may be good reasons for favouring the professional-led model, but that will have trade-offs and tensions with the marketing view, placing the user at the centre of the organisation instead. Most X-ray departments, in practice, will produce parts of each version, but this does not detract from the tensions present within each element of the service delivery when considered from competing perspectives.

A home visit

A second example, this time from social care, will support this further. A home visit for an older person can be a valuable support mechanism as it allows people to stay in their own homes for longer rather than being relocated to a home specialising in care for the elderly, and therefore allows greater independence and can be a valuable way of preserving dignity. This is not to say that elderly homes do not provide this, but that many people, given a choice, would prefer to remain in their own home if they are able to receive support to allow this happen.

A visit organised around a professional would occur at a time that suited the professional, again with no guarantee that it will occur at exactly that time. The user would be expected to be ready to receive the visit, which could cause stress and concern that sleeping or visiting the toilet might mean the professional is missed. The home visitor might never have met the older person before, as carers might be regarded as substitutable, and would not have telephoned ahead to let the client know they are on their way.

The visit would then be organised according to what the professional believed needed to be done, probably in line with standardised best practice, and would be efficiently organised to make sure that work is done in an accurate and clinical fashion. The visit would end when the home visitor needed to move to the next appointment, and a further appointment scheduled according to his or her professional expertise. The home visitor would then leave after making sure that their client is safe.

A contrasting view of the home visit would be where the visitor has been booked according to the schedule of the older person. This may have been at short notice, with the home visitor's organisation making sure that spare capacity is available from their staff to make sure this can happen. The home visitor would be expected to turn up at the agreed time, but with an open agenda as to what needed to be done. The older person and home visitor will agree what needs to be done together, and there may be not only elements of care delivered by the visitor, but also more mundane tasks performed, such as a shopping trip or a visit to a friend, neither of which might be possible for the client alone if they are relatively immobile. The appointment might therefore need to be more open-ended, and the home visitor work organised flexibly on a 'pool' basis with appointments met by trained staff who expect to fit around their clients' needs. Where clients require particular members of staff for continuity of care, or where they have specifically requested them by name, they may have to wait a little longer, but when the home visitor sets of to visit they will ring the older people to let them know they are on the way and be given an estimated arrival time. The visit ends when the requirements of the older person have been met, and when he or she is back safely in his or her own home, having had the agreed goals for the visit met. A further appointment might then be arranged at a mutually agreeable time, or via a telephone call at a later date to the home visit organisation.

Again, the contrast here is great. Home care delivered by professionals will be more flexible if user-led, both in terms of time and also in terms of the type of care delivered. Professionals may feel that supporting users to go shopping or to visit friends is demeaning to their skills, but if that is the type of support the user needs, then a marketing view would dictate that this is the type of care that should be delivered.

The marketing view of public organisation places the needs of the user at the centre of organisation, rather than the needs of professionals (be they doctors, or social care workers, or managers). It becomes the role of managers to make sure that services are reorganised on this basis and to survey users to make sure that their needs are met.

Difficulties with the marketing view in public organisations

There are a range of dilemmas that come from the marketing view that public managers need to find answers they are comfortable with.

First, where service users demand an unreasonably high level of service, what should managers do? If public managers are responsible for refuse collection, for example, and users suggest that daily collections are most appropriate as they remove the need for them to store unhygienic and unpleasant rubbish outside of their homes, should they go along with this request? The subject of how often rubbish should be collected from people's homes is a universally contentious one. In the United Kingdom attempts to move rubbish collection from a weekly to a two-weekly basis have proven unpopular, even when local authorities have attempted to justify the service on the grounds of persuading users to recycle more of their waste. There seems to be a tendency, feared by the tabloid press, towards weighing the amount of rubbish generated by homes in order to charge for its collection in line with the actual effort involved in collecting it, but this will not be popular as it requires households to change their behaviour. A marketing-oriented refuse collection service would be very different from a socially responsible one. Where end users are demanding high levels of service, it might require a considerable investment in educating them to substitute the values of responsible disposal of refuse for those of high customer service, and even then, some individuals may not accept that the local authority has any right to tell them what to do with their rubbish. Refuse collection is an area dogged particularly by the free-rider effect where individual service users may believe that recycling rubbish is not their problem because someone else will do it on their behalf.

In the Simpsons episode 'Trash of the Titans', Homer Simpson is put in charge of refuse collection for his home town of Springfield with an agenda of offering extremely high-quality service, but ends up spending the entire annual budget in one month. As public services are often offered within a fixed budget, the spectre of funding always has the potential of limiting the level of service available. A possible way of offering a higher standard of service is to offer everyone weekly or two-weekly collections, but charge for additional collections if they want a higher standard of service. Where this is economically viable it may square the circle of cost and service, but at the price of allowing those with higher incomes to be less responsible with their rubbish, which may go somewhat against the grain of social and environmental responsibility. Placing the needs of local users at the heart of delivery can mean that other important agendas are missed out. The case of refuse collection is covered in greater depth in the case study at the end of this chapter.

A second potential clash is between safety and user need. If local park users want the local authority to set up an adventure playground for their children, then the children themselves might want climbing frames that go very high, swings with long chains on them to allow both greater speed and height, skateboard areas with big ramps and slides going from the top of trees down to the floor via ropes and pulleys. If examined from a health and safety perspective however, the local authority may feel that these proposals are likely to result in children being injured and so want less exciting facilities. But if the users, with the support of their parents, want more risky, more exciting playground rides, should this override the safety concerns of the local authority, even when they know that the proposals are likely to result in injured children?

A third difficulty, and a variation of the tension between safety and user need, is where evidence and user need appear to work in opposite directions. Healthcare provision is a good example of this. Where a patient demands an untested treatment, perhaps one from homeopathy or another alternative therapy, should this be funded from public funds or the more conventional version given instead? Should public funds be used to support treatments that cannot be shown to have a scientific base, or which do not have randomised controlled trial data to support them? Medical opinion is often split.

Many writers argue that using public funds for unproven treatments is a waste of money as it uses up funds that could be used to help patients that could benefit from evidence-based care (Tallis, 2005). Medical practitioners increasingly, however, seem to be taking a more view that what supports and helps patients should be paid for by the state even if the treatment itself does not meet the same standards of evidence as other funded treatments. This can be illustrated by a patient approaching a local health authority or insurance company to be treated for HIV entirely using complementary medicine. According to a strict evidence-based regime, the patient would be refused public money for this. But several patients appear to have managed to prevent his HIV from developing into full-blown AIDS for several years by using a complementary medicine regime, and so, even though there is little scientific data supporting this treatment, they have been funded through the UK NHS on the grounds that it seemed to work for that individual. Whether this decision could be generalised across a population is, however, very debatable.

Next, it may be unclear in many public organisations exactly who the customer is (Christy and Brown, 1996). Do the police serve the public as a whole (in which case, how is this even possible?), or do they serve the members of the public who have been victims of crime specifically (which would exclude crime prevention as being part of their role) or, if they have a member of the public in custody, is he or she their customer? In a blood trans-fusion service, are the donors customers or are they the recipients of the blood donated instead? Giving simple answers to these questions never really works – almost invariably public organisations must treat all members of the public as customers or potential cus-tomers, but this does not mean that they always have to do exactly what the customer wants. Some clear thinking needs to take place in each service as to what the public gen-erally should expect from it, as well as to what specific interactions with particular public groups mean.

Graham (1994), writing in a mainstream marketing journal, suggests that the applica-tion of marketing to the public sector tends to reveal it being used appropriately where private sector values are already dominant. Where, however, the environment, mission and ethos are very different in the public sector, effective use of market communications only may be appropriate because a more integrated approach to marketing will not work. As such, the context of the particular public organisation needs to be carefully considered before attempting to implement the marketing approach as a whole. Walsh (1991) argues along similar lines, suggesting that marketing presents few challenges to the public sector if it is seen only as a series of techniques, but if it presumes a market and exchange then, because of the different values between the two sectors, it presents significant difficulties as private sector marketing will not be straightforwardly translatable. Kearsey and Varey (1998) go further, arguing that marketing management differs in both theory and practice between for-profit and pubic organisations, but is especially problematic in relation to the democratic process in the latter. Marketing may be used as an 'operational' tool, with the public sector making better use of market research and customer service techniques, but they argue that the potential for an integrated marketing approach in the public sector is limited. The root of this problem is perhaps most clearly stated by Ventriss (2000), who writes that the NPM, with its often concern with private sector values and market-driven approaches, is 'often 'too silent on the "publicness" of the field's role in society and the subsequent obligations we have to the citizenry' (p. 514).

Last in terms of the problems of utilising marketing in the public sector, there is the clash between user need and resource, perhaps the most pervasive dilemma of all. The case of refuse collection already intruded into this territory, but there are more specific cases that illustrate it. One resource in short supply, as noted above, is public professional time. Doctors take time to train and are expensive to employ. As such, demanding doc-tors are available to see patients entirely at the patients' convenience, funded from public monies, would appear to be unreasonable as this would suggest a great deal of doctor time is presently redundant, and this is simply not the case. Another good example is the 'places' available in high-quality, higher education institutions. If students had a com-pletely free choice of the university they could attend, then the most prestigious sites of learning would become overrun with students whilst those less well known might struggle to fill their places. Given a choice, would not most US and UK students prefer to go to an

'Ivy League' University or to 'Oxbridge'? However, these universities simply could not take everyone who would like to go to them, and their prestige may well be tied up with them being able to be extremely selective in their intakes. Allowing everyone to attend would reduce the quality of the student experience for everyone, as facilities would become over-crowded and standards fall as a result, as well as meaning that the badge of being a graduate of those institutions would not carry the status it held before as far more students would be able to claim it.

In these circumstances where user wants and capacity clash, other ways of organising services need to be found. In the case of doctors, most people would agree that patients with greater clinical need should be seen first, and in the case of universities, the ability of the student (or at very least the potential ability of the student) would seem to override the demand that users in each service should get what they want. Hospitals and universities not only will still want to market their service to attempt to make clear what distinctiveness they offer, but will also want to preserve their ability to make decisions on criteria other than user need.

How can a marketing approach be adopted in public services?

A middle way in considering the use of marketing in the public sector attempts to organise services, where practicable, around the needs of users, but with the competing claims of professionals and with wider societal goals firmly in mind as well. Public managers have to be extremely careful in their choices – there may be very good reasons why services are organised in a way that appears at first glance to be working against rather than with user need.

However, there are also many cases where services are more about the convenience of professionals being preserved through arcane rituals and rules. The difficult task is working out whether services that are less than user-friendly are in need of reform, and if so, how professionals can be brought on board to reorganise services without remov-ing the user voice completely. Public managers often have the tricky task of representing the user voice in service redesign against vested interests who are firmly entrenched in the professional view of how services should be delivered. Equally as often, however, they may become the bulwark between state-led attempts to reform services to become more user-responsive and the need for organisational stability (Schofield, 2001).

Many of the problems highlighted above with using the marketing approach in the public delivery or services are based on tensions between what is good for the individual and what is good for the whole public as a whole. When wanting an improvement in a service to me, thinking as an individual, I may not take into account the need to deliver that service to the rest of those needing it. If I am prescribed an expensive new drug, it might mean that there are insufficient funds to treat patients with other conditions (or even the same condition). If my bins are collected weekly, it might mean that those in more remote locations are unable to have their rubbish collected more than every two weeks. Public services, as they tend to occur within relatively fixed budgets, have to deal with the tension of the individual versus that of the group.

Vigoda (2002) suggests that treating citizens as clients (by which he seems to mean customers or consumers) of public services has worked for the benefit of bureaucracies by forcing them to take greater responsibility towards citizens (in the sense of customers collectively), increasing public service accountability in and transparency, and has emphasised that government must be continuously monitored to ensure high efficiency, effectiveness and good economic performance. It has also, according to Vigoda, made clear that government power must depend upon citizen support, especially with regard to the services they receive. However, in line with Fox and Miller (1995), Vigoda suggests that citizens are 'unwilling – perhaps incapable – of becoming practical owners of the state even if they are the real owners by all democratic and business criteria' (p. 538). They seek 'practical flexibility' between the role of citizen and client, and that public administration must rely upon a conception of greater collaboration and partnership with the citizenry in order to increase the authenticity of the relationship between the state and the citizenry (turning the 'they' view of customers into 'we', where service managers, politicians and service users work together). Market-type modes of governance increase the potential risk of 'citizen alienation, disaffection, scepticism and increase cynicism toward governments' (p. 538), and will require a high level of co-operation that fosters mutual effort.

The risk of the alienation of service uses through the use of market-type mechanisms in the public sector comes because organising public services around a marketing view effectively makes them accountable to individual users, where the danger of collective publics might disappear in the rush to have individual needs met. In this circumstance, individuals may find services unresponsive or unhelpful and be unable to understand why their needs are not being met, when public managers are simply trying to make provision fair to everyone. Where services refuse to collect rubbish more frequently or to prescribe the latest drugs, individuals may feel aggrieved, but there may be good collective reasons for them not receiving the level of service they are demanding. But, as seen in previous chapters, public service accountability can be achieved not only through customer-type relationship, but that the traditional approach to public administration argued that services should be democratically accountable instead. Organising public services on a marketing basis makes them accountable to individuals, rather than accountable to the public more generally as democratic accountability attempts to achieve. It may also be the case that many of the public resist considering themselves customers or consumers of public services, and that they explicitly reject this language because they favour alternative discourses about public provision based on partnership between providers rather than competition (Clarke et al., 2007).

Given the problems associated with attempting to make services accountable to individuals, or making them democratically accountable, what other means can be found for public service users to participate in the running of services?

Achieving greater local accountability for public services

A first method of getting greater local accountability for public services is to get users involved in the running of services themselves. User representatives might be appointed to help public managers make decisions, and to give the 'user' view when required. In education, students are invited to decision-making meetings to try and make sure that services are organised with them in mind, or at least to allow students to feel that they are part of debates around service provision.

However, it can be difficult to get users to volunteer to be involved in the running of services, and those that volunteer may not be representative of the public as a whole (if this is, indeed, even possible). Equally, user representation can sometimes become tokenism where users in decision-making meetings have one or two votes compared to the 20 or so assembled representatives of professional and management groupings. Lay membership (as it is often called) does, however, lead to professionals at least having to listen to user views in meetings, which is no bad thing in itself, and may lead to support for managerial initiatives to change services more in line with the needs of the public.

The difficulty with getting local people involved in public organisations comes in achieving membership that is at all representative of the public at large (if such a thing is even possible), especially with regard to groups that may find dialogic debate difficult, and so could be marginalised by it. Even those members of the public that are comfortable with participating in the running of public services can become effectively incorporated or institutionalised into them, risking losing the point of bringing in members of the public in the first place (Barnes *et al.*, 2003).

A second approach to public participation is for groups of users (which again ideally should be representative of the public as a whole in some way) to be empowered to make decisions that affect their public services. A panel of local people might be given two or three days of briefings from interested groups and professionals, and then be asked to make a decision for what happens next. In social housing estates, user groups (or 'citizens' juries') have sometimes taken control of the future of their housing by working out strategies for dealing with social problems in their areas and working collaboratively with the police and social services to try and come up with innovative new ways of tackling long-standing problems where conventional approaches have failed. Equally there have been experiments in attempting to prioritise what public funds should be spent on by involving the public in decisions about local amenities, inviting them along to local halls and explaining the possible decisions. Votes can then be taken as to what the priorities for public funding in the local area should be.

This kind of initiative, however, is not without its difficulties. Where users take decisions on behalf of their local communities they may enter the decision-making processes with particular prejudices, with the end result be based more on the pre-existing views of those that are able to organise themselves to participate in the decision-making process than of the views of the public that have to live with the decision more generally. Tenants might have opinions that are racist or sexist, or which even involve illegal acts.

In the circumstances where user's views are illegal or dangerous some limits might have to be placed on the ability of the decision-making body to come to the conclusions it wishes to, but this, in turn, might be experienced as an attempt by managers to prevent the popular will from being carried out. Equally, holding decisions in local halls that decide priorities for expenditure may be dominated by groups that manage to organise to attend the meeting, crowding out other opinion, or users may feel that the decisions delegated to the local level are too trivial and so not worthy of their attention. Local meetings may become dominated by discussion about the relocation of bus stops within a 20 metre stretch rather than more important issues such as crime or the availability of other public amenities.

Equally, public participation can be extremely expensive. Irvin and Stansbury (2004) present a range of 'ideal conditions' when citizen participation in agency decision-making might work, and when it might not. They ask key questions such as whether citizens care enough to actively participate in particular decisions or service areas, or would resources devoted to participatory processes be better directed elsewhere? They ask if participation offers the opportunity for economically motivated special interests to dominate decision processes, and whether public managers can indeed avoid some level of interest dominance over public decision-making processes. They emphasise that 'talk is not cheap – and may not even be effective' (p. 63).

The role of public managers, if it has been decided that decisions will be delegated to local people, is to make sure that the decisions delegated are meaningful and that the solutions created are both legal and viable. This last point may involve extremely careful work in trying to steer users away from particular solutions and creative work in attempting to come up with alternatives. Equally public managers will also have the responsibility for making sure that the decisions are carried out and that successful implementation occurs. If local people have made a decision which has cost them time and energy, but nothing is seem to come of it, then they will be reluctant and understanding suspicious of becoming involved again.

Co-production

A third approach attempts to steer a middle path between professionals and users towards achieving a 'co-production' model. Co-production can mean a number of different things, depending upon the exact public context where it is being used, but usually means the service users take responsibility for some aspects of the delivery of the public service himself or herself (Pestoff *et al.*, 2006). This can be done in a number of ways. At the minimum, professionals might be required to demonstrate that they have had meaningful consultation with users before decisions have been made, with users given the opportunity to scrutinise the decisions made by local professionals and to have their say.

In local authorities co-production might mean decisions about the allocation of land or local authority budgets are made recursively, as decisions made by professionals might be passed for consultation with local people, and then passed back to the professionals to see how they respond to the problems or criticisms made by local people. This clearly requires local people to be extremely engaged with local decision-making, and for their views to be taken seriously by professionals rather than simply rebuffed or ignored. Bovaird (2007) suggests that co-operation between public professionals and service users needs pro-active management even to the point of appointing a 'coproduction development officer' (p. 858) to oversee it. Achieving a high level of public engagement can be extremely difficult, but the increased use of online consultations and of local authorities having to justify their budgetary decisions to their local populations points to possibilities where it can become more widespread.

Alford (1998) takes a slightly different approach to co-production, presenting techniques such as web-based tax assessment as an example of co-production, but also including definitions more in line with those of Pestoff in his discussion of tenants' councils on high-rise estates – a far more collectivist and activist model of co-production.

If involving local people in decisions on an occasional basis represents the minimum end of the scale of time and effort in terms of co-production, a far greater role is also possible. In childcare, co-production models have led to parents becoming more involved in looking after children, brought in as a source of additional labour and expertise by the state (Pestoff, 2006). As such, parents become the deliverers of childcare as well as the clients of it, with childcare coming to represent an employment possibility as well as a need.

Co-production can also take place in a more intimate setting where professionals are encouraged to consult with the users of their services on a one-to-one basis, such as when they visit the doctor. The conventional model of doctor diagnosis and prescription is one where the doctor fires off a series of questions and then informs the patients what is wrong with them, and what the doctor thinks should be done about it. A co-production model attempts to give the patient alternative treatments, along with their possible advantages and disadvantages, and to involve the patient more in decisions such as where they should be referred for further treatment (if necessary) or how the patient might go about making changes to their lives required by ill-health. The co-production model in these circumstances should lead to greater patient compliance with the diagnosis and treatment, as it has been decided together, and so clearly has advantages from an implementation perspective. However, it also means longer consultations between doctor and patient, and so a greater resource commitment. Patients can also find such a process disorienting where they are used to the doctor simply telling them what is wrong and what they should do.

Collectivised individualism

The above approaches attempt to try and bridge the gap between the individual user and the general public, through public organisations incorporating individuals or groups of individuals into their decision-making processes. However, there is another possibility. This is where individual user feedback is 'collectivised' and patterns sought in order to try and find lessons through which services can be improved for everyone.

User complaints are often regarded by public managers with a sense of dread because they can mean having to investigate professionals who may feel they are being deliberately targeted by both users and managers because they do not go along with organisational reform. Equally, in an increasingly litigious world, complaints can be attempts to try and extract money from public organisations where no wrong has been done. There will always be a small minority of people attempting to claim compensation fraudulently. However, complaining often takes up time and effort, and can provide public managers with detailed feedback about user experience of services offered. It can therefore be a valuable means of finding ways which those services might be improved. If this feedback is routinely collected and analysed by public managers responsible for the delivery of that service, then it can at least give them a clear idea of what is going wrong with their service.

An alternative to managers reviewing feedback is for it to be passed on to citizen advocacy groups. This allows individual complaints to be effectively combined and for the citizen groups to lobby public organisations for improvement. Individual patients are often unaware that patient groups exist that can represent them and drive for service improvement, and may also not want to be bothered themselves to complain as they may never need the particular public service they are unhappy with again.

If public feedback can be collected and passed to independent patient organisations, this would allow recurring problems to be identified, for providers to be held to account for it and for opportunities for service improvements to be made. Complaints are a powerful source of feedback about what is going wrong with particular services, and public organisations are often extremely poor in dealing with them. Of course, where the public write to congratulate public organisations for their high standards and good performance, this can also form the basis for working out what is being done well, and how to achieve more of it.

In either system, where public managers collect complaints or where public advocacy groups utilise them, this allows the possibility for individual responses to be collectivised, patterns examined, and services which are experiencing systemic difficulties (or successes) investigated further to see what can be learnt from them, and what can be improved. This 'collectivised individualism' has the advantage of being potentially a routine part of service delivery, requiring no additional work on the part of service users, who do not have to attend additional meetings or have to confront professionals with problems directly, which they may find intimidating or difficult. It cannot work in all areas of public service, but can be viewed as a potentially fruitful way of bridging the gap between consumerist, individualistic notions of service delivery, and the collective need for public services to be accountable to the public more generally. Table 7.2 summarises different approach to local involvement in public services along with their advantages and drawbacks.

Table 7.2 Different ways of achieving local accountability

	Advantages	Drawbacks
Get users involved in the running of public services	Potential for public to be directly involved	Can be difficult to get individuals to volunteer
		Individuals that volunteer may not be representative of public
		Users on committees may be treated as 'tokens'
Empower users to make decisions	Informed, sensitive decisions can be reached by those that have to live with their consequences	Pre-existing prejudices might inform decisions
		Limits may have to be placed on scope of decisions and public resent this
		Representativeness of those making decisions
Co-production	Collaborative approach between professionals and users stressed	Users may feel they are not able to participate on equal terms and defer to professionals
	Public may provide extra capacity by providing services themselves	Public may become cheap source of poor-quality services
Collectivised individualism	Routine feedback is acted upon and service change occurs as a result	Does not engage public deliberatively and this may create a different result from individual-only responses
	Has some sense of collectivity as all feedback can be examined	

Conclusion

This chapter began by asking what the implications of a marketing-based view of public organisations were, and how the public could become more involved in the running of public services. The two questions appear separate, but are very related to one another. When considering a marketing view of public services, the central problem is how to meet individual service users' expectations within the resource constraints available to public organisations, without sacrificing the needs of the public to the needs of the individual. Where particular individuals demand very high standards from public services that mean significantly increased resources will need to be deployed, should they receive a much higher level of service, even if it means services reductions for other members of the public? What about the needs of the public collectively?

It is hard to see how a marketing approach can be taken without regard to resources. This applies to every organisation, but is particularly appropriate within the resource-constrained world of the public sector. It means that public managers cannot rely upon the legitimacy of providing high customer service standards to everyone and meeting all of the public's needs. As such, managers need alternative ways of engaging with the public in order to make their services accountable to them. Various mechanisms for getting the public involved in services exist, with the two least problematic being the co-production and collectivised individualism models. In the first, the public themselves become more involved in service provision. This covers a wide variety of positions from the public running the services entirely themselves (as in childcare) through to professionals being required to demonstrate adequate consultation with service users has occurred, as might be the position in healthcare. The collectivised individualism model attempts to find ways of collectivising individual feedback, either by public managers or by citizen advocacy groups, and that services are required to find a response to systemic problems identified by it. This has the advantage of being potentially a part of everyday feedback collection by public managers (whether they analyse the results themselves or not), and so does not require members of the public to attend specific meetings or confront professionals themselves. It cannot work in all circumstances, however, and will not engage members of the public with the dynamic of negotiating their views with others. It therefore does not get users involved in the process of deliberative debate that other means of public involvement can achieve.

CASE STUDY

Marketing, the environment and refuse collection

Refuse collection is one of the least glamorous aspects of public provision, but is a service that is universally needed, and has the potential to cause considerable unpleasantness if things go wrong with it. It is an area often subcontracted or passed from public to private providers, but has proven to be rather more complex than it might first appear. In the United States, Brown and Potoski (2004) have shown that, even though refuse disposal appears to be a remarkably simple area to administer in principle, it requires managers prepared to actively manage market relations in order to improvements in service delivery to occur.

Refuse collection is also interesting because it brings together a number of the tensions and debates present within this book. The increased recognition of the need to protect the environment, and to recycle rather than simply disposing of waste, give public managers a significant number of problems. There seems to be little doubt that the world is warming because of the human activity, with potentially disastrous consequences if it is allowed to progress too far. There is therefore a moral duty on us all to do things to try and prevent this from happening, and to protect the planet for future generations.

However, at the individual level, making the decision whether to throw away rubbish or to recycle can seem incredibly trivial. Individual citizens may believe that their own actions have very little effect upon the environment, and in that, they are largely correct. However, the problem is that if everyone comes to the same conclusion that little can be done through individual action, then a self-fulfilling prophecy occurs where little will be done by many communities to address their impact upon the environment. There is what economists call a collective action problem – where individual actions may have perverse affects upon the community as a whole.

An additional problem is that it is easy, if someone in my community is already concerned with their affect on the environment, and is taking a great deal of time and care to recycle their rubbish, for me to believe that there is no need for me to do so. I do not need to recycle because my neighbour does. This is the free-rider effect, where I rely upon others to do the right thing without bothering to do so myself in the belief that others' actions get me off the hook.

Given these problems, what can be done? One answer is for individuals to have to pay for rubbish that they wish to dispose, rather than recycle, with rubbish being weighed and a charge levied on individual households based upon its weight. This makes some sense, but would probably lead to some odd behaviour in communities as people try and dump their own rubbish into their neighbour's bins to avoid the charge themselves. Bins would probably therefore have to be locked, and additional time have to be spent by refuse collectors unlocking bins in order to empty them. Equally, it will also require a great deal of administrative time and effort to create a billing structure to weigh and charge individual houses for rubbish collection, and one that would potentially be subject to endless appeals and complaints from the households. Finally, there would be a strong incentive for households to engage in fly-tipping of their rubbish and to claim that they were not generating any household refuse at all, and so incurring no charge for it, but probably doing more environmental damage and costing the local authority a great deal to address with the problem.

If policymakers introduce the system of weighing and charging for rubbish, it becomes the public manager's job to try and administer this rather cumbersome system as efficiently as possible. Local authorities in the United Kingdom have allegedly put microchips in rubbish bins as a means of determining who owns which bin, so providing a system where rubbish can be weighed, but this has prompted a popular outcry in the media that appear not to link weighing bins with helping the environment. Clearly a great deal of public education would be required in this system, as well as strong procedures to monitor fairness and penalise fly-tippers. Weighing rubbish and charging for it would be an expensive system, as the extra income brought in from the charges would be unlikely to cover its additional running costs, but if the cost to the environment of not using the system were included, it may be shown to be financially viable.

Two alternatives to the system above suggest themselves. First would be for refuse collection to be wholesale privatised, and for private contractors to be given targets for recycling. Privatising the system would mean that it was run on a contract basis, with clear accountabilities set up for who was responsible for recycling at each stage, and what was to be done where too much waste was classified as rubbish rather than recycling. Such a system would be complex, but not necessarily unviable, even though it would require a great deal of care and thought to make it work.

Managers within the system would have clear targets for recycling and have to find ways of meeting them. Were the system decentralised it could provide an intriguing melting pot of alternative approaches to the problem of local recycling, with firms offering private individual incentives to modify their behaviour, such as rebates or even cash payments. Such a system would require regulation and policing though, as it would be subject to considerable gaming potential by both private providers and households.

A final alternative would be for the public sector to take full responsibility for all refuse collection and sorting of refuse into what is recyclable and what is not. Public managers would then be responsible for hitting recycling targets, and for sorting rubbish as effectively as possible. Households may have to pay higher refuse collection charges to make this possible, but might receive rebates where they recycle sufficient amounts of material – although again this would require weighing and so might produce an over-complex system.

As such, the issue of refuse collection brings together a range of debates in this book – should the public be treated as consumers and be allowed to throw away what they like, or given a more citizen type role and be expected to recycle in the name of saving the planet on behalf of their community? Should public managers incentivise individuals to try and recycle more, or are there community-based methods that might work better? What can marketing a marketing approach do to make people aware of the implications of their behaviour both publicly and privately?

Further reading

One of the earliest books fully exploring the use of marketing in public organisations was by Rod Sheaff (Sheaff, 1990) in his examination of marketing concepts to healthcare organisations. Sheaff's book, however, is remarkable in that many books that purport to be about public marketing more generally do not achieve its scope or depth. Kieron Walsh also wrote a great deal about the subject in both books (Walsh, 1996) and papers (Walsh, 1991). Any undergraduate studying marketing is likely to have come across textbooks by Philip Kotler, who has also written about the application of marketing concepts to the public sector (Kotler and Lee, 2006), and are worth a look, as is the chapter by Christy and Brown (1996) in Farnham and Horton's *Managing the New Public Services*.

Part 3

Contemporary issues
in public management

8

Performance management

Introduction

Previous chapters have shown how, along with the growth in the use of markets and market mechanisms, performance management has also become an increasingly central issue in the public sector. There is something of a paradox in this. On the one hand, markets are often used and invoked as a means of decentralising public service delivery. Their advocates claim that markets take the politics out of public services by forcing them to become more responsive to user need, rather than being the product of political design. On the other hand, however, performance management is often a strongly centralising force in public service delivery. It is often used as a means of getting local organisations to be more accountable to central or regional government bodies. Performance management is often portrayed as a neutral set of tools for planning and monitoring public service activity, but is inherently political in that it makes public organisations accountable to government (Spicer, 2004). The chapter asks the question, 'what is the role of performance management in public organisations?'

The chapter proceeds as follows. First, a brief section outlines the importance of performance management in today's public services, and gives some reasons for its increased usage. Next, the chapter explains the difference between performance management and performance measurement before discussing the problems that result from performance management in the public sector. After giving examples of how performance management plays itself out in specific services, it explores the implications of performance management for professional groupings in public services, especially in terms of the role of the HR function. It concludes by summarising the tensions found in the chapter and discusses their implications for public managers.

Performance management in context

There are a number of reasons why performance management has become so important in public services. A few of these are presented in Table 8.1 and are summarised below.

Table 8.1 Reasons for the growth of performance management in the public sector

Fiscal crisis and concerns about lack of public service measurement	As public budgets got tighter from the 1970s onwards, performance management became a more relevant tool for scrutinising public organisations, especially in relation to finance
Implementation gap	Policymakers became increasingly concerned that the plans were not being carried out at the local level – performance management gave them a way of trying to bridge this gap
Failure of democracy	If public services were not directly democratically accountable to the people, then a greater central accountability through performance management might provide an alternative
Concerns that decentralisation will mean loss of control for government	If markets and decentralisation are being carried out, how does the state continue to guarantee quality standards and accountability without greater use of performance management?
Wider availability of information technology	Wider use of IT means that more complex information systems can be constructed upon which performance management systems depend

For much of the history of public services central or federal government has struggled to measure or control what happens at local levels as the organisations responsible for the delivery of services can be hundreds of miles away, and policy can be mediated heavily through the activities of public professionals. Performance management has been seen by many in government as a means by which the stronger implementation of central policy can be achieved through the active measurement and the rewarding of local performance that meets centrally designed targets. Performance management can be seen as the solution to the 'implementation gap' between the ideas of policymakers in central governments and the delivery of public services on the ground.

Attempting to bridge the implementation gap is not the only reason for increased significance of performance management in public services. First, there is perceived failure of democracy as a means of achieving accountability (Fox and Miller, 1995). This results in a deficit that stronger performance management can narrow by making sure that services at least correspond to the standards prescribed of it, standards that are monitored ultimately by politicians, making public services at least accountable to democratically elected figures, if not the public itself. Second, in an era where public policy advocates have argued for the greater decentralisation of public services (Osborne and Gaebler, 1993), governments have felt the need to try and retain some central control whilst decentralising through the use of market mechanisms. They have decentralised the allocation of public services through markets, but tended to simultaneously centralise the accountability of their delivery through performance management systems. There has been a simultaneous decentralisation (of allocation) and centralisation (of accountability measurement) (Peckham *et al.*, 2005). Third, performance management systems depend on high-quality information systems. Public sector information systems have often struggled to meet the needs of their users or of central governments, but the wider availability of IT more generally has led to the potential for far greater information collection and analysis than in the past, and so to a far greater potential for some degree of performance measurement.

Performance management is not an entirely centralising force – this is only the case if performance standards put in place are decided centrally and local organisations are penalised if they do not meet them. It is equally possible for performance standards to be delegated to the local level, and so for them to become a means by which services might become more decentralised. However, the temptation has always been for central policymakers to use performance management as a means of achieving greater control over public services rather than delegating greater responsibility.

Performance management and performance measurement

Performance management is often equated to performance measurement, when the two are not the same, as the measurement of performance is only one aspect of its management, even if it tends to become the most contentious. A basic performance management feedback loop suggests a first stage where a plan for what needs to happen is constructed. Second, measurements are taken against that plan to establish whether performance is developing in line with the plan or not (the performance measurement stage). Third, corrective action is taken where performance is falling short of targets (negative feedback) or perhaps to push it even further from the target where the target is being exceeded (positive feedback). Finally, the cycle starts again, with a new plan being drawn up as necessary to reflect changes in the situation within which the service finds itself, such as the introduction of new policies or a change in the service's environment.

Management theory based on a simple systems approach, such as the performance management loop, treats performance as a control mechanism, suggests that learning can occur as adjustments are made to the organisation if its measured performance falls short or exceeds the standards of the plan (called 'single-loop' learning, as it occurs within the standard feedback cycle in the manner of a simple closed system like a thermostat and radiator). Further learning can also occur as planners look to see how realistic their expectations were in the light of actual performance and changes in the wider environment of the organisation (called 'double-loop learning' as it means that the plan upon which the performance plan was based is itself called under question (Argyris and Schon, 1995)).

As such, performance measurement is an important part of the cycle of performance management, but it also involves planning, taking action to deal with good or bad performance, and making sure that plans are still relevant. As such, it can be regarded as a strategic process in which all of these elements must be considered. 'Strategy' is a term that is much used and abused, and needs to be treated with caution because it has been somewhat 'naturalised' in the management literature as representing an objective series of processes when, especially in the public sector, strategies will fall upon organisational actors (especially public professionals) in different ways (Llewellyn and Tappin, 2003). Where it falls on actors who are inexperienced in strategic processes (or represent 'unculti-vated ground' (p. 978)) there is a danger of a lack of debate over the meaning and purposes of strategy occurring. Bearing this in mind, how does performance management work in the public sector?

Performance management in the public sector

Planning

In order to performance manage, a plan is necessary. The first question is establishing actually how a plan should be put together and who should contribute to it. One obvious answer is that it is for the government to put together plans for public organisations – in the past this has often been how things worked. In order to try and achieve a unified hierarchy of control, government put together plans that were then worked out in greater detail at each level down the hierarchy, being broken down into more specific and precise goals.

However, the view that central policymakers are solely responsible for the setting of plans has come increasingly under question. The role of the user has become more impor-tant as consumerist agendas have become more significant in public organisations, and the public more generally have demanded the politicians pay closer attention to their needs and aspirations. Politicians have increasingly found themselves engaged in consultation and 'listening' exercise before constructing plans, having to show that they are not simply constructing plans according to their own understanding and prejudices. Equally, there are several other bodies that have had considerable influence over the policy process at vari-ous times in the history of public organisations. Trades unions have sometimes demanded inclusion where plans for public services significantly affect their members, with corpo-ratist models of policymaking more common in Europe than elsewhere, but attempted at various times in the United Kingdom as well. Strong professional groups in public organ-isations have also demanded inclusion in policy formulation, particularly those with high prestige and status, such as the doctors. The influence of professional groups often goes beyond their expertise and to a level where they may have attended the same schools and universities as policymakers, thereby creating an administrative 'elite' where under-standings are reached outside of the formal policy process itself (Wright Mills, 1956). This means that the plans that finally emerge for public services might be the result of informal discussion and consultation that is not at all transparent to the public at large. This is a more pluralistic view of policy than the assumption that politicians alone put together plans, but not one that is particularly democratic or very accountable to the public.

The fact that many societal groups are interested in being a part of the plan-setting for public organisations is because their scope is often so wide, and because their activities have so many implications for so many people. School provision does not just impact upon parents of children of school age and their children, but can also significantly affect property prices in the area, meaning it potentially affects all householders, has the potential to cause planning issues because of traffic problems when children are arriving or leaving, can reduce crime (by taking young people off the street) or increase it (creating a concentration of young people who might try and 'bunk off' or 'shirk' classes), as well creating a potential market for local business suppliers and local businesses themselves, who may come to rely upon school children spending money in their stores. The knock-on effects of public organisations are considerable, leading to local communities and businesses wanting a say in how they are run as well as the service users and general public.

As public services have so many interested parties (or, in contemporary parlance, 'stakeholders'), any plan must attempt to work through the competing interests of those parties to attempt to create goals and targets that as many as possible can sign up to. This requires public managers to be able to work across several different groups, to listen to their concerns and to show that they are being treated seriously, even if they cannot all have what they want. This also means that long-term relationships must be formed as not all the goals put forward by interest groups can be achieved quickly – patience and mutual understanding are important virtues in public service planning (Stoker, 2006).

Plans and measures

If planning is a complex process, then establishing reliable measures that can assess the success or failure of the plans is perhaps harder still. There is now a considerable literature on the difficulties of performance measurement in the public sector (Greener, 2003b; Pollitt, 1986; Sanderson, 1998; Talbot, 2000). It is difficult to summarise the findings of research in just a few words, but a particularly important theme is that public organisation's output can be very difficult to measure. This problem is clearly a part of both the planning and the measurement elements of performance management – it relates not only to planning as plans must be broken down into objectives, at least some of which need to be measurable, but also to the measurement element of performance management as actual performance needs to be compared with the plan in order to measure progress.

Boyne and Gould-Williams in one of their studies of local government planning (Boyne and Gould-Williams, 2003) found that plans can work well where favourable perceptions of the planning process are already held within the organisation but that a 'proliferation of precise quantitative targets is associated with poorer performance' (p. 130). Their best guess, however, is that planning does lead to service improvement overall, suggesting that it has a valuable role in the performance management cycle.

The measurement of public organisations is difficult because finding variables that capture their activities can often prove elusive. Nicholson-Crotty and his collaborators (Nicholson-Crotty et al., 2006) found, in an examination of educational organisations in Texas, that managers' perceptions of their organisations depended significantly upon the choice of performance measures that they used. An example of the difficulties of finding appropriate measures in the public sector should make this clear.

Road planning and performance management

Road planning is usually carried out in urban areas by members of local authorities. Planning departments will work to try and deal with the problems of increased traffic flow through towns, at the same time trying to make sure that people are attracted into urban areas because of the increased commercial opportunities afforded business as a result. They therefore have to balance the needs of commerce (and often tourism) in local areas, which want as many people as possible to visit, with the need of local residents, who probably just want to get to and from work as quickly as possible. Road planning also does not happen without regard to the road infrastructure of the past – today's planners inherit the decisions of previous planners and cannot simply rip up all the roads and start again. Some cities have heritage landmarks that may mean that the road infrastructure is very limited in where it can or cannot go, as demolishing buildings of historic significance is clearly off-limits

The measure of the effectiveness of road planning is therefore a function of several factors. Clearly traffic flow is important, with higher volumes being better for business (up to a point where traffic simply stops moving or pollution get very bad, perhaps deterring people from visiting) and lower volumes better for residents (but not to a point where towns become so empty that property prices start falling and local amenities move away). Coming up with an agreed level of traffic that planners should be aiming for might therefore be a highly political, or even arbitrary exercise. Equally some areas of town might be traffic blackspots with either exceptionally slow moving traffic or a number of accidents, but road planners unable to do much about this because the causes are due to the location of an historical monument (that means there is limited space for roads) or a school (which may be the responsibility of the education department and so outside the scope of their influence) or an employer with a large workforce all trying to arrive and leave at the same time (which might be the result of decisions from the local authority's commercial department).

As such, the road planning department might find themselves having to come up with measures of traffic flow that are likely to be both highly contested and contestable, and which are thwarted by decisions made in other departments, but then being held to blame for them. This highlights the need for public managers to be able to work across areas of their organisations (and even to work across organisations), but if each department or organisation has its own performance management goals then this may become impossible as the relationship might become competitive and insular rather than collaborative and outward looking.

Table 8.2 Some problems with performance measurement

Measuring the measurable only	Instead of attempting to capture the complexity of outputs of public organisations, over-simple measures are put in place that do not really represent them
Target focus	Managers become so concerned with meeting particular targets that they do not manage the service for the good of the public any more
Gaming	Managers manipulate systems in order to try and present their performance as being better than it is, even giving fraudulent returns of their activities

Measurement

Moving on to the measurement stage of the performance cycle, a range of additional problems become apparent. These are summarised in Table 8.2, and again, discussed at greater length below.

Measuring what can be measured

One problem that overlaps with the planning process is where planners find it impossible to find a variable that measures the performance of their organisation, and so instead of trying to find innovative ways of measuring activity, base their planning decisions on what they can measure. It may seem odd planning on the basis of what can be measured rather than on what the public organisation really does, but this is surprisingly common. Healthcare is a good example. Working out how healthy a person is can be a remarkably difficult thing to do. Many doctors will ask 'healthy for what?' if confronted by the question, as the standards required by a regular exerciser will be very different from those of a dedicated fast food consumer. In the former case not being able to run for an hour because of joint pain might be seen as a major problem, whereas in the latter this would hardly impinge upon the individual's daily activities, which might be more about being able to consume particular types of food without feeling sick. Objective measures can be constructed in terms of blood pressure and heart rate, but these again may simply not apply to many people, so long as they are able to meet their home and work needs they may not care if they are a little overweight or if their cholesterol level is too high.

How we measure how healthy we are is a function of our expectations and the environment we find ourselves in. If working this out for an individual can be hard, then working out how healthy a whole local population is can border on the impossible. However, there are a range of simple indicators that can be used to measure the health of both individuals and populations. The body mass index (BMI) can measure a person's weight to height, and give an indication of whether they are obese or not. However, the weight part of the measure does not differentiate muscle from fat, and so, famously, Hollywood stars such as

Brad Pitt appear obese according to the index. Equally, finding a baseline from which to apply an index to assess healthcare can be very difficult, as much of the data upon which these baselines of healthiness are based are by their nature historic, and so may not be relevant in a world that has changed considerably since those measurements were originally taken. Attempting to measure health based on these variables might be deeply flawed, but public managers may find that they have no alternative where they are faced with governments demanding that increased state investment in their service delivers an improvement in the area required, and that improvement is measurable.

Target focus

A related problem is where public managers become focused not on improving their service, but instead upon the variables used to measure the improvements in their service. To continue with the example of healthcare, doctors might be told, for example, that they must see a patient within 30 minutes of their arrival for an appointment. This seems sensible – patients should not be kept waiting for unreasonable amounts of time. However, it also creates space for public managers to 'game' the system. Looking at the target, doctors do not have to treat the patient, but merely to 'see' them. As such, an easy way of meeting the target would be for doctors, in-between treating patients, to periodically (every 30 minutes) to emerge from their treatment rooms, greet all the patients waiting, and then to return to their room again. They will have 'seen' the patients, and so met the target. If this sounds far-fetched, then readers should be assured that I did not make it up.

A second example might be where policymakers become aware of the 'seeing' patients ruse, and change the target to say that all patients should have their treatment begun within 30 minutes of arriving for an appointment. A devious public manager might again look at the exact wording of the target, and put in place a system whereby, because the new target does not specify a doctor will treat the patient, a triage nurse instead will be tasked with meeting every new patient as they arrive, interviewing them, and where possible dealing with patient problems without the doctor. The hospital might argue that diagnosing the patient is a crucial part of treatment, and interviewing the patient is an important part of diagnosis. Although no doctor has been near a patient, the process of treatment therefore has begun as soon as the triage nurse sits down with the patient, and the target has been met.

Performance gaming

Where public managers find themselves in a regime where they stand to lose performance-related pay or even their job should they fail to meet their required target level, things can get even worse. In these situations there can be strong incentives to go beyond target focus of the type described above and to descend into blatant gaming of the system. If patients cannot be seen quickly enough, bogus patients have sometimes been entered onto computer databases to make it look like services are treating more patients than they actually are. Where managers are responsible for several areas of a service and some are falling behind targets whereas others are well in front, there will be a temptation to try and 'reallocate' numbers to try and artificially bring up the performance of the poor areas where this might lead to sanctions against the managers or service. If public managers are on short-term contracts requiring high performance, or where promotions depend upon hitting particular targets, then these sort of temptations will be great.

Where public managers do not expect to stay in organisations very long before moving on to new posts, it will always be tempting for them to try and conceal the situation within their organisation where things are not going well rather than to try and actually deal with their underlying problems, which may be much more time-consuming work that does not necessarily deliver the boosts to performance measures that gaming the figures might. Where public managers are given incentives that lead them down the path of focusing on numbers rather than actual performance, they will, like any other human being, have to be strong to do what is easy rather than what is right for their service. In these circumstances public management performance literally becomes a performance (Talbot, 2000) – an attempt to present a view of the organisation that may bear only a tenuous reality to its actual state, and to periodic crises before which managers attempt to move on before the underlying situation becomes apparent.

Hood (2006), in his summary of gaming problems coming from the UK Blair government's reforms, suggests that their extensive use of targets appears to lead to three classic gaming responses; ratchet effects (the tendency of target setters to fix next year's targets a little above this year's, leading to providers deliberately reining back on this year's production); threshold effects (where uniform target leads to no incentive for those that exceed targets); and output distortion (the deliberate manipulation of results). Hood also suggests that policymakers have been too quick to accept good news from their performance measurement systems uncritically, taking reported gains at face value, and having no coherent antigaming strategy.

Taking action

After performance measurement, the next stage of the performance cycle is taking action when measured performance appears out of line with reported performance. Where performance is less (or more) than hoped for, managers should be intervening to find ways of addressing the difference.

If too few patients are seen (or treated) by a hospital or if exam results in schools are below those expected, managers should be coming up with strategies to try and resolve the problems the performance system has brought to their attention. This asks a fundamental question of public managers – can they actually make a difference to the service they are responsible for? The answer can often be quite sobering and quite difficult.

The example of road planning above suggested that public managers might be held responsible for the results of decisions of other departments, and the only way for this to be resolved is for cross-boundary working and close collaboration across the whole of delivery. But what if the problems identified as preventing targets from being met go beyond the limits of local public organisation? What if they are due to more general societal forces such as poverty or demography? A local manager might be held accountable for smoking cessation in the local area, or at least for persuading local people to enrol in smoking cessation programmes. The problem is that local people may not perceive smoking to be a problem – their social backgrounds might be such that their friends, relatives and parents smoke, and smoking might be a part of the fabric of social life. Cigarettes might be purchased in collective trips to the local shops, smoked together, and the habit becomes something regarded as a defining feature of a particular group. In this situation, if people do not regard themselves as having a problem, and they are not doing anything illegal, is it really the job of public managers to attempt to persuade them otherwise? What chance do public managers have in particular social settings where smoking is part of the embedded culture, compared to other areas, where it might be seen much more as an unacceptable act, and individuals come forward willingly to attempt to give up? The social setting for a particular public manager might make a considerable difference for the measured success of his or her activities, as well as for the potential to change behaviour.

Equally, if a public manager is engaged in trying to improve services for older people in their local area, they are substantially more likely to be successful where a strong network of representatives for that age group are already in place and can be mobilised. A seaside retirement town is much more likely to back changes that mean more services for older people than a town where predominantly young people reside. Ironically, of course, the former town is likely to already be well endowed with facilities for older people, and the latter town having a shortage. Breaking through the existing infrastructure is difficult enough because of its very physical presence, but public managers will also have to deal with the vested interests that seek to protect it and persuade them, often in a situation where budgets are a zero-sum game (where an increase in funding for one service means a reduction in funding for another), that spending money in an under-resourced area is required.

Interest groups and professional groups

This takes us on to the subject of interest groups more generally. Many public organisations, because of the nature of the services they deliver or the complexity of the organisation required to deliver those services, have strong professional groups within them. Professionals will demand the ability to express their own judgement of what is required based on their specific expert knowledge. Public managers are placed in a difficult situation where they want to change things as the result of a performance management system demonstrating low levels of achievement. Where professionals agreed the original plan, they may have 'buy-in' to the achievement of higher levels of performance, and so agree to do more to try and improve things. However, the situation is often more difficult than this. Managers may have to rely upon the professionals to formulate their own improvement plans and to attempt to implement them within a specific time frame in order to demonstrate that improvements are being made. However, if professionals do not regard the original plan as being viable or sensible, then they may equally regard a deviation of measured performance compared to the plan as being irrelevant, and so no further action to be needed. Public managers therefore have to try and make the original plan appear viable and important, even if the particular professionals now refusing to take action were not involved in its formulation.

Public managers therefore have both a selling job and a telling job in relation to performance management. The selling is needed to show that conforming to the plan is necessary in order to secure the service's improvement, or even its future. A sense of shared destiny can overcome professional backgrounds remarkably quickly. In this case public managers will have to show that they have the support of central or regional policymakers, and that there are sanctions for non-compliance (as well as hopefully, rewards for meeting the plan's targets). A telling job might be necessary where managers can find no way of persuading professionals that a change in their behaviour is necessary. This can be remarkably difficult, as professional groupings often have their own hierarchies and loyalties, may not regard public managers as holding any authority over them, even where this is, in fact, the case. Faced with the complexities of having to 'tell' professionals to change their behaviour, public managers often engage in a complex range of strategies for trying to achieve this goal without direct confrontation, such as scheduling meetings to give professionals minimum preparation time to oppose changes, setting agendas to conceal contentious items of business, and attempting to fill meetings with their own supporters so that professionals are bound by decisions taken collectively, but with the odds rigged heavily in their favour (Greener, 2005).

These strategies of avoiding direct confrontation with public professionals are not exactly above-board, but are a part of organisational life where change can be difficult to achieve. It is not entirely unknown for professionals to engage in similar kinds of behaviour to preserve the status quo. An interesting situation appears where professionals take on managerial responsibilities, and attempt to straddle the two roles. The evidence suggests that in a conflictual situation, professionals tend to revert back to their professional rather than their managerial role (Kitchener, 2000), but this will depend upon the particular professional in question, and some of the most evangelical managers of public organisations are former professionals who have become frustrated by the constraints of their previous identity.

Public managers and HR

The problems of the relationship between public managers and professionals can often be traced back to the poor development of the HR function in public organisations. One of the differences between the old public administration and the new public management was that in the past, personnel functions were in place that were primarily concerned with making sure that legal requirements were met for the organisation, and for dealing with any legal disputes that arose around employment (Boyne et al., 1999). These are clearly important roles within an organisation, but is a rather passive use of the organisational function responsible for overseeing and supporting those working within it.

Contemporary human resource management is a more pro-active process, embracing the functions of the old personnel departments, but attempting to increase its range of activities across the organisation. It takes a greater responsibility for the proactive recruitment of outstanding individuals into the organisation, as well as their development once recruited. It tries to improve the productivity of those working within the organisation by assessing their training needs and making sure that their skills and professional knowledge are kept up-to-date. Human resource management is regarded as one of the key ways that an organisation can achieve a competitive edge over its rivals and to make the most of those working within it. It therefore corresponds with contemporary notions of achieving competitive advantage through the human capital of an organisation, such as the resource-based view of the firm (Barney, 1996). Performance management is therefore a crucial part of human resource management.

HR and change dissenters

Faced with performance management pressures to deliver services at higher standards, public managers have increasingly called upon the human resources function to help them deal with professionals unwilling or unable to conform with change agendas. Professionals unwilling to change their practices have been requested to update their skills or acquire new ones, such as customer-orientation, and have found themselves drawn into standardised employment practices from which they had previously enjoyed considerable freedom. Professionals might be required to attend a certain number of management development courses each year in order to show their commitment to improving the standards of customer focus. HR functions have taken a lead in developing standardised job profiles for professional groupings that specify the roles required of them, and once these roles have been standardised further, have developed the means by which the performance of individual professionals can be measured and assessed.

The promotion and development of professionals is no longer the exclusive concern of the professional groupings themselves, but instead involves public managers and HR professionals, who have become increasingly involved in making sure that professionals are meeting the roles required of them. Bonuses and merit awards, previously given by professionals to professionals through sub-committees that were based on professional expertise, have found themselves under the scrutiny of both public managers and user representatives in the name of increasing accountability and transparency. If they are to be promoted, professionals increasingly find themselves required not only to meet just the standards of their professional organisations, but also to have shown a commitment to their managerial development through attending organisational development courses and understanding budgets and marketing principles.

Where professionals repeatedly fail to come up to performance standards, or where they refuse entirely to co-operate with performance management systems, this might ultimately lead for public managers to be supported in a decision to dismiss them from their posts. Because of the high status of many public professionals and the prestigious professional support groups that they may belong to, this can be a time-consuming and difficult process for everyone involved. It is likely to result in a legal case, with HR functions increasingly having to call upon in-house or external specialist legal services, as well as making sure that the cases public managers bring to them where dismissal is necessary are well supported by documentation and procedurally correct. The problem is that the sanction of dismissal is still relatively (compared to the private sector at least) under-used in most public organisations, which means that public managers are still relatively inexperienced in dealing with it. They will therefore need a great deal of support and help from HR functions, which are themselves often under-resourced and ill-equipped to deal with complex cases. As HR in the public sector expands its role, it is becoming regarded as a service for public managers to utilise in their organisations, and it needs to raise its game to make sure that it is one they regard as valuable to them rather than as a central overhead that generates no useful return.

Completing the performance management loop

Having worked through the stages of agreeing a plan, measuring performance against it, and trying to change professional behaviour where necessary in order to meet performance standards, this takes us back to the beginning of the performance management cycle again, the process of reassessing the validity of the present plan amongst the many available stakeholders. At this stage, those responsible for planning have something of a conundrum. If they throw out the existing plan, opting for a range of new goals and targets, then they can be seen as acknowledging the problems with past plans and accepting the need for change. This may be embraced by public managers and those responsible for the delivery for public services as a positive step if the problems of the past have been overwhelming. However, it can also be seen as 'moving the goalposts' and a demoralising process within which public workers have to constantly reset their goals depending upon which plan has been put in place this year.

Too much change can result in 'redisorganisation' (Smith *et al.*, 2001) as reform programme comes after reform programme and little or no stability is ever granted for services. Equally, it is hard to measure whether a service is actually getting better or not if the variables used to measure them are changed every year, taking validity away from any claims of reforming services in the name of improvement because it becomes almost impossible to demonstrate that such improvement has actually occurred. The argument for the stability of measures on the other hand is that it allows continuity of measurement, and at least some indication of whether services are getting better or not. However, it will also be unpopular if poor measures, or difficult to achieve measures, are in place that lead to public managers being removed from their jobs for a failure to demonstrate success. Given this problem, it seems hardly surprising that politicians find it almost impossible to resist changing performance measures frequently, and that they may even want to try and revisit the entire basis of the performance management system in order to find a new solution to the many problems involved in attempting to assess how well public services are delivered.

Conclusion

Performance management is about setting plans, measuring progress against them, taking any necessary action, and then assessing the plan to make sure that it is still relevant. It is a simple process in principle, but its application in the political environment of the public sector leads to a number of difficulties and problems.

Agreeing a plan between multiple stakeholders is a complex process because it may lead to those with very different values and goals attempting to try and find ways of sharing sufficient common ground to come up with a plan of what should be done. The goals of business leaders will often be very different from the goals of local residents, and public managers must find some process by which an agreement can be reached that they all can respect. Where stakeholders are consulted and their views are rejected, they may not wish to re-enter the planning process again, and so public managers will have to work extra hard to include groups whose views have been sought but not included in their present plans. Even if stakeholders can reach agreement, public managers must still work together to achieve their stated goals; middle-level managers may not share the same goals as those higher up their organisations, and often have a key role in modifying strategy rather than simply carrying it out (Currie, 1999).

Once a plan has been put in place, the problem will often come in coming up with appropriate measures to determine whether or not it is being met. The difficulty of measuring public sector output is a recurring theme throughout the book because it can lead to some rather perverse outcomes. Good examination results are not the same things as providing a good education service (although the two are related) and high user ratings are not the same thing as a good public service. Public managers need to find the best possible measures of their service's success, and be flexible enough to realise that any measure is unlikely to do the job forever – as contexts and services change they must be alert to both 'hard' and 'soft' indications (Goddard et al., 1999) of whether their service is working. As well as hard numbers of those things that are measurable, other softer forms of intelligence will be available that will be more opinion-based, but may well be crucial in assessing how well organisations are performing. A distinction is sometimes made between outputs (the measures to be implemented) and outcomes (the end results of reform programmes) – the first are picked up by specific performance measures, whereas the second are often not (Polidano et al., 1998), and may be both intended and unintended (Mannion et al., 2001). Public managers must also avoid the temptations of gaming their performance measures, even where policymakers put tremendous pressure on them to achieve results that may not be realisable.

If action is necessary because public organisations are under-performing, then managers will often have to deal with strong professional groups and get them to change their practices. Where professionals believe that public managers have no authority, or that they lack legitimacy because they are not as well educated or as prestigious as them, this will be difficult. In this situation public managers often employ a range of strategies to get professionals on side with change, but where these do not work, they may have to go down disciplinary routes. In these circumstances, the HR function of the public organisation will become important, but it is still often the case that both managers and HR professionals are ill-equipped at dealing with low performing professionals, making the problem of raising the performance of public organisations an entrenched one.

Finally, public managers must be resilient in that, once they have completed a cycle of the performance loop, little else remains other for them to have to start again and begin the planning process once more. They need to occupy a number of different roles during the whole process; facilitating between a range of stakeholders to get them to agree to 'buy in' to a plan and so being able to both 'sell' and 'tell' it; being realists in the process of performance measurement by recognising that some targets, if not met, might lose them their jobs; being able to support professionals who are prepared to work with new ways of working as well as trying to persuade and cajole that are not; being assertive and able to face up to professionals who are systematically under-performing; and having a considerable amount of stamina in the knowledge that once the performance cycle is over it must be begun again the following year. Table 8.3 summarises public management roles during a cycle of performance management.

Public managers must therefore look to the future and be able to build long-term relationships that go beyond any particular planning cycle, but will possibly exist in an environment that encourages the meeting of short-term performance targets by any means necessary, with possible sanctions for those that do not meet them. Ackroyd, Hughes and Soothill (1989) suggest that the imposition of prescribed managerial practices, of which

Table 8.3 Public manager roles during performance management

Planning	Liaising between stakeholders
	Finding ways of setting shared goals
	Including all groups with a right to voice
Measurement	Ensuring that targets are reflective of actual performance
	Dealing with hard and soft information
	Avoiding gaming
Action	Selling and telling
	Utilising appropriate change strategies
	Working with HR
Completing the loop	Keeping the process going
	Deciding between change or continuing with plans

centrally prescribed performance management systems are perhaps the most visible example, end up taking away discretion from public managers and reducing their autonomy and ability to manage their organisations. It is somewhat paradoxical that, at exactly the time the state has demanded that public managers take greater control of their organisations, the careless imposition of centrally imposed managerial strategies might actually remove their capacity to manage.

Behn (2003) suggests that performance measures are helpful in achieving eight different managerial purposes (evaluation, control, budgeting, motivating, promoting, celebration, learning and improvement), but that no particular measure is appropriate for all eight purposes. Public managers therefore need to think carefully about the managerial purpose performance management that might contribute in order to deploy measures appropriately, and to be aware that performance measures are not objective, neutral tools, but instead need to be treated with caution as each measure may fit some purposes well, and other purposes rather badly.

CASE STUDY

Performance management in higher education

Higher education is an interesting area of public service for a number of reasons. First, most of the managers in higher education are academics or former academics, so the tension between professionalism and management is extremely strong – when under pressure do academic managers revert to their professional or managerial type? Second, higher education is not insulated from the market in that students have a reasonably wide choice of where they study for a degree or postgraduate qualification. But equally, higher education institutions also choose their students; any country has a hierarchy of providers with some reckoned to be the best (Ivy League, Oxbridge) and others, who do not have such elevated reputations, taking students with less strong academic qualifications. If students choose universities, then universities also tend to attract particular kinds of students – this is a long way from a free market. Third, the traditions of academic freedom lead to universities having a range of staff in place from internationally recognised research stars through to staff in teaching-only roles, all of whom, upon being granted a permanent contract in the United Kingdom, or tenure in the United States, have a relatively (compared to most private industry) protected position in terms of job security. If staff believe their job is safe, how do you motivate them?

These problems combine to create a fascinating environment to manage in. In the United States the problem of incentivising staff is dealt with in a very front-loaded way. New academics are often employed in University Departments without having been granted a permanent position, and are expected to show that they are worth keeping or of 'making tenure'. To this end, more staff might be initially employed than there are permanent positions available, and some expected to fall by the wayside on the way to developing an academic career. Academics are expected to achieve high-impact research that is cited by their peers, and, depending on the institution they are employed in, increasingly to show they are good teachers and competent administrators as well. Getting tenure can be a cut-throat business, with several websites existing which contain advice from experienced staff giving clues as to how it might be achieved.

Once staff have achieved tenure though, there is an assumption (which is being brought under question in some institutions, although largely appears still in place) that they have a job for life at their university if they wish it. The public management problem is therefore how to incentivise staff after they have achieved tenure. In the case of low performers, academics who publish very little and make little effort to continue to achieve their pre-tenure standards, managers have a significant problem in performance managing staff. Promotion and appraisal systems need to be introduced to try and move staff on in their careers, or to capture their lack of achievement and to try and find ways of addressing it.

In the United Kingdom academics are often appointed to permanent positions on a probationary basis, although with the assumption that their contract is in little danger of not being renewed unless they demonstrate a high degree of incompetence. However, they are often initially appointed at a very junior level, and so are incentivised through trying to reach higher grades and more pay.

The UK government has attempted to performance manage research through the Research Assessment Exercise (RAE), which offers funding for the best performing universities in this area. The problem is assessing what research is to count as the best, and presently involves a substantial peer review system that has attracted a great deal of criticism because it is unwieldy, that it forces academics to write before they might be prepared or ready and that it can damage an academic's career if he or she is not included in the exercise. This might occur if they have not produced enough research, or enough research of a high enough quality. Career progression for research-active academics certainly depends on being included in the RAE, but whether asking for them to produce four pieces of research to be included in the process (which occurs every five or six years) is fair remains a vexed question.

The RAE has had some perverse outcomes for managers of University Departments. Academics with strong publication and funding records become very attractive to other universities, and so as the date of assessment nears, a transfer market of those perceived to be 'research stars' appears. The task for managers becomes about retaining high-quality staff, even though the HR strategies of most universities tend to be relatively inflexible about what can be offered in terms of pay or promotions.

They therefore often have to find non-pay or promotion means of retaining staff, such as offering research leave or teaching relief.

The transfer market that occurs as a result of the RAE creates the problem that it is often easier to be promoted in the United Kingdom by moving job than by staying in the same institution. Applying for promotion often involves a lengthy process of submitting a case, it being peer-reviewed by international experts, and internally assessed by the university. It can often take in excess of six months. Applying for a new job, in contrast, typically involves filling in an application form, submitting a CV, getting friends to provide good references, and doing well in an interview. Despite the upheaval, it can be easier to get a new job at a higher level than get promoted, and this can result in academics getting new jobs only to try and persuade their present universities to promote them as a special or emergency retention case. In all, the academic job market tends to get a little silly as the date of the RAE approaches, and some odd appointment and retention decisions can be made.

The problem of what to do about low performing Professors is a problem in the United Kingdom as well as the United States. Once staff have been promoted to professorial level, it can be extremely difficult to remove them, even if they do very little, and Departments might have to 'carry' some professorial staff who make little contribution to academic life there. The relative under-development of HR in many UK universities contributes to this, as does having academics as managers, as this can make them reluctant to challenge their underperforming colleagues. This is because academic managers often have little knowledge of HR practice or employment law, and so they may think it is easier to ignore low performing colleagues than to try and performance manage them.

Further reading

Performance management and performance measurement have practically become industries in their own right over the last ten years. Among the earliest studies of performance measures were those conducted by Christopher Pollitt (1985) in the United Kingdom (1985), who has revisited the subject in his recent *The Essential Public Manager* (Pollitt, 2003). The strategic approach to performance management is presented in a number of contexts by Johnson and Schoes in their edited book *Exploring Public Sector Strategy* (Johnson and Scholes, 2001).

A great deal of the work on performance management attempts to link it to variables that assess other aspects of public organisations, such as their organisational culture (Mannion *et al.*, 2004), and to try and find prescriptions for improvement as a result. The confusion over the use of performance management is perhaps best summarised, however, by Colin Talbot (2000) in his piece 'performing performance'.

Professionals in public management

Introduction

This book has suggested that public service are often characterised by having a strong professionalised presence within them. Local government services have planners, hospitals have doctors (perhaps the most revered public service profession), schools have teachers and universities have academics. They are a distinctive part of public service organisation, although of course not an exclusive one, as many of these professional groups work within the private sector as well.

Where services have to be organised using professionals this brings an additional level of complexity to public management. This chapter explores the challenges that professionalised services offer to public managers, raising questions of their relationship with both managers and users. It also examines the question of who should run public services – should it be managers brought in from the private sector or from other successful public services – suggesting that management is something of a generic skill? Should public services be run by the professionals themselves because of the specialist nature of their contribution to those services? Before it is possible to tackle these questions, however, it is important first to define what exactly professionals are, and to explore the implications of the dimensions of professionalism for those seeking to manage them.

The nature of professionalism

There is a well-established literature exploring professionalism (Ackroyd, 1996; DiMaggio, 1991; Gillespie, 1997; Haug and Sussman, 1969; Klein, 1990; Kirkpatrick and Ackroyd, 2003; Wilding, 1982). From these studies, it seems important to consider what the nature of professional work is, and to try and work out what difference it makes to organisational life. A number of dimension of professionalism recur as being important to these questions. They are shown in Table 9.1 and discussed in greater depth below.

Table 9.1   The dimensions of professionalism

Dimension	Problem to managers
Expert knowledge	They know things managers don't – so how can managers assess their work?
Socially powerful	They are often well-connected and powerful – so how can managers challenge them if necessary?
Autonomous	They are trained to work autonomously – so how can managers hold them to account?
Have confidential relationships with their clients	Their work often cannot be directly observed by managers, so how can they see if it is being done well or not?
Outputs difficult to measure	Their activities may be difficult to measure, so how can managers tell good from bad performers?
Have discretion over their work	Their actions are not programmable, so how can managers tell when professional decisions are poor ones?
Can do extraordinary things	They may necessary to get the job done, so what do managers do when professionals refuse to work with them?
Are self-regulating	Professional discipline may be asserted in the first instance by their regulatory body, so how do managers control professionals where their first allegiance may always be to their professional association?

Professionals have expert knowledge

First, professionals have expert knowledge. This means that they have often been through long periods of training and have acquired high-level skills that are often not available to the general population. These skills might be based in the knowledge of complex laws, as with planners or those in the legal profession, or in the understanding of complex systems, such as the workings of the human body in medicine. Expert knowledge means that professionals have a special status in an organisation and are able to argue that managers without their specialist knowledge cannot understand their work. How is a manager who lacks this expertise supposed to organise and direct a professional to do their work better when they do not necessarily understand the nature of the work? This is an age-old conundrum, to which there are a few answers.

One way of dealing with the problem of the management of expert knowledge is for managers to measure not how work is done, but the outcomes or outputs of the work, and to ask professionals to account for significant differences there. Where one surgeon has a very high success rate for a procedure, and another surgeon a low rate, this would seem to require an explanation. The problem is that the manager may not be able to assess whether the explanation given by the professionals is a sensible one or not, as this may too depend upon expert knowledge. This carries with it parallels with the kind of work often done by traders in complex financial instruments in the private sector, where it often seems as if managers have little or no understanding of what it is those they are meant to be responsible for are doing (Greener, 2006; McLean and Elkind, 2004).

An alternative is for professionals to be brought in to assess the work of their peers; professionals might be given managerial roles and so be asked to oversee other professionals, or regular reviews put in place where teams were brought in to assess the quality of work independently. The difficulty with the first approach is that professionals, when also given managerial roles, may tend to revert back to their professional identity where conflict between the two arises (Kitchener, 2000). This is hardly surprising – professional/managers will have to spend considerably longer time as professionals than as managers, and may be considering that they will have to return to their professional role once their time as a manager has passed. Under these circumstances, making an enemy of other professionals by being seen to side with managers may be thought of as unwise long-term career move.

Equally, in review groups designed to review professional work, there is a danger that those professionals chosen bring into the review norms and standards to judge their peers that would not be shared by managers or service users, and so decisions which appear extraordinary to those other groups might be made. Medical regulation procedures, for example, sometimes lead to doctors being allowed to continue to practice by their peers when user groups campaign outside hearings for their licenses to be removed. In these circumstances the clashes between user understanding of services and professional understanding are brought out into the open, often with the media making an inflammatory contribution. Professional hearings and reviews are accused of being 'old boys clubs' which are designed more to protect professionals than to prevent bad decision being made or harm to users occurring, and public misunderstandings abound (Tallis, 2005). In this situation managers are often caught between the demands of users for professionals to be removed and the demands of professionals that their colleague be allowed to practice or to be reinstated. This kind of dispute highlights the question of who should have the final say in how services are run – should it be service users, expert professionals, politicians or managers attempting to get services to work as a whole?

Professionals are socially powerful

The second key characteristic of professional status is that professionals often come from extremely well-connected backgrounds. This is not always the case – in more recent times professional groupings have become far more diverse than in the past, with increased educational mobility meaning that professionals are more likely than ever to come from both genders and a range of ethnicities. However, they are still most likely to come from the middle classes of a society, and from the ethnic group that is economically dominant within it. This has a knock-on effect for many professionals, who may have attended the same schools together (or at least the same universities), are likely to have been educated with other powerful figures (particularly politicians) and so have influence beyond even that which professional status affords. Equally, professional groupings tend to have their own membership organisations, with those organisations having high-level access to politicians and other important decision-makers because of their social background and professional importance.

The leaders of professional organisations may regard themselves as having a right to contribute not only to the running of their own organisations, but also towards national policy formulation and to government debates around their professional area. They may also expect to be able to lead and participate in high-profile media campaigns against the government of the day where they believe that their particular public service is not being well supported. Some professional groups, such as doctors, will be able to make these claims rather more strongly than others because of their public popularity and ability to generate stories that will be interested to the media (with headlines of the type 'Health services in crisis, say leading doctors').

The challenge that the influence professionals hold in society raises for public managers is that they can be powerful supporters but extremely difficult opponents. Professionals can often be strong allies where managers are seen to be supporting the profession's interest, but where they challenge it can find themselves attacked in the media, by professional organisations, and even subject to legal challenge. Where legal action is threatened and management decisions are brought under the scrutiny of well-organised and influential professional bodies, managers who dare to challenge professional behaviour, or who threaten to remove professionals they perceive as under-performing, may find themselves under considerable pressure to reconsider their position.

Professionals are autonomous

The next characteristic of professional groupings is their autonomy. Professionals have often organised themselves into separate hierarchies within public organisations based on their professional standing and status. The most extreme version of this occurs in healthcare where a doctor's position in the medical hierarchy is usually regarded by a doctor as the only factor worth considering in terms of their importance. A doctor might be in a position of managerial authority over another doctor, but where they both are of the same clinical grade, the doctor manager will often find his or her peer refusing to respect his or her managerial authority. Doctors who take management positions may even be regarded as failures by their peers, viewed as having opted out of the medical hierarchy because they are unable to be successful there – that they must be second-rate doctors as a result. In India it is not unknown for doctor-managers not to tell their families that they have taken on managerial roles, so strong is the prejudice against those choose to work outside of their professional area.

Professionals then, expect considerable autonomy in their work. They often regard managers as being irrelevant bureaucrats, and even where the managers are practising professionals, they may be thought of as traitors or failures for 'crossing-over', with what matters their location in their professional hierarchy rather than their organisational position. Many doctors have little or no respect for managers. Two solutions to this problem present themselves; for managers to show their ability to support doctors and build relationships of trust, or to challenge doctors and confront their prejudices.

Where managers attempt to work with clinicians, they often frame their role in terms of attempting to help professionals overcome the barriers to them achieving success; perhaps showing them how their budgets might be managed better to reach higher professional standards, or by reorganising work so that the professionals are given greater space to pursue their goals. This effectively reinforces professional autonomy, but tries to get professionals to regard managers as people to be worked with rather than enemies, and may foster trust and so eventually an ability to work together. This is very much a long-term project however, and in public organisations where managers may change their jobs frequently, far more frequently than the professionals they must work with, it can be extremely difficult to achieve.

A second strategy is simply to try and exert managerial authority over professionals. This is likely to lead to a great deal of unpleasantness and requires the strong support of senior managers as well as an active human resources department to make sure that any challenges are legal and enforceable. This second approach is increasingly being used as professionals have their job descriptions standardised, and as their performance is increasingly tightly measured. However, its obvious downside is that it is trying to make relationships more straightforward in the future by causing conflict today. This requires a long-term commitment from both the managers challenging the professionals and the senior managers of the organisation. If this commitment falters, or if professionals being to win appeals against managerial decisions, then managers may find that they are able to exert influence through neither trust nor authority. Under these circumstances, a severely dysfunctional organisation is likely to be the result. In hospitals and universities, professional groups have launched campaigns to have senior managers sacked, using all of their influence and power to disrupt board meetings and organise votes of no confidence.

Professionals often have confidential relationships with their clients

A fourth important aspect of professionalism is the confidential relationship professionals often have with their clients. Again law and medicine represent the archetypes of this, but it is also found in other settings. In this situation, managers may find themselves in a situation where it is extremely difficult to examine a professional's work as that individual can argue that they are not able to discuss their confidential relationships with individual clients. If managers can neither measure nor control what occurs between a professional and a user, it is difficult to establish whether it is being done well (or badly).

There are various means for attempting to deal with the problem of confidentiality. One is for professionals to have their work overseen by other professionals who share the principle of confidentiality, and so are able to view professional performance first hand in a way a manager cannot. This, however, can lead to accountability structures where professionals can engage in mutual favours (if you assess me, I will assess you) rather than creating the opportunity for genuine performance feedback to be given. Equally, managers may still find themselves completely excluded from the process, and that the peer review processes is extremely frustrating if not taken seriously by those involved in it.

An alternative means of addressing the confidential relationship is for managers to measure not individual cases, but the results of several cases and to ask for individuals to be held to account (by either themselves or their professional group) for cases that appear to be statistically or substantively unusual. If a particular doctor takes five days to discharge patients where others seem to take three, this might need some investigation to see if resources are being deployed appropriately. Managers might go further than this, calling multi-disciplinary teams together to examine case notes of users who have been anonymised (so not breaching client confidentiality) to see if anything can be learned from those cases and improvements made in the future. This can be supportive if professionals believe that the process is about learning and improvement rather than allocating blame. However, where everyone on the panel knows, despite the anonymity in the case notes, exactly which case they are talking about and who the professional involved was, this process clearly fails and can degenerate into being perceived by professionals as a personal attack. High-profile medical cases tend to fall into this category, where despite case notes having all personal details are removed, all the participants in the review know exactly which patient is really being talked about, and who the doctors involved were. As such, the pretence of removing client confidentiality is removed, and a more difficult situation emerges. In cases such as this, and where high-profile problems have emerged, there is clearly a need for managers to approach reviews far more carefully, and to perhaps bring in reviewers with no personal ties to the case to make sure that the process is as independent and objective as possible.

Professional outputs are difficult to measure

The difficulty in measuring the 'output' of public professionals has been mentioned several times in this book already. If public managers find themselves in the unenviable position of being able to measure neither the process through which professionals engage with their service users (because of confidentiality) nor their output (because it is so difficult to measure), then the management role appears to be more about trying to motivate and support their professional peers than trying to control and measure their performance. This seems to have been largely the role associated with the old public administration approach so under fire since the 1980s, but in the terms described above, there appears to be good reasons why this approach have to be adopted in the first place. Of course this is something of a simplification. There are means of examining the processes involved in public professionals interactions with clients and there are at least some measures of a public professional's output, even if they are imperfect. The problem comes, as Chapter 8 suggests, in trying to choose indicators that capture the nature of the particular service rather than allowing what can be measured to dominate what the service comes to be about. It is relatively easy to measure waiting lists, but they may not be a good indicator of the performance of the agency for which people are waiting.

Professionals have discretion in their work

Perhaps the defining feature of professionalism, however, is that professionals have discretion in their work. They are able to apply their expert knowledge and judgement to the particular problem they are encountering, and to come up with a solution that, in information systems terms, is not 'programmable'. This means that the decisions professionals make can be not only a mix of knowledge, existing evidence, experience, but also perhaps instinct and gut feeling. This means that such complex decisions are not easily captured in the terms that allow them to be replicated by machine – the relationship between decision and inputs is not always easily explained. As decisions get more complex and where the variables within them become more inter-related, the need for professional discretion grows ever greater. This clearly has implications for public managers.

First, it creates 'wriggle room' for the occasional public professional who wishes to try and opt out of management systems by simply arguing that his or her work is too complex to be assessed because they must be able to retain their discretion in order to be able to retain their professional identity. This chapter has already looked at several ways this difficulty can be overcome, but they will all involve public managers putting themselves in the position of having to ask questions that professionals may prefer not to answer. However, just because professionals have discretion, it does not mean that they do not have to be accountable. Some public professionals have used their expert knowledge and professional discretion to allow themselves to be unaccountable in their work (Marquand, 2004), but this position is getting harder and harder to sustain. Public managers have to find ways of ensuring that professionals are accountable without resorting to mindless target setting and bullying, or attempting to standardise their work to a point where professional judgement is no longer trusted.

Professionals are extraordinary

The next characteristic of professionals is their ability to often be able to do something extraordinary, or at least, because of their position in society, to be positioned so that certain tasks are only accomplishable with their help. The clearest case of this is that of the doctor – few other groups can literally save lives. Modern medicine can appear almost magical at times, being able to bring sight to the blind and to intervene to bring people back from the most horrendous injuries and illnesses to have reasonably normal lives again. This means that doctors are often extremely popular, with the public recognising their extraordinary abilities. Equally, however, other professionals gain considerable power from their ability to be the only ones who can make particular things happen. It is extremely difficult to pursue a legal case without a solicitor or barrister (although not impossible) and businesses may find their entire future plans hanging on the decision made by a town planner. University staff may have to make decisions about whether students pass or fail their degrees, potentially leaving them to come away from three or four year's study with little to show for it.

Professionals often hold considerable power; be that over life and death, or over our future. They can therefore do extraordinary things. The role of public managers in this relationship is, again, to try and make sure that accountability comes with this power. Many readers will have come across doctors who have perhaps become a little too aware of their power over life and death, and have so become rather arrogant and patronising. It is perfectly possible to have the powers of a professional without needing to belittle others who do not hold them. Public managers need to get professionals to keep their feet on the ground, and despite their extraordinary powers, to remember that they are dealing with the hopes and fears of human beings. The very best professionals, no matter how exalted in their standing, tend not to lose sight of this. For the cases where professionals believe they have become a law unto themselves, managers clearly need to find ways of intervening.

Professionals are self-regulating

Finally, professionalism is often associated with self-regulation. This means that professionals are not held to account by managers or by the organisation that they work for, but instead by the professional organisation they are affiliated to. Doctors will be allowed to practice as the result of their membership of a professional body which can refuse them their right to practice if they are found to be dangerous or incompetent. This decision is not taken by the organisation employing the doctor, but by a separate regulator such as the American Medical Association or the General Medical Council of the British Medical Association. If a doctor is removed from the list of practitioners, his or her employer will probably also have to sack the member of staff concerned because they will be unable to carry out their duties, but it is unusual for the organisation concerned to take permanent action against a member of staff before their own regulatory body has met to decide their future. An organisation might suspend that member of staff, but not dismiss them until the regulatory body has made its recommendation. Were a professional to be sacked by a public organisation and then subsequently cleared by their professional body, it would probably lead to a claim of substantial damages by the member of staff affected.

Self-regulation is a means by which public managers are able to allow professionals to settle their disputes 'internally', but can also cause problems. Where a professional is cleared of wrongdoing by its own regulatory body, but there are numerous user complaints about that individual, should managers side with the regulatory body and support their member of staff, or side with the users and still attempt to dismiss them? In this situation it is not unusual for further investigations to be made and for issues around professional competence to drag on for very long periods of time indeed, often with the member of staff suspended on full pay. This may be occasionally necessary, but it is clearly not a good use of public money to employ an expensive professional and to not allow him or her to fulfil their duties.

Given the many difficulties that professional status seems to cause, this leads us to the question – if professionals are so difficult to control, who should manage them?

Who should manage professionals? Should professionals be managers (or managers professionals)?

A recurring problem in the above analysis is trying to work out who should be in charge of professionals. There are three generic answers to this.

Putting managers in charge of professionals

Option one is for public managers, trained primarily as managers, to be put in charge of professionals. This means that management takes place independent of the professionals present in the service. The advantage of this is that managers will be able to bring a different set of priorities to the process of organising the public service, being grounded in different thinking, and creating the opportunity for a wider discussion of the issues before the organisation than is likely to otherwise take place. Managers may believe that they can better act on behalf of the public interest if they do not come from the same background as the professionals they are placed in charge of (but professionals will often dispute this – who speaks for the public is an extremely contentious topic), and be better able to represent the public interest than professionals who may have a vested interest in preserving the status quo.

However, this approach has the potential to be conflictual. If managers are being brought in especially because they have a different background to doctors, and because they are there to represent users to create changes to services, then they are creating the potential for disputes over who is best placed to run public organisations. Professionals may regard managers as being ignorant of the complexities of their work, and not fit to be placed in charge of them, and refuse to co-operate with managers or even campaign to have them removed. Managers may be left wondering after every meeting with professional groups exactly what it is they have done wrong to be so roundly attacked when all they wanted to do was to try and make the organisation better.

Putting managers alongside professionals

The alternative logic of putting managers into public organisations is that they work alongside professionals rather than trying to be in charge of them, in line with the professional support role envisaged by the public administration school. The irony in that approach pointed out by some of the leading British writers in public management (Harrison *et al.*, 1990) is that it positions managers in what, according to management theory, is a remarkably contemporary, facilitation-type role, at exactly the time it has become unfashionable in the public sector. In the coach or facilitator role of public management, a distributed leadership approach is taken by attempting to get behind those that deliver services to users rather than get on top of them (Conger and Kanungo, 1998). At the same time as the public administration approach became unfashionable, many of its virtues have been held up as extemporary and cutting in the private sector. This is not to say that public managers adopting this role is not without its problems – a brief review of the problems of managing professionals will make clear that this is far from the case (see above). However, it does suggest that management thinking can often be as much a function of prevailing fashion as it is about 'what works' (Greener, 2005a).

Professionals managing professionals

The alternative to managers managing professionals is that professionals take over the job. Perhaps the clearest expression of this came in the NHS Management Inquiry of the early 1980s where the Chairman of a successful supermarket was asked to examine how the NHS could be better managed, and went as far as suggesting that doctors were the 'natural' managers of the health service (Department of Health and Social Security, 1983). If professionals can be persuaded to see the problems of their organisations from perspectives other than their own, where they place a high priority upon financial responsibility and user-responsiveness, and can be persuaded to become accountable for their decisions, there is no reason why this cannot work. The difficulty is that the transition to this position can often be a difficult one, with many professionals believing that thinking in a managerial way represents the very antithesis of professionalism. This is unfortunate and unnecessary. There are clearly flash points around which services will always have to navigate (professionals having to navigate the problem of providing services within fixed budgets rather than according to need, for example), but these problems are unavoidable, and need careful dialogue and thought from all sides rather than confrontation and dispute.

Where professionals are able to see perspectives other than the one native to their own training, however, they can find the process of 'selling' change to their professional peers to be rather debilitating, being seen to have 'gone native' as a manager by the professionals and regarded with some distrust by other managers as a former professional. In these circumstances it is hardly surprising that many professional-managers regard themselves on loan to management, and that in situations of conflict their professional identities reassert themselves (Kitchener, 2000). It may also be that, by pursuing their professional careers, they are able to secure superior financial rewards by avoiding taking on managerial roles, and so this hardly provides an incentive to take the additional responsibilities of managing.

In all, when managers attempt to tell professionals what to do, even though may they have the authority on paper, this is likely to lead to conflict. Professionals may spend their entire careers working for a particular organisation and regard newly appointed managers as under-qualified and ignorant of the realities of running public organisations. The administrative approach of supporting professionals has much to commend it, but may fail to hold professionals to account, and this lack of accountability detracts from the legitimacy of public organisations and may lead to public managers being positioned so that professionals are forced to report to them. Finally, there is the option of professionals managing professionals, but the danger that professionals taking on this role will be isolated from their peers, or that they will simply side with them whenever a conflict situation appears. Given the lack of clarity over who should manage professionals, is there at least an answer to the question of to whom they should be accountable?

To whom should professionals be accountable?

The question of accountability is key for public services. To whom should professionals be accountable? Several answers suggest themselves, but perhaps the four most likely will be discussed here; to managers; to service users; to their peers and to politicians.

Accountability to managers

Holding professionals accountable to managers does not necessarily mean that managers have to be placed in line-control relationships with the professionals. It does mean, however, that professionals are required to report back on their activities and to be scrutinised in relation to them. Because of the specialist and confidential nature of professional work, its results are often easier to examine than its processes, but, as noted in Chapter 8, it is often difficult to find appropriate measures on which to base these results. Even so, given the huge amount of information now connected in relation to public sector performance, managers can be expected to find the reasons for unusual results. It is also possible to examine feedback results from users and to ask professionals to account for poor feedback ratings or for poor results from peer review processes.

Examining performance and feedback results for statistically significant deviations from output or outcome measures allows managers to argue that they are not victimising particular professionals, but are instead using objective measures to identify good and poor performance and requiring professionals to account for their activities. Capturing both good and bad performance is still political in that the boundary of the category labelled as 'bad' will still need to be decided, and will be open to contestation, especially where activity measures are primarily linked to financial measures (Broadbent and Laughlin, 2002) instead of elements professionals might regard as more important, such as public service. Once it has been established, managers will need to work out an action plan with the professional to either try and avoid the problem from occurring in the future or provide an adequate explanation for the deviation that both professionals and managers can accept. Despite its contentious and difficult nature, the process can at least give managers some legitimacy for asking professionals questions about accountability, and give them a route into a more regular dialogue that has often been missing in the past. Managers can try and position themselves as being part of a multidisciplinary team put in place to examine unusual outcome results, and who take the lead in organising a response to the findings of reviews, as well as putting forward action points, hopefully with the support of professionals, for how the difficulties will be resolved.

Accountability to service users

Making professionals accountable to service users suggests another different approach. In this situation, accountability systems will attempt to try and achieve direct or indirect accountability. Direct accountability is where professionals regularly meet the representatives of service users face-to-face to discuss their concerns and to attempt to agree in consultation with users what needed to be done as a result. This is most common perhaps in education where teachers or lecturers will meet regularly with student representatives, as well as inviting them to committee meetings so that they can contribute directly to the running of their university. Indirect accountability is where professionals are required to respond to the feedback taken from service users through surveys or complaints. In this case an intermediary will be necessary to record the professionals response and to pass it on to user representatives to make sure that, where necessary, something is done in response to user concerns.

In either case, making professionals accountable to users means a different form of responsiveness compared to the outcome approach where professionals are accountable to managers. In the latter case, user feedback will be one aspect of the way that professional performance is measured, but will be combined with other outcome measures that are appropriate to try and get a fuller view of performance. In the case where user accountability is favoured, different elements are likely to become more important such as politeness and friendliness (nurses sometimes complain of face pain from smiling all day in this type of regime (Bolton, 2001)), with the inherent danger that incompetent professionals with nice dispositions can be favoured over their brilliant peers with fewer social skills. Good public service requires a mix of both professional and personal skills, but most of us would still probably be cured by a surly doctor than made more ill by his polite colleague.

Balfour and Grubbs (2000) suggest that, when made accountable to individual service users rather than collective publics, civil servants become focused on a continuous quest for change and innovation rather than providing good services. They suggest that the 'values of the marketplace must be balanced with other values such as equity, justice and human dignity' (p. 581), not only reminding us of earlier debates about public service values, but also pointing to the difficulties of identifying exactly who public professionals should be accountable to.

Accountability to other professionals

Making professionals accountable to other professionals has been the means most often taken in public services. In this model, professionals are accountable through either disciplinary mechanisms that come through self-regulation, through professional development and updating, through internal promotions procedures, through anonymised case reviews or through peer-review.

The disciplinary mechanism model usually only applies to cases where allegations of incompetence have been made of a professional, and the regulative body responsible for that group has decided that there is a case to answer. This is a form of accountability designed to prevent incompetent practitioners from being allowed to practice, but does little for the vast majority of practitioners that are between the extremes of competent and brilliant. Professional development and updating makes professionals accountable for keeping their skills up to date, and may mean that they are required to demonstrate, in order to keep their registrations, that they have participated in a certain number of accredited training days and practised for a minimum amount within the specified timescale. This puts in place some basic safeguards that appeal to the professional's identity to prevent them from getting too out-of-date, but clearly attending an updating meeting is very different from understanding all that goes on within it. If disciplinary hearings are meant to address incompetent practitioners, personal development and skills updating are meant to try and prevent practitioners from becoming incompetent in the first place.

If the emphasis moves away from incompetence and its prevention, then there may be an attempt to try and reward good behaviour through promotions procedures. In this case professionals will often review the work of other professionals to see if they are worthy of better pay or more elevated position. The academic world offers itself as a model here, where tenure or promotion to a higher grade is usually based upon the member of staff being able to demonstrate expertise to his or her peers. This may be through high teaching scores (often measured not only through student feedback, but also through peer review), but is more likely to come through achieving peer-reviewed journal articles in prestigious publications. Peer review of research means that papers are scrutinised by other academics, and it is then other academics that judge the importance of the publications – a kind of double academic review, or double accountability. Promotions are given to staff judged to have achieved good publications in highly rated journals, and those that do not achieve this are asked to try again, or even have to face performance reviews where they fail to meet minimum standards of achievement.

Professional to professional accountability can also be achieved through case reviews. Professionals here, often brought in from outside of the institution, or at least the department, under review, come and go through the anonymised notes pertaining to a particular case to try and see if there is anything to be learned from them, or at worst, whether there were failing in procedures or judgement from the professionals involved. In hospitals particular kinds of death are subject to this kind of review routinely, with a panel being convened made up primarily of other doctors, although other professional groups and managers may also be involved, to try and work through the circumstances leading to the death. There are good reasons for this activity; it can foster learning and try and improve handling of difficult cases for the future. But as well as this, it can also protect the institution from subsequent legal claims against it by demonstrating that the organisation is serious about reviewing its processes and procedures, and that it is taking action to try and achieve the best possible outcomes for service users.

Peer review is perhaps the most common form of professional to professional account-ability and can take a number of forms. Peer review of work has already been mentioned in relation to academic promotions criteria above, but any professional work that produces an object that might be assessed can be reviewed in this way. Where it is more difficult to assess a final object, peer review will typically take the form of assessing process; so for academics their research can be assessed as an object in terms of their research papers and books, but their teaching will usually be peer reviewed as it happens as it does not produce as clear an end object.

Political accountability

Finally, there is political accountability. Politicians are elected in order to represent the citizens of their local areas and to represent their views. As such, political accountability is a kind of democratic accountability, albeit an indirect one. Most public organisations have a strong political element in that elected politicians may be given the specific role of overseeing a particular service, or in some states there may be elections held to decide who runs particular public services. In the first case the aim of the politician may be to improve the service, but according to public choice theorists, it may also be to maximise the oppor-tunities for both public managers and politicians as well (Boyne *et al.*, 2003). Reasoning that public managers often progress by showing they are effective, and politicians become popular by demonstrating that they have improved public services for the better, the pub-lic choice view suggests that public managers will be trying to demonstrate effectiveness, even if what they do is not necessarily in the interest of the service they are managing, and politicians will want to demonstrate improvements in public services in order to achieve a bigger and better portfolio and get a more important job.

The public choice view presents a rather cynical view of the motivations of public managers and politicians, but has something to commend it because both groups can be subject to the kinds of incentives that public choice theorists suggest. Public managers may be as much interested in creating the illusion of success (engaging in gaming or even mis-representation, see Chapter 8) and success itself, and politicians may be keen for them to do so, as this might mean, in turn, that they too are judged to be performing well. What the public choice view highlights, even if it is not the case in practice, is that there are strong incentives under political accountability for an awful lot of misrepresentation of organisa-tional performance borne of the need of both managers and politicians to show that they are making a difference. This can create perverse incentives such as the maximisation of the budget the manager or politician is responsible for, rather than the improvement of the public service they have been tasked to run.

In the case where officials are elected to run particular public services, they will have a strong incentive to make as much difference as quickly as possible. This can lead to an incentive structure where periods of frantic change occur upon the changing of the leadership of a service changing (as can sometimes happen when governments change as well), followed by a period where services settle back down before another election (perhaps also punctuated by an attempt to secure quick improvements before the election, in-line with the theory of the 'political' business cycle). In this environment public managers may face some difficult choices between short-term maximisation in order to satisfy their elected official leaders, and long-term maximisation which they might deem to be in the best interests of the service. If they adopt the second view they risk being portrayed as having 'gone native', and may come to regard themselves as the guardian of the service, attempting to shield it from the whims of political masters. This problem also occurs where political accountability is to be achieved by elected officials, where the politicians behave according to public choice theory but managers attempt to preserve the goals of the service instead.

As such, there are a range of different means of achieving greater accountability for public professionals, but they all carry with them particular problems. The question of how professionals should be accountable is not quite as difficult as the one of who should manage them, but is still far from straightforward.

Conclusion

Professionals are a distinctive part of a great deal of public service provision, but there are significant problems in answering both who should manage them and to whom they should be accountable.

The nature of professionalism means that they have expert knowledge, that they are socially powerful, that they are autonomous, that they often have confidential relationships with their clients, that their outputs are difficult to measure, that they have discretion in their work, that they are capable of extraordinary things and that they are self-regulating. All of these aspects of professionalism create particular challenges for public managers as it means that they are often dependent upon professionals to deliver the service, but may find it difficult, without the professional's co-operation, to influence the way the service is delivered directly.

The question of who should manage professionals has three generic answers. Managers can try and take on the role, but professionals have often strongly resisted this answer, and because of the nature of their professionalism, pubic professionals have often been able to insulate themselves from managerial reforms. If managers work alongside professionals this provides a compromise answer, but this goes against contemporary ideas in public management based around managers being the leaders of their organisations. Finally, professionals can try and manage other professionals, but stepping outside of their professional role, especially in times when managerial and professional agendas conflict, can be extremely difficult.

The question of to whom professionals should be accountable is also a difficult one to provide a straightforward answer. Accountability to managers can possibly be best achieved where managers and professionals work together, but this can be seen to be working against contemporary new public management ideas. Making professionals accountable to service users has much to commend it, but carries with the danger of confusing popularity with high professional standards, when the two may not be at all the same. Achieving accountability to other professionals can be achieved through a number of means, but with the concern that professionals will tend to protect their own rather than conform to management reforms where a potential conflict occurs. Public professionals are all politically accountable in some way or another, as their salaries are often paid for by public funds and carries with it the problem of the public choice critique that combining self-seeking professionals with self-seeking politicians is a recipe for public services being run badly.

Public management of professionals

As the main concern of this book is with public management, then some kind of conclusion about the relationship between public managers and professionals is needed. The dynamics of the likely relationships can be summarised in a grid that considers the possibilities where the status of managers and professionals are strong and weak respectively. This will be, to some extent, culturally specific as the standing of managers and professionals varies between countries, but some generalisations can be made. The combination of the strength of professional and management groups gives a situation a 'situational' logic (Archer, 1995) that does not determine what happens, but does create a tendency towards a particular kind of relationship that may be difficult on either side to overcome. These logics are summarised in Table 9.2.

Where there are weak management groups and weak professional groups, neither will find it straightforward to challenge the inherited organisational form. This will tend to result in inertia, and tends to occur where professional groupings are not well regarded in the organisation, and management is poorly organised. A situation with weak managers and strong professionals will tend to mean that professionals dominate, with it being difficult to manage them, or to make them accountable. This has often been the case within public management, and to the public administration approach that dominated for much of the post-war period. Where managers are strong but professionals are weak, then this will mean that professional expertise can be challenged and managerial agendas become dominant, unless the professionals become better organised. Finally, where there are both strong managers and strong professionals, this might lead either to continual conflict where neither group is prepared to back down or to a situation where both groups seek to protect themselves, recognising their mutual strength. In this situation, a kind of

Table 9.2 Relationships between managers and professionals

	Weak professional group (poor organisation, gender bias, e.g., nursing)	Strong professional group (highly organised, highly educated, e.g., lawyers/ barristers)
Weak management group (low status, low qualifications)	Inertia – neither group able to challenged inherited organisation	Professionals dominate and self-organise
Strong management group (higher status, higher professional qualifications)	Management able to challenge professional power and organise professionals around their agenda	Two scenarios Conflict – where neither group able to back down Protection – where both groups acknowledge their mutually dependent status

mutual respect can be possible where managers and professionals are prepared to work alongside one another.

CASE STUDY

Managing doctors

As has already been mentioned in the chapter, the archetypal professionals are doctors and lawyers, and in the public sector, the growth in state provided health-care in the 20th century means that doctors have become hugely important public professionals.

Managing doctors presents a number of challenges for public managers. They belong to highly prestigious professional groupings such as the American Medical Association, or UK Royal Colleges and British Medical Association, meaning they have access to peers in elevated social positions holding significant power. Winston Churchill's doctor, Lord Moran, was not only used to occupying the corridors of power but also of being in charge of doctor organisations. The organisational details present in the NHS Act of 1948 were largely the result of informal negotiations between Aneuran Bevan, the first post-war Minister of Health, and the Medical Lords, in the period leading up to the NHS Act (Rintala, 2003).

The relationship between the state and the medical profession in the United Kingdom has been characterised as a 'double bed', in which mutual dependence exists because the state needs the doctors to run the NHS and make difficult decisions about who gets cared for and in what order, and the doctors need the state because, with the creation of the NHS, it effectively became a monopoly employer of medical expertise (Klein, 1990). Although in other countries the state does not have the monopoly employer status, the double bed is a powerful metaphor for the way politicians and medical leaders have often worked together.

Managers enter the hospitals, the bastions of medical expertise, characterised as being 'corporate rationalisers' (Alford, 1972, 1975), put in place by the state to challenge the dominant interest, the doctors, to achieve greater efficiency and effectiveness with public funds. A variety of management tools and techniques have been employed by health managers and the state to try and give them greater leverage. Management information systems have been used to scrutinise clinical performance, and ever-more elaborate coding systems employed to try and measure clinical activity in greater and greater detail (Bloomfield and Best, 1992; Bloomfield and Coombs, 1992). Budgeting systems have been put in place to attempt to make clinicians aware of the resource implications of their decisions (Buxton and Packwood, 1991). HR practices have attempted to become more pro-active to find ways of removing medics who do not conform to reform agendas or are shown to be poor performers through the new measures.

At the same time as this, however, managers have also found themselves increasingly scapegoated by the state for poor organisational performance (Greener and Powell, 2008) and come to regard the state's need to frequently reorganise health systems as 'redisorganisation' (Smith et al., 2001) in which they find managing increasingly hard as the parameters and structures they have to work in are continually changed. Instead of being rather one-dimensional figures, put in place by the state to act upon its agendas and close implementation gaps, health managers are far more interesting figures, often having clear ideas of what needs to be done in their organisations outside of central agendas, and having to make choices about what their priorities will be. They may even come to identify more with their local health organisation than with the national targets and goals set for them, and so become, in the state's eyes, as difficult to control as the professionals they were introduced to challenge in the first place.

At the same time as this, health managers have found that the difficulties of managing professionals have led to them using a range of tactical behaviours that mean that they are able to take decisions and implement government agendas where necessary, but avoid direct confrontation with medics. To this end, they may attempt to shape meeting agendas so that they are able to carry votes over decisions unlikely to be popular with their clinician colleagues, and engage in other forms of 'negative power', where they try and control what is spoken about (and not spoken about) rather than trying to argue face-to-face with doctors. By doing this, they are able to restrict arguments to times and places where they have a chance of getting their own way (Greener, 2005). Equally, the framing of many public management techniques as being objective by the state means the use of performance management and budgeting can be presented by managers as being outside of their control and necessary evils rather than being attempts to move power relationships away from clinicians. Whether doctors accept these limitations, however, is open to question.

Doctors have also faced pressures from their patients to improve services, asking difficult questions of the nature of professionalism in even its most elite settings. Worryingly, Dent (2006) suggests that this can lead to a situation where consumerism, because it leads to some patients becoming more demanding and less deferential to doctors, and to a situation where they may try and impose their own interests upon medical relationships, can lead to patients undermining trust in doctors more generally. Giving patients more choices over healthcare can therefore lead not to them being more satisfied with their care, but to greater disaffection (see also Bauman, 2007). In this situation, public managers have to find ways of challenging professionals to improve their services, but also accepting their expertise and not undermining public confidence in their ability to deliver it.

The extent to which government health reforms have created change over the last 20 to 30 years is difficult to assess. In the United Kingdom, budgetary pressures have led to hospital managers having to drive health reform faster than at any time in the NHS's history, and this has led to doctors rated as poor performing or surplus to requirements losing their jobs. Whether health managers hold any greater power in the long term, however, remains to be seen (Greener, 2005).

Further reading

The classic studies of the relationship between health managers and doctors in the United Kingdom are those conducted by Stephen Harrison, David Hunter and Christopher Pollitt (Harrison, 1982, 1988; Harrison and Wistow, 1993; Harrison *et al.*, 1990, 1992). Equally, there are numerous studies of medical power, with perhaps those by Turner (1987), Illich (1977) and Ehrenreich (1978) offering the most powerful critiques. A good edited collection exploring professionalism in a range of contexts was edited by Laffin (1998).

Part 4

Conclusion

10

Putting it all together — managing contradictions in public management

Introduction

Given the previous chapters the reader might by now feel rather confused. This book has not tried to give the right answers to the many problems facing public managers in the contemporary world. Instead it has attempted to explore the kinds of issues they are likely to face with the view that being forewarned might not exactly forearm, but it might at least make clearer the nature of the challenges to be faced. This last chapter will attempt to summarise the difficulties and tensions present in public management to try and allow the reader to work through these issues and develop their own understanding of them. These are, by definition, difficult problems, but that does not mean they should be ignored and filed away under the 'too hard' heading. Instead I hope that by encouraging readers to think about these 'disjunctures and dilemmas' (Newman, 2002) a deeper knowledge of the nature of public management might be achieved. This chapter asks the question 'how can we make sense of public management given the tensions and contradictions contained within this book?'.

The tensions explored below are listed in Table 10.1, and then discussed each in turn below it.

Table 10.1   Tensions in public management

Public and private	Public and private management are often characterised as very different, but are these differences narrowing?
Professionalism and customer-focus	Should public services be organised around professionals or customers?
Control and entrepreneurialism	Should public managers be primarily concerned with control or with being entrepreneurs?
Provision for the public or provision for the individual	Should public provision be concerned with serving the public as a whole, or individual users?

Services accountable to the public as citizens and services accountable to the public as consumers	Should public services be accountable to the public at large, or to individuals as they receive the service?
Centralisation and decentralisation	Should public services be controlled by government, or decentralised and allowed to become more locally diverse?

Public and private

The first tension is between the public and the private. This is a neat division, but one that often crumbles under scrutiny in today's world. Public managers can be working for private organisations, and private managers working within the public sector. Does this mean that the terms are therefore meaningless? Boyne's work suggested that the differences between public and private management are not as widespread as is often believed, but also that many of the taken-for-granted assumptions about the nature of public management remain just that – taken-for-granted. They have therefore not been scrutinised, and it would seem an important job for research to be conducted that attempts to compare a range of factors between public and private management to better understand whether or not differences exist. In the meantime, however, some general tendencies appear to be present.

For much of the 1980s onwards, public management has been encouraged to be more like private management, to become more 'business-like'. Private management is regarded as entrepreneurial, customer-centred and efficient. This is, if you like, the taken-for-granted assumption about private management. However, how often is this actually the case? Business book shelves groan under the weight of case-study style books (traceable back to titles such as Peters and Waterman's *In Search of Excellence* (Peters and Waterman, 1982)), but what seems to unite the organisations featured in such books more than their business practices is their unerring ability to drive themselves into serious trading trouble almost as quickly as books celebrating their success hit the shelves. One of the most celebrated organisations (in the business press at least) of recent times also became its biggest corporate bankruptcy – Enron (McLean and Elkind, 2004).

This is not to disparage private management. There are extraordinary managers out there in both the private and the public sectors. However, the important thing is surely to explore what works, where, how and when, rather than assuming there is an automatic fix-all for any managerial situation. Today's management theory is tomorrow's discredited fashion, be it organisational excellence, organisational learning, business process engineering, total quality management, corporate culture or leadership. Instead of jumping on management bandwagons it would surely be better to try and form context-sensitive theories of what structures, incentives, practices and policies seem to work, and to argue for extremely careful transplantation away from their original contexts. Both private management and public management have much to learn from one another; private management can be more dynamic and entrepreneurial, but public management can offer greater continuity and stability, and in a situation where lives might be at stake and futures risked, these values can suddenly seem enduring and important.

Instead of demanding that public managers become more like their private peers, it would surely make sense to ask what values we want our services to hold at their core. Public managers often argue that they are there to preserve a public ethos, a set of values that are based around notions of public service and fairness. Many private organisations also seem to suggest that they also hold these values. Values do make a difference, and instead of debating which organisational processes work best, perhaps it is necessary to start by asking what our organisations are for. It may well be that, in particular circumstances markets can deliver a fairer outcome than public bureaucracies. However, this cannot be taken for granted, and must be subjected to careful testing, and sometimes for policymakers and public managers to admit that they have made a mistake where things are not working.

In sum, although the terms 'public' and 'private' both hold considerable explanatory power, perhaps when working out what needs to be done it is more important to analyse the values, context and goals of the circumstance rather than coming with a set of presumptions that either public or private methods are automatically best. There is something of a paradox here – despite the words 'public' and 'private' being so loaded in values and holding such emotion, neither may actually be that useful in working out what needs to be done or how. This book has written about public organisations and public managers because, at present, they are just about identifiable despite all of the change that has occurred over the last 30 years. In the future, it might be necessary to find words other than 'public' or 'private' to describe our organisations.

Professionalism and customer-focus

A second tension present in the book is between professionalism and customer-focus. Professionalism tends to lead to services having a producer-focus and professional self-regulation, two of the enemies of many of those in positions of power who believe instead that customer-focus brings individual accountability to pubic services and requires professionals to rethink their approach to work to drive up standards and improve user responsiveness.

However, what often gets lost in this debate is that professionals are often self-regulated for good reason (that their job is so complex that only other professionals can often understand what they have done) and that producer-focus may actually be an efficient way of organising resource-poor services, as the professional's time could be the public organisation's most valuable asset. It would be wonderful to be able to visit a doctor entirely at my own convenience, and to organise rubbish collection not once every one or two weeks, but when my rubbish bin is full. However, neither of these options, where public services are trying to achieve efficiency and have to operate on a large scale, are particularly efficient. To be able to see a doctor whenever I like, that doctor has to have a great deal of redundancy in his or her schedule, and employing public professionals on high salaries to wait for my convenience does not seem an efficient strategy. If I am not seen by a doctor until half an hour after my appointment time, this was probably due to a case appearing before me that was more urgent than mine, rather than because the doctor was sitting around drinking coffee.

This is not, however, to offer a universal apology for all the time public organisations keep their users waiting, or all the times that professionals seem rude to them. Public professionals often work under tremendous pressure and resource constraint. However, it does not seem much to ask that the dignity and privacy of service users is always kept in mind. It costs little for an administrator to monitor how far behind with appointments the professional is getting in order to be able to tell arriving users how long they are likely to have to wait, but this is still not routinely done. If it is necessary for queuing and waiting to occur, then those having to give up their time should at least have an indication of how long their wait is likely to be, and in what order they are being seen. This costs nothing. Practices such as booking users in for appointments at the same time in order to maximise professional time take the efficiency argument outlined above to the extreme, but clearly cross the boundary of common courtesy and so should be stopped. In return for users accepting that public professionals are busy and overworked, professionals must make sure that they are treated with dignity and courtesy in return. Professionalism and customer-focus can appear to be contradictory where both are defined at the extremes, but they also have a great deal in common, and it is the job of public managers to try and find a meeting in the middle. However, policymakers must make sure that they do not stoke up expectations of public services delivery to levels that cannot possibly be met.

Equally it is the job of public managers to find appropriate ways of scrutinising public professionals to make sure that, where services can be redesigned to improve their service to users without diluting their professionalism, this should happen. Techniques such as business process re-engineering (McNulty and Ferlie, 2002) can be dismissed as management fads, but carry at their root an important message about services being designed around the needs of their service users. This can never be achieved completely within finite resources and with the safeguards necessary for professional work to be carried out safely and fairly, but public organisations should regularly ask the question of how they could better meet the needs of their users. This job seems a good one for public managers to have.

Finally in terms of the tension between professionalism and user-focus comes the difficulty of what to do about complaints. Complaints are an important part of public management as they represent a situation where someone, for good motives or bad, has taken the time to go through a time-consuming process and instead of simply grumbling and walking away having received service they are not happy with, they have put pen to paper or been prepared to engage with the organisation in some other formal way. The effort sometimes involved in making a complaint in public organisations should not be under-stated. Complaints procedures can be confusing, elusive and worded in obscure language. In Douglas Adams' book *The Hitch Hikers Guide the Galaxy*, a planning department required a ridiculous series of acts be performed for the local council to take user voice or complaints into account. Adams was parodying local government, but most parody contains a grain of truth.

Complaints are an index of how well an organisation is doing. Simply counting complaints can reveal very little – complaints may go up because new systems are in place that make it easier for users to make their voice heard, or go down because staff become efficient at intimating users into leaving before they have a chance to complain. The important thing is that complaints are treated seriously by both users and public managers, who will often have the job of investigating them. Public managers need to have robust processes in place to show that full investigations have occurred, and that they are able to explain clearly what action they have taken to service users at the end. There should be an assumption that users do not complain because they have nothing else to do, and their complaints treated, as a result, in good faith. Users, in turn, need to understand that wasting a public organisation's time in an attempt to drive up a degree classification which they do not deserve or trying to achieve an unfair amount of resources compared to other users by complaining regularly are not acceptable. Public organisations are universal in nature, and have to treat complaints seriously because of their fairness brief (private organisations, in contrast, can ban individuals from their premises relatively easily), but where complaints procedures are being abused, it surely needs to be possible to warn particular users that any further complaints are likely to strain credibility.

It is a sad state of affairs where the motives of user complaints have to be questioned, but where significant amounts of compensation and preferential treatment might be attained, there will always be small majority of users wishing to 'game' the system. The important thing seems to be that complaints are treated seriously and fairly by managers, but that users understand that complaints do not necessarily mean that there is a case to answer, and that they do not abuse the processes in place.

Control and entrepreneurialism

A third tension present through the book is the one between control and entrepreneurialism. The standard critique of the bureaucratic organisational form is that its impersonality is a sham – all it does is legitimise and disguise pre-existing power structures under the guise of providing objective rules (Foucault, 1977). Feminists and disability rights campaigners were instrumental in showing how public policy and public organisations preserve pre-existing power relationship by making women dependent upon men for their welfare payments and how those with disabilities found themselves having to endure 'normalising' policies that attempted to make them more like more prevalent members of society. If bureaucracies were not neutral and independent, what use did they serve?

Recent scholarship, however, has come strongly to the defence of bureaucracy, emphasising the importance of control and the need for the objective administration of rules (Du Gay, 2000). Many public organisations' legitimacy depends upon them administering rules fairly, and if this is shown not to be the case, there also exists the possibility of making the bureaucracies work better rather than simply abandoning them. Equally Lynn (2001) has argued persuasively that the caricatures of bureaucracy often presented in critiques of it often fail to capture its complexities and that 'traditional' thought is far more sophisticated than painted by contemporary critics, exhibiting 'far more respect for law, politics, citizens, and values than customer-oriented managerialism or civic philosophies that, in promoting community and citizen empowerment, barely acknowledge the constitutional role of legislatures, courts and executive departments' (pp. 154–155).

Entrepreneurial discourses, as Lynn suggests, point at their extremes, directly away from the bureaucratic form. They suggest that for public management to work better, managers need to be freed from constraining rules in order to give users the services they need and deserve. The term 'entrepreneurialism' is commonly used in two ways. First, there is the notion of the dynamic entrepreneur creative new services and adding value to existing ones by being able to anticipate user need. This type of entrepreneurialism is strongly linked to market notions around placing the user at the heart of the organisation's activities. Second, and more commonly in the social science literature on the subject, there is the notion of the entrepreneur as the filler of 'structural holes' (Burt, 1993), linking together the offerings of professionals and the needs of users, recombining professional services and marketing them to meet user need. This usage is distinctive from the first sense of the term because it focuses on entrepreneurialism as a structural phenomenon, as a process whereby under-demanded services can meet presently unmet user need through managers (and others) overcoming information or service delivery problems through their organisational abilities (Garud *et al.*, 2002; Hwang and Powell, 2005). The problem is that entrepreneurship is often used as a word in ways that empty of it of meaning – if it is to have value in public management it must be clear exactly what usage is being evoked by the term.

The first sense of entrepreneurship, used effectively as a short cut for the marketing approach, does clearly have tensions with notion of a bureaucracy. If the organisation is driven to meet user need, this will tend to mean a more relaxed approach to rule interpretation. Advocates of the marketing approach often make the claim that customer-driven organisations need only two rules. Rule one is that the customer is always right. Rule two is for situations where managers believe rule one does not apply, and refers the manager back to rule one for reference. If the user is always right, it is hard to see how bureaucratic organisation can work. However, the second sense of entrepreneurship does not necessarily conflict with the idea of the bureaucracy. Managers recombining existing services to overcome information or delivery problems does not necessarily mean conforming only to what users want, but could instead be about providing a wider range of services through their new combination, or simply publicising pre-existing services better. Even in non-market environments, public services need to be used or they serve no purpose. Publicising services is often associated with a market environment, but this does not have to be the case – it could simply be about gaining additional referrals for a new medical service, or getting local authorities to make use of a pre-existing facility that improves service efficiency, but is presently being underutilised.

As such, the tension between bureaucracy and entrepreneurship depends on what is meant by the terms, especially with regard to its second, service-combination-based usage. It also depends on those organising services being careful enough not simply to dismiss notions such as bureaucracy because they are presently ill-regarded by many management theorists, as well as often by the public at large. There are circumstances where rules and regulations are important, and where bureaucracies might be the most efficient way to deliver services.

Provision for the public and provision for the individual

A fourth tension exists between the provision of services for the public and the provision of choice for the individual user. This tension is based on the assertion that what is good for us individually may not always be the best use of resources for everyone. The most extreme example of this occurs where an ill individual finds notice that a new, very expensive drug has become available, without which he or she feels might die. That individual clearly has a strong motivation to get the state to pay for their treatment with the drug, and whether or not that money could be better spent on treatments that provide bigger collective gains will not be a particular concern to them. As new drugs are developed, this situation appears increasingly regularly in healthcare systems across the world. Who is right, the individual wanting potentially life-saving treatment or the health manager arguing that the resources could be better spent on activities such as getting people to give up smoking, or by testing people's cholesterol levels to try and reduce their chances of heart disease?

Inevitably, neither position is without its problems, but both are understandable. The individual in need of treatment has a pressing case to try and save his or her own life, and any healthcare system must have systems for dealing with this kind of need. The history of healthcare shows a bias towards acute medicine, treatments which deal with the health problems of those suffering today, rather than fully utilising treatments and promotional activity that might improve the health of the population as a whole tomorrow. This does not seem at all surprising – it takes a strong person to postpone the needs of those sick today in order to secure better care for others tomorrow, even if this will result in a net health gain in the long term. Those most in need clearly need to have public managers prepared to take up their cases and to try and find resources to allow their treatment. Equally, however, difficult decisions also need to be made about investing in services that are more long-term in duration. It takes a brave manager to advocate and organise services that he or she might never receive the credit for, but it is also a necessary job.

The important thing is that the values of organisational systems are reviewed to make sure that the balance between the present and the future is justifiable, and that it reflects the wishes of sufficient members of the public to make it legitimate. Public services are there for both their specific users, but also the general public. If they become so focused on user views that they forget the public at large, they lack the legitimacy to continue to regard themselves as serving the population as a whole.

Public services accountable to the public as citizens, and services accountable to the public as consumers

This takes us on to the fifth public service tension, between services that are accountable to the public as citizens and services that are accountable the public as consumers (Flynn, 2002). Accountability to services users as consumers takes place primarily on the individual level, with users being offered choices and being able to say whether they have been offered high standards of service through feedback mechanisms. The most immediate mechanism for offering feedback where services are consumed frequently is through the strategy of 'exit' (Hirschman, 1970), through which they can choose another service provider if they are unhappy with the offerings or service levels of their present provider. Exit is an individual choice, but has collective implications – if enough users exit a service its future might be called into question. Public managers find out about exit by examining whether service users return and by trying to work out why some leave and some come back. In addition to this, consumers also have 'voice' mechanisms through which they may try and improve services either for themselves or for others. Voice can therefore be either individual or collective, but at least gives public managers more information than exit alone. Of course, some users may exit with voice, or persist with their choice and try and achieve change by challenging their organisation. In these circumstances they are exhibiting a kind of loyalty, not exiting but instead trying to change things. This also brings service users closer to citizen-type roles in which they participate in services and try and improve them for all.

In public service delivery in the past, the primary means by which users have been involved in services is through voice mechanisms, as choices simply have not existed (except for the choice to use private facilities instead). However, voice mechanisms, such as complaints procedures, have often been weakly implemented in public organisations (Allsop and Jones, 2008).

The danger of relying too much upon choice to achieve accountability is that it often gives public managers little idea about how good their services are, as exit information might come too late to change things. However, most people prefer exit to voice because it creates an easy way out without having to explain their decision. It therefore seems an important part of public management work to try and get voice from those that choose to exit a service, perhaps routinely attempting to capture a sample of all service users (some of which will subsequently exit). This may have the by-product of actually increasing the loyalty of service users, impressed that someone is asking for their views (but only if managers show that they are actually listening). Loyalty can lead to citizen-type behaviour by giving managers regular engagement with service users that can result in an improvement in services for everyone.

However, the term 'citizen' is more usually used in two other senses; in terms of the voice of the public more generally and in terms of user representation specifically. Where 'citizen' becomes another way of referring to 'the people', it is used in the sense of attempting to make public services accountable to those they are meant to be serving collectively. This can be achieved through a variety of different routes, but is most likely to occur during political election campaigns where politicians campaign, either locally or nationally, to improve services for all citizens. Using the word 'citizen' can therefore be shorthand for political accountability, with all of the strengths and weaknesses this can bring (see Chapter 9).

An alternative is to use the term 'citizen' in the sense of those users who offer themselves as representatives of other users. Citizens might be invited to give the views of others at government-held events where new policies are outlined, or even where which policies are to be pursued is decided. This mode of citizen-representation has cycles of popularity and unpopularity. It is clearly useful in that it means that politicians or managers are being held to account direct to user representatives, and so this increases the engagement of public representativeness and the transparency of the running of public services. Citizen-juries and other co-production methods can be empowering for local people who contribute directly in decisions about the future of public services in their areas. However, the issue of the representativeness of those that put themselves forward is always a problem. By definition, those that are able to attend frequent meetings and make a substantial time commitment to public service are not representative of most of those in a local area, and alternatives such as randomly selecting individuals, or using stratified samples to try and get representative groups together, often do not work where the majority of people in a local area are too busy, or simply do not wish to get involved. The notion of citizen decision-making is also haunted somewhat by the danger that the majority of people in many populations might hold views that might lead to minority groups being ignored, or of decisions such as the wider use severe punishments such as the death penalty being taken, even though they may fly in the face of the best available evidence. Greater democracy and public accountability is clearly a laudable goal for public managers to pursue, but it is not a panacea that means that the public can make all the decisions from now on.

Centralisation and decentralisation

A final tension is one that has not been extensively covered in this book, but builds upon many of those described above. This is the tension between decentralisation and centralisation. Should public services be different from place to place based on local need, or conform to national standards, positioning public managers as implementers in a chain of command reaching to the centre? The former option gives public managers more responsibilities than the latter. In this case they will be responsible not only for implementing plans, but also establishing what local priorities ought to be, and then producing plan upon which work is to be based. In a centralised system, public managers will also have to devise their own performance management system. A decentralised approach means that there is far greater scope for managers to innovate, but they will also have to confront the problem of users comparing what is on offer with other areas and feeling they are being short-changed. Different local plans in different geographical areas mean different levels of service, and the potential for accusations from users that they are not receiving services they would receive elsewhere. In the United Kingdom the language used by the media to make this criticism is that of the 'postcode lottery', the suggestion that where you live (your postcode) makes a lottery of the public services you receive. This goes directly against the grain of the public administration approach that suggested public services should be universal and uniform. However, following the logic of user-responsiveness leads to locally differentiated services and locally differentiated priorities, compromising fairness in the name of greater responsiveness. Accountability is therefore primarily to local users and local people more generally, with national accountability less prevalent.

Centralisation leads in the opposite direction. In this approach public managers are responsible for the implementation of plans set elsewhere. As such, they are likely to have performance management systems imposed from the centre, and the system of accountability will be to politicians nationally. Local accountability will still be necessary, but public managers will always have the get out of saying that their hands are being forced by nationally made decisions. Centralised systems more closely resemble the bureaucracies so resented by advocates of the new public management approach, with the need for local managers to occupy more clearly defined roles to fit within national frameworks.

Again, however, the differences between centralisation and decentralisation may be more theoretical than actual. What is centralising from one perspective may be decentralising from another; it depends on what you regard as being the centre of an organisation, and from where in the organisation you are looking. The centre of an organisation moves whether you are talking about geography, resources or power. A geographical centre may be the hub of an organisation through which all communications flows, but hold little power. The resource centre may be where money, head office staff or decision-making expertise resides, and may be entirely different from the geographic centre, but have little idea of what is going on in public organisations locally. The power centre of an organisation may be something different again; in many public organisations it might be where the dominant professional group have their headquarters, or there may be many local power headquarters where professionals organise and dominate. Whether the various centres are in the same place or not varies tremendously from organisation to organisation, but the more centres there are in one location, the greater overall centralisation exists. A reform that is centralising from the point of view of a user might be dencentralising from the point of view of a public manager if the latter gains power or resource that previously resided with users instead. The issue of decentralisation and centralisation depends, to a considerable extent, exactly what resource is being examined and from whose perspective.

Finally, recent reforms have attempted to square the circle of centralisation and decentralisation by creating new hybrid forms such as the one used in the United Kingdom of 'earned autonomy'. In the earned autonomy approach public managers are promised greater discretion and the ability to locally manage but they must first demonstrate that they conform to national standards set in areas policymakers regard as being necessary. This approach therefore attempts to balance the need of local managers with the needs of national policymakers. Local managers are allowed discretion but only if they first demonstrate their ability to meet national standards. How the dynamic of this works out will depend upon how many central targets are set, and how successful public managers are in meeting them. The more targets, and the least success of local managers, the more centralised the system will end up being. If, however, nationally set targets are minimums rather than maximums, they are more likely to be met and greater local discretion will be achieved. In the United Kingdom so far, it seems that earned autonomy has been more centralising than decentralising because of the number of targets put in place, but the rhetoric of government suggests that greater decentralisation may still yet occur.

Conclusion

A simple summary of the contents of this chapter is that the role of public managers has become increasingly more complex over the last 20–30 years. The criticisms that led to the decline of the public administration approach, that they lacked democratic legitimacy and developed unresponsive bureaucracies, do have some credibility. Public administration was based on principles of fairness, accountability, probity and service. These are fine virtues that form the centre of the public service ethic, and it is wrong to always assume that bureaucracies are self-serving and inefficient. The administrative role of mediating between professionals rather than trying to provide strong leadership can appear both simultaneously old-fashioned and able to correspond to a great deal of modern management theory positioning managers as coaches and enablers of others (Harrison *et al.*, 1992).

In the 1970s and 1980s, there was a strong suggestion from the state that public managers could learn a great deal from their private counterparts, that that they should become more 'business-like' in their approach. In the views of politicians, public organisations had become too expensive, and economic difficulties led to demands for them to reduce their costs, whilst simultaneously, because of the growing consumerist movement (Haug and Sussman, 1969), to improve the services they offered. Public managers were therefore, as well as facilitators, required to be corporation-style managers, running services efficiently and according to their customers' needs.

In the 1980s managers were also told that their job was to implement government policy on the ground. They were the corporate rationalisers of Alford's model (Alford, 1975), there to do the state's work and challenge entrenched in professional groupings and make sure that the policy-implementation gap was filled. Managers that achieved this were to be celebrated, and those that did not comply were labelled as belonging to the past – dinosaurs who did not support reform agendas.

More recent reforms have demanded that public managers become more financially aware, having to gain an understanding of the complexities of contracting in the new market environments, and of working in public – private partnerships. Public managers therefore had to become competent accountants, able to balance their books (or even generate a surplus), as well as run a service that added value for the public.

'Entrepreneur' is a notoriously slippery word, but in the sense of acting as brokers to link together services, it is particularly apposite. Public managers are required to be able to take a view across the networks of available local services and find ways of combining separate services into a seamless pathway. Managers therefore also need to be entrepreneurs.

Managers, however, must also be leaders. They are required not only to comply with centrally imposed government targets (as corporate rationalisers) but also to come up with new ideas for how services can be better run at the local level. They must then lead their organisations towards those goals, taking their employees with them. The leadership literature often has competing notions of what the term 'leadership' actually means, through from trait-based models to approaches that stress the transformational potential of leaders to delegate and empower those that work with them. The analysis presented here suggests that transformation leadership is a more appropriate model in public services because of the need to work closely with professionals, but it is still often unclear exactly what is required by policymakers.

Public managers are also required to be accountable for the service they are tasked with running. This means that they are often cast, not least by managers themselves, as heroes or villains (Greener, 2005a). When public organisations work well and are high performing by government measures, public managers become heroes, responsible for delivering high achievement. When things do not work out, where services have budget deficits or deliver service measured as being of low quality, it is the manager's fault. There are certainly good reasons for blaming managers when things go wrong – it is they are meant to be responsible for the governance of their organisations. However, it is also politically expedient. It is a lot harder to sack doctors than it is to sack public professionals. Professionals are often a lot harder to replace than managers, as they have expertise in short supply, and powerful professional bodies to support them in any legal action. Getting rid of a manager, however, is relatively easy, as a replacement can usually be readily found, and there is unlikely to be much public sympathy for the removal of a poor-performing Chief Executive.

Then there is the role of being the public service guardian. Many public managers do not do their jobs for financial betterment or for career advancement, but instead because they wish to make a difference. They may closely identify with the goals of their public organisations, and regard attempts to reform them as crude and clumsy attempts by politicians to interfere in something they do not really understand. In many ways, they

Table 10.2 Public manager roles

Role description	Characteristics
Administrator	Probity
	Fairness
	Service
	Enabling
Corporation manager	'Big picture' management
	Efficient
	Customer focused
Corporate rationaliser	Challenger of professional interests
Accountant	Balancer of budgets or creator of surpluses
Entrepreneur	Care pathway creator
	Adder of value
Leader	Goal setter
	Inspiration
Hero or villain	Accountability taker
Guardian	Preserver of the good of the past
	Stabiliser against unnecessary reform

have a point. Public policy has a tendency towards being somewhat circular in nature, with periods of centralisation and decentralisation following one another, and the use of markets rising and falling in popularity. With all of this meddling it is often a wonder that public services work at all. As such, the role of public manager as guardian appears to be an important one, trying to keep the waters within an organisation relatively still compared to the raging torrents that may surround it. Table 10.2 summarises these roles.

The quality of public management matters profoundly (Meier and O'Toole, 2002), but public managers therefore have incredibly demanding and janus-faced existences. They must 'acknowledge multiple levels of managerial accountability – to citizens, to elected officials, to public employees – and to their own professional standards' (Kelly, 2005:82). They are almost guaranteed, because of the variety of stakeholders they must deal with on a day-to-day basis, to be failing on some front or another. They also risk, because of the variety of roles they are required to adopt, to appear to at least some of those that work with them, to be inconsistent at least some of the time. How is it possible to be both guardian and corporate rationaliser? To be both an administrator of probity and an entrepreneur? This seems to be the challenge public managers are now required to meet – squaring the incompatible and extraordinarily difficult roles now demanded of them by the state.

Two main answers seem to appear as to how public services should be reformed. First, there is the greater use of markets, stressing entrepreneurial roles and making public managers increasingly accountable to individual service users rather than to collective publics. The extent to which the market can ever be allowed to run without any state hindrance, with the danger of inequalities between users resulting (which would seem to undermine key principles of public service) and concern that greater use of the private sector might result in greater measured efficiency, but also 'gaps' in provision where services cannot be supplied profitably, or where widespread, collective responses are needed (the most obvious example being when confronting natural disasters). Markets will result in the private sector making profits from public services (which readers may or may not be comfortable about), to a stressing of contractual relationships and the need for managers to work across networks of providers to avoid the fragmentation of services, and to the problem of who holds public services, as a whole, to account if they are extensively privatised and so democratic processes impinge less and less upon them.

The alternative is for the state to accept that there are some services that it must play a role in providing (see Greener, 2008 for an attempt to begin to work out how this might be done), and to accept that such services must be made more democratically accountable than is presently the case, putting place a collective accountability measure to the public as a whole. Roberts (2002) suggests, in line with some of the ideas of Fox and Miller (1995), that public officials need to be accountable through 'dialogue' because the benefits of such a system outweigh the costs. In Minnesota, an attempt was held to have a wide-ranging dialogue on education that was covered by local, state and national press, reinforcing traditional accountability mechanisms by making them more transparent and visible. The publicness of the dialogue also made participants more accountable to one another, building relationships based on mutual listening and learning, and leading to adversarial politics becoming less attractive as working together had become far more attractive. However, it could also be isolating for those that call for a decision to be quickly made, and time consuming and resource demanding, and required public managers to learn new skills to make the process work. However, greater democracy does not come cheaply, and may not work in every situation (Irvin and Stansbury, 2004).

Where services are recognised as being public, the tension between the state attempting to run services so that they are run as fairly as possible, individual user responsiveness, and collective local democracy come to the fore. Should services be standardised as much as possible, or should local variations be allowed? How do you manage the tensions between services being delivered to individual users, but collective democratic decisions having to be made about what is provided and to whom? Even with extensive dialogue processes there are no easy answers to these questions. Public organisations, however, must find them if they are to claim their legitimacy based on collectivity and democracy. As Denhardt and Denhardt (2006) suggest, 'Only when our commitment to democratic principles and ideals is clear to all will we once again be able to establish public service as the highest calling in our society' (p. 446).

Is it not possible to try and find hybrid forms that allow both markets and extensive state formations, as the Third Way discourse (see Chapter 3) attempts to achieve? This would seem to make some sense as a pragmatic response to the problems of both the market-led and the democracy-led models described above. However, such a combination may have significant difficulties.

Jane Jacobs, the author of the public administration classic *The Life and Death of American Cities*, considered the issue of the moral foundations of commerce and politics in her book *Systems of Survival* (Jacobs, 1992). In it, in the form a platonic dialogue between a range of characters, an agreement is reached that trying to combine the moral systems of the two is likely to produce hybrids that are subjects to corruption and abuse. Jacobs' characters suggest that there is room for 'ingenuity and improvements' (p. 158) in both systems, but that it is essential to be aware of the moral principles underpinning each and to make sure that they are not compromised. Jacobs' work has far-reaching implications for both public and private managers – if she is right they must know what it is they stand for, and for public managers to only go along with reforms that make public organisations more market-oriented where they can show that their principles will not be diluted or compromised as a result.

This book began by asking whether there is a difference between public and private management, and public and private organisations. Jacobs' work would suggest that the two are based on different moral foundations (those of commerce and politics) and that, even if differences can be difficult to establish empirically at times, the rationale for the two different types of organisation differs sufficiently for us to have to think about reforms not only on instrumental grounds, but also on moral grounds. Students often say that they might consider working in the public sector because they might be able to 'make a difference' or 'do good'. Those working in public organisations often claim that their choice of work was driven by the same beliefs (Buelens and Van den Broeck, 2007; Khojasteh, 1993). This is not to derogate those working in private organisations, but to argue that there may be different underlying moral reasons why the two kinds of organisation exist, and that considerable care must be taken in both identifying and mixing the two. The quality of public services is crucial both for our individual futures and for the future of all our economies. The quality of public management within those public services is hugely important. It is crucial that we give public services the resources and status they deserve, and that the public managers within them understand their role, and the principles for which they stand. Then we can begin to get the services, that we as the public, both expect and deserve.

Bibliography

Aberbach, J. and Christensen, T. (2005) Citizens and Consumers: An NPM dilemma. *Public Management Review*, 7, 225–245.

Ackroyd, S. (1996) Organization Contra Organizations: Professions and Organizational Change in the United Kingdom. *Organization Studies*, 17, 599–621.

Ackroyd, S., Hughes, J. and Soothill, K. (1989) Public Sector Services and Their Management. *Journal of Management Studies*, 26, 603–619.

Aitkenson, G. and Olseon Jr, T. (1998) Commons and Keynes: Their Assault on Laissez-faire. *Journal of Economic Issues*, 32, 1019.

Aldcroft, D. (2001) *The European Economy 1914–2000*. Routledge, London.

Aldridge, A. (2005) *The Market*. Polity, Cambridge.

Alford, J. (1998) A Public Management Road Less Travelled: Clients as Co-producers of Public Services. *Australian Journal of Public Administration*, 57, 128–137.

Alford, R. (1975) *Health Care Politics*. University of Chicago Press, Chicago.

Alford, R. (1972) The Political Economy of Health Care: Dynamics Without Change. *Politics and Society*, 12, 127–164.

Allsop, J. and Jones, K. (2008) Withering the Citizen, Managing the Consumer: Complaints in Healthcare Settings. *Social Policy and Society*, 7, 233–243.

Archer, M. (1995) *Realist Social Theory: The Morphogenetic Approach*. Cambridge University Press, Cambridge.

Argyris, C. and Schon, D. (1995) *Organizational Learning II. Theory, Method and Practice*. Prentice Hall, London.

Asenova, D. and Beck, M. (2003) The UK Financial Sector and Risk Management in PFI Projects: A Survey. *Public Money and Management*, 23, 195–202.

Bacon, R. and Eltis, W. (1978) *Britain's Economic Problem: Too Few Providers*. Macmillan, London.

Balfour, D. and Grubbs, J. (2000) Character, Corrosion and the Civil Servant: The Human Consequences of Globalization and the New Public Management. *Administrative Theory and Praxis*, 22, 570–584.

Ball, S., Bowe, R. and Gewirtz, S. (1995) Circuits of Schooling: a Sociological Exploration of Parental Choice of School in Social Class Contexts. *The Sociological Review*, 43, 52–78.

Barber, M. (2007) *Instruction to Deliver: Tony Blair, the Public Services and the Challenge of Achieving Targets*. Portoco's Publishing, London.

Barnes, M., Newman, J., Knops, A. and Sullivan, H. (2003) Constituting 'The Public' in Public Participation. *Public Administration*, 81, 379–399.

Barney, J. (1996) The Resource-based Theory of the Firm. *Organizational Science*, 7, 469.

Bauman, Z. (2007) *Consuming Life*. Polity Press, Cambridge.

Behn, R. (2003) Why Measure Performance? Different Purposes Require Different Measures. *Public Administration Review*, 63, 586–606.

Birnbaum, N. (1999) Is the Third Way Authentic? *New Political Economy*, 4, 437–446.

Blaug, M. (1997). *Economic Theory in Retrospect*. Cambridge University Press, Cambridge.

Bloomfield, B. and Best, A. (1992) Management Consultants: Systems Development, Power and the Translation of Problems. *Sociological Review*, 40, 3, 533–560.

Bloomfield, B. and Coombs, R. (1992) Information Technology, Control and Power: The Centralisation and Decentralisation Debate Revisited. *Journal of Management Studies*, 29, 459–484.

Bolton, S. (2001) Changing Faces: Nurses as Emotional Jugglers. *Sociology of Health and Illness*, 23, 85–100.

Bovaird, T. (2007) Beyond Engagement and Participation: User and Community Coproduction of Public Services. *Public Administration Review*, 67, 846–860.

Boyne, G. (1999) Editorial: Markets, Bureaucracy and Public Management. *Public Money and Management*, 19, 4, 3–4.

Boyne, G. (2002) Public and Private Management: What's the Difference. *Journal of Management Studies*, 39, 97–122.

Boyne, G., Farrell, C., Law, J., Powell, M. and Walker, R. (2003) *Evaluating Public Management Reforms*. Open University Press, Buckingham.

Boyne, G., Jenkins, G. and Poole, M. (1999) Human Resource Management in the Public and Private Sectors: An Empirical Comparison. *Public Administration*, 77, 407–420.

Boyne, G. and Gould-Williams, J. (2003) Planning and Performance in Public Organizations: An Empirical Analysis. *Public Management Review*, 5, 115–132.

Bozeman, B. (1988) Exploring the Limits of Public and Private Sectors: Some Boundaries on the Maginot Line. *Public Administration Review*, 48, 672–674.

Bozeman, B. (2002) Public-Value Failure: When Efficient Markets May Not Do. *Public Administration Review*, 67, 145–161.

Bozeman, B. and Bretschneider, S. (1994) The 'Publicness Puzzle' in Organizational Theory: A Test of Alternative Explanations of Differences between Public and Private Organizations. *Journal of Public Administration Research and Theory*, 4, 197–223.

Bozeman, B. and Kingsley, G. (1998) Risk Culture in Public and Private Organizations. *Public Administration Review*, 58, 109–118.

Bradley, L. and Parker, R. (2006) Do Australian Public Sector Employees Have the Type of Culture They Want in the Era of New Public Management? *Australian Journal of Public Administration*, 65, 89–99.

Brinton Milward, H. and Provan, K. (2003) Managing the Hollow State: Collaboration and Contracting. *Public Management Review*, 5, 1–16.

Broadbent, J. and Laughlin, R. (2002) Public Service Professionals and the New Public Management. In *New Public Management: Current Trends and Future Prospects* (Eds. McLaughlin, E., Osborne, S. and Ferlie, E.) Routledge, London, pp. 95–108.

Brown, T. and Potoski, M. (2004) Managing the Public Service Market. *Public Administration Review*, 64, 656–668.

Buelens, M. and Van den Broeck, H. (2007) An Analysis of Differences in Work Motivation between Public and Private Sector Organizations. *Public Administration Review*, 67, 65–74.

Burt, R. (2000) The Network Entrepreneur. In *Entrepreneurship: The Social Science View* (Ed. Swedburg, R.) Oxford University Press, Oxford, pp. 281–307.

Burt, R. (1993) The Social Structure of Competition. In *Explorations in Economic Sociology* (Ed. Swedburg, R.) Russell Sage Foundation, New York, pp. 65–103.

Buxton, M. and Packwood, T. (1991) *Hospitals in Transition: The Resource Management Initiative*. Open University Press, Buckingham.

Callon, M. (1999) Actor-network Theory – the Market Test. *Sociological Review*, 46 S, 181–195.

Callon, M. (1998) An Essay on Framing and Overflowing. In *The Laws of the Markets* (Ed. Callon, M.) Blackwell, Oxford, pp. 244–269.

Chapman, R. and Dunsire, A. (Eds.) (1971) *Style in Administration: Readings in British Public Administration*. George Allen and Unwin, London.

Cho, K. and Lee, S. (2001) Another Look at Public-Private Distinction and Organizational Commitment: A Cultural Explanation. *International Journal of Organizational Analysis*, 9, 84–102.

Christensen, T. and Laegreid, P. (2001) New Public Management: The Effects of Contractuaralism and Devolution on Political Control. *Public Management Review*, 3, 73–91.

Christensen, T. and Laegreid, P. (2002) A Transformation Perspective on Administrative Reform. In *New Public Management: The Transformation of Ideas and Practice* (Eds. Christensen, T. and Laegreid, P.), Ashgate, Aldershot, pp. 13–39.

Christy, R. and Brown, J. (1996) Marketing. In *Managing the New Public Services* (Eds. Farnham, D. and Horton, S.) Macmillan, Basingstoke, pp. 94–112.

Clarke, J., Cochrane, A. and Smart, C. (1992) *Ideologies of Welfare: From Dreams to Disillusion*. Routledge, London.

Clarke, J. and Newman, J. (1997) *The Managerial State*. Sage, London.

Clarke, J., Newman, J., Smith, N., Vidler, E. and Westmarland, L. (2007) *Creating Citizen-consumers: Changing Publics and Changing Public Services*. Paul Chapman Publishing, London.

Clarke, J., Smith, N. and Vidler, E. (2006) The Indeterminacy of Choice: Political, Policy and Organisational Implications. *Social Policy and Society*, 5, 327–336.

Cockett, R. (1995) *Thinking the Unthinkable: Think-tanks and the Economic Counter-Revolution*. Fontana Press, London.

Cole, A. and Jones, G. (2005) Reshaping the State: Administrative Reform and New Public Management in France. *Governance*, 18, 567–588.

Conger, J. and Kanungo, R. (1998) *Charismatic Leadership in Organizations.* Sage, New York.

Currie, G. (1999) The Influence of Middle Managers in the Business Planning Process: A Case Study in the UK NHS. *British Journal of Management*, 10, 141–155.

Dean, H. (2002) *Welfare Rights and Social Policy.* Pearson, London.

Denhardt, R. and Denhardt, J. (2000) The New Public Service: Serving Rather than Steering. *Public Administration Review*, 60, 549–559.

Denhardt, R. and Denhardt, J. (2006) *Public Administration: An Action Orientation.* Thomson, Belmont.

Dent, M. (2006) Patient Choice and Medicine in Health Care: Responsibilization, Governance and Proto-professionalization. *Public Management Review*, 8, 449–462.

Department of Health and Social Security. (1983) *NHS Management Inquiry.* HMSO, London.

DiMaggio, P. (1991) Constructing an Organizational Field as a Professional Project: U.S. Art Museums, 1920–1940. In *The New Institutionalism in Organizational Analysis* (Eds. Powell, W. and DiMaggio, P.) University of Chicago Press, Chicago, pp. 267–292.

Du Gay, P. (2000) *In Praise of Bureaucracy: Weber, Organization, Ethics.* Sage, London.

Dunleavy, P. and Hood, C. (1994) From Old Public Administration to New Public Management. *Public Money and Management*, 14, 3, 9–16.

Dunsire, A. (1999) Then and Now: Public Administration 1953–1999. *Political Studies*, XLVII, 360–378.

Edwards, B. and Fall, M. (2005) *The Executive Years of the NHS: The England Account 1985–2003.* Radcliffe Publishing Ltd, Oxford.

Ehrenreich, J. (1978) *The Cultural Crisis of Modern Medicine.* Monthly Review Press, Boston.

Enthoven, A. (1985) *Reflections on the Management of the National Health Service: An American Looks at Incentives to Efficiency in Health Service Management in the UK.* Nuffield Provincial Hospitals Trust, London.

Esping-Anderson, G. (1990) *The Three Worlds of Welfare Capitalism.* Princeton University Press: New Jersey.

Exworthy, M. and Halford, S. (Eds.) (1998) *Professionalism and the New Managerialism in the Public Sector.* Open University Press, Buckingham.

Exworthy, M., Powell, M. and Mohan, J. (1999) The NHS: Quasi-market, Quasi-hierarchy or Quasi-network? *Public Money and Management*, 19, 15–22.

Farnham, D. and Horton, S. (1996) *Managing People in the Public Services.* Macmillan, London.

Ferlie, E. (1992) The Creation and Evolution of Quasi Markets in the Public Sector: A Problem for Strategic Management. *Strategic Management Journal*, 13, 79–97.

Ferlie, E., Pettigrew, A., Ashburner, L. and Fizgerald, L. (1996) *The New Public Management in Action.* Oxford University Press, Oxford.

Flynn, N. (2000) Managerialism and Public Services: Some International Trends. In *New Managerialism: New Welfare?* (Eds. Clarke, J., Gewirtz, S. and McLaughlin, E.) Sage, London, pp. 27–44.

Flynn, N. (2002) *Public Sector Management*. Pearson Education, Harlow.

Flynn, N. (1989) The 'New Right' and Social Policy. *Policy and Politics*, 17, 97–109.

Flynn, N. and Strehl, F. (1996) France. In *Public Sector Management in Europe* (Eds. Flynn, N. and Strehl, F.) Prentice Hall, London, pp. 112–131.

Forbes, I. (1986) *Market Socialism: Whose Choice?* Fabian Society, London.

Foucault, M. (1977) *Discipline and Punish: The Birth of the Prison*. Penguin, Harmondsworth.

Fox, C. and Miller, H. (1995) *Post-modern Public Administration: Towards Discourse*. Sage, London.

Friedman, M. and Friedman, R. (1990) *Free to Choose: A Personal Statement*. Thomson, London.

Galbraith, J. (1958) *The Affluent Society*. Penguin, London.

Garud, R., Jain, S. and Kumaraswamy, A. (2002) Institutional Entrepreneurship in the Sponsorship of Common Technological Standards: The Case of Sun Microsystems and Java. *Academy of Management Journal*, 45, 196–214.

George, V. and Wilding, P. (1994) *Ideology and Social Welfare*. Harvester Wheatsheaf, London.

Giddens, A. (1994) *Beyond Left and Right: The Future of Radical Politics*. Polity Press, Cambridge.

Giddens, A. (1998) *The Third Way: The Renewal of Social Democracy*. Polity, Cambridge.

Giddens, A. (2002) *What Now for New Labour?* Polity, Cambridge.

Giddens, A. (2003) Challenge of Renewal. *Progressive Politics*, 1, 36–39.

Giddens, A. (2007) *Over to you, Mr. Brown*. Polity Press, Cambridge.

Gillespie, R. (1997) Managers and Professionals. In *Perspectives in Health Care* (Eds. North, N. and Bradshaw, Y.) Macmillan, Basingstoke, pp. 84–109.

Goddard, M., Mannion, R. and Smith, P. (1999) Assessing the Performance of NHS Hospital Trusts: The Role of 'Hard' and 'Soft' Information. *Health Policy*, 48, 119–134.

Graham, P. (1994) Marketing in the Public Sector: Inappropriate or Merely Difficult? *Journal of Marketing Management*, 10, 361–375.

Granovetter, M. (1985) Economic Action and Social Structure: The Problem of Embeddedness. *American Journal of Sociology*, 91, 481–510.

Granovetter, M. (1973) The Strength of Weak Ties. *American Journal of Sociology*, 78, 1360–1380.

Gray, A. and Jenkins, B. (1995). From Public Administration to Public Management: Reassessing A Revolution. *Public Administration*, 73, 75–99.

Greener, I. (2005) Health Management as Strategic Behaviour: Managing Medics and Performance in the NHS. *Public Management Review*, 7, 95–110.

Greener, I. (2008) Markets in the Public Sector: When Do They Work, and What Do We Do When They Don't? *Policy and Politics*, 36, 93–108.

Greener, I. (2006) Nick Leeson and the Collapse of Barings Bank: Socio-technical Networks and the 'Rogue Trader'. *Organization*, 13, 421–441.

Greener, I. (2003a) Patient Choice in the NHS: The View from Economic Sociology. *Social Theory and Health*, 1, 72–89.

Greener, I. (2003b) Performance in the NHS: Insistence of Measurement and Confusion of Content. *Public Performance and Management Review*, 26, 237–250.

Greener, I. (2001) Social Learning and Macroeconomic Policy in Britain. *Journal of Public Policy*, 21, 133–152.

Greener, I. (2005a) Talking to Health Managers About Change: Heroes, Villains and Simplification. *Journal of Health Organisation and Management*, 18, 321–335.

Greener, I. (2005b) The Role of the Patient in Healthcare Reform: Customer, Consumer or Creator? In *Future Health Organisations and Systems* (Eds. Dawson, S. and Sausmann, C.) Palgrave, Basingstoke, pp. 227–245.

Greener, I. (2003) Who Choosing What? The Evolution of 'Choice' in the NHS, and its Implications for New Labour. In *Social Policy Review 15* (Eds. Bochel, C., Ellison, N. and Powell, M.) Policy Press, Bristol, pp. 49–68.

Greener, I. and Powell, M. (2008) The Changing Governance of the NHS; Reform in a Post-Keynesian Health Service. *Human Relations*, 61, 5, 617–636.

Grimshaw, D., Vincent, S. and Willmott, H. (2002) Going Privately: Partnership and Outsourcing in UK Public Services. *Public Administration*, 80, 475–502.

Hall, P. (1993) Policy Paradigms, Social Learning and the State. *Comparative Politics*, 25, 275–296.

Harrison, S. (1988) *Managing the National Health Service: Shifting the Frontier?* Chapman and Hall, London.

Harrison, S. and Wistow, G. (1993) Managing Health Care: Balancing Interests and Influence. In *Dilemmas in Health Care* (Eds. Davey, B. and Popay, J.) Open University Press, Buckingham, pp. 12–26.

Harrison, S. (1982) Consensus Decision-Making in the National Health Service – A Review. *Journal of Management Studies*, 19, 377–394.

Harrison, S., Hunter, D., Marnoch, G. and Pollitt, C. (1992) *Just Managing: Power and Culture in the NHS*. Macmillan, London.

Harrison, S., Hunter, D. and Pollitt, C. (1990) *The Dynamics of British Health Policy*. Unwin Hyman, London.

Haug, M. and Sussman, M. (1969) Professional Autonomy and the Revolt of the Client. *Social Problems*, 17, 153–161.

Hayek, F. (1944) *The Road to Serfdom*. Routledge and Kegan Paul, London.

Hennessy, P. (1997) *Muddling Through: Power, Politics and the Quality of Government in Post-War Britain*. Phoenix, London.

Hennessy, P. (1994) *Never Again: Britain 1945–1951*. Pantheon Books, London.

Hirschman, A. (1970) *Exit, Voice and Loyalty: Responses to Decline in Firms, Organizations and States*. Harvard University Press, London.

Hoggett, P. (2000) *Emotional Life and the Politics of Welfare*. Palgrave, London.

Hood, C. (1991) A Public Management for All Seasons? *Public Administration*, 69, 3–19.

Hood, C. (1998) *The Art of the State: Culture, Rhetoric and Public Management*, Clarendon Press, Oxford.

Hood, C. (2006) Gaming in Targetworld: The Targets Approach to Managing British Public Services. *Public Administration Review*, 66, 515–521.

Hutton, W. (1996) *The State We're In*. Vintage, London.

Hwang, H. and Powell, W. (2005) Institutions and Entrepreneurship. In *Handbook of Entrepreneurial Research* (Eds. Alvarez, S., Agrawal, R. and Sorenson, O.) Springer, New York, pp. 179–210.

Hyman, P. (2005) *1 out of 10. From Downing Street Vision to Classroom Reality*. Vintage, London.

Illich, I. (1977) *Limits to Medicine*. Penguin, Harmondsworth.

Irvin, R. and Stansbury, J. (2004) Citizen Participation in Decision Making: Is it Worth the Effort? *Public Administration Review*, 64, 55–65.

Jackson, P. (2003) The Size and Scope of the Public Sector: An International Comparison. In *Public Management and Governance* (Eds. Bovaird, T. and Lofler, E.) Routledge, London, pp. 25–39.

Jackson, P. (1990) Public Choice and Public Sector Management. *Public Money and Management*, 10, 13–20.

Jacobs, J. (1992) *Systems of Survival: A Dialogue on the Moral Foundations of Commerce and Politics*. Hodder and Stoughton, Kent.

Jenkins, S. (2006) *Thatcher and Sons: A Revolution in Three Acts*. Allen Lane, London.

Jessop, B. (1992) Fordism and Post-Fordism: A Critical Reformulation. In *Pathways to Industrialisation and Regional Development* (Eds. Storper, M. and Scott, A.) Routledge, London, pp. 46–69.

Jessop, B. (1990) *State Theory: Putting the Capitalist State in its Place*. Polity Press, Cambridge.

Jessop, B. (1993) Towards a Schumpeterian Workfare State? Preliminary Remarks on Post-Fordist Political Economy. *Studies in Political Economy*, 40, 7–39.

Jessop, B. (1994) The Transition to Post-Fordism and the Schumpeterian Workfare State. In *Towards a Post-Fordist Welfare State?* (Eds. Burrows, R. and Loader, B.) Routledge, London, pp. 13–37.

Jessop, B. (1999) The Changing Governance of Welfare: Recent Trends in its Primary Functions, Scale and Modes of Coordination. *Social Policy and Administration*, 33, 348–359.

Jessop, B. (2002) *The Future of the Capitalist State*. Polity Press, Cambridge.

Johnson, G. and Scholes, K. (Eds.) (2001) *Exploring Public Sector Strategy*. Pearson Education, Harlow.

Johnston, J. (2000) The New Public Management in Australia. *Administrative Theory & Praxis*, 22, 345–368.

Kearsey, A. and Varey, R. (1998) Managerialist Thinking on Marketing for Public Services. *Public Money and Management*, 18, 2, 51–60.

Kelly, D. (1999) The Strategic-Relational View of the State. *Politics*, 19, 109–115.

Kelly, J. (2005) The Dilemma of the Unsatisfied Customer in a Market Model of Public Administration. *Public Administration Review*, 65, 76–84.

Kernaghan, K. (2000) The Post-bureaucratic Organization and Public Service Values. *International Review of Administrative Sciences*, 66, 91–104.

Kessler, I. and Purcell, J. (1996) Strategic Choice and New Forms of Employment Relations in the Public Service Sector: Developing an Analytical Framework. *The International Journal of Human Resource Management*, 7, 206–229.

Keynes, J. (1997) *The General Theory of Employment, Interest and Money*. Prometheus Books, New York.

Khojasteh, M. (1993) Motivating the Private vs. Public Sector Managers. *Public Personnel Management*, 22, 391–401.

Kickert, W. (2005) Distinctiveness in the Study of Public Management in Europe: A historical-institutional analysis of France, Germany and Italy. *Public Management Review*, 7, 537–563.

Kickert, W. (1997) Public Governance in the Netherlands: An Alternative to Anglo-American 'Managerialism'. *Public Administration*, 75, 731–752.

Kickert, W., Klijn, E. and Koppenjan, J. (Eds.) (1997) *Managing Complex Networks: Strategies for the Public Sector*. Sage, London.

Kirkpatrick, I. and Ackroyd, S. (2003) Transforming the Professional Archetype? The New Managerialism in UK Social Services. *Public Management Review*, 5, 511–531.

Kirkpatrick, I. and Martinez Lucio, M. (1996) Introduction: The Contract State and The Future of Public Management. *Public Administration*, 74, 1–8.

Kitchener, M. (2000) The 'Bureaucratization' of Professional Roles: The Case of Clinical Directors in UK Hospitals. *Organization*, 7, 129–154.

Klein, R. (1990) The State and the Profession: The Politics of the Double-bed. *British Medical Journal*, 301, 700–702.

Kotler, P. and Lee, N. (2006) *Marketing in the Public Sector: A Roadmap for Impoved Performance*. Wharton School Publishing, Upper Saddle River.

Laffin, M. (Ed.) (1998) *Beyond Bureaucracy? The Professions in the Contemporary Public Sector*. Ashgate, Aldershot.

Larson, P. (1997) Public and Private Values at Odds: Can Private Sector Values be Transplanted into Public Sector Institutions? *Public Administration and Development*, 17, 131–139.

Le Grand, J. (1991) *Equity and Choice: An Essay in Economics and Applied Philosophy*. Routledge, London.

Le Grand, J. (1997) Knights, Knaves or Pawns? Human Behaviour and Social Policy. *Journal of Social Policy*, 26, 149–169.

Le Grand, J. (2003) *Motivation, Agency and Public Policy: Of Knights, Knaves, Pawns and Queens*. Oxford University Press, Oxford.

Le Grand, J. (2007) *The Other Invisible Hand*. Princetown University Press, Woodstock.

Learmonth, M. (1999) The National Health Service Manager, Engineer and Father? A Deconstruction. *Journal of Management Studies*, 36, 999–1012.

Lee Potter, J. (1998) *A Damn Bad Business*. Orion, London.

Lindblom, C. and Woodhouse, E. (1993) *The Policy-making Process*. Prentice Hall, Englewood-Cliffs.

Llewellyn, S. and Tappin, E. (2003) Strategy in the Public Sector: Management in the Wilderness. *Journal of Management Studies*, 40, 955–982.

Lynn, L. (1999) Public Management in North America. *Public Management*, 1, 301–310.

Lynn, L. (2001) The Myth of the Bureaucratic Paradigm: What Traditional Public Administration Really Stood For. *Public Administration Review*, 61, 144–160.

Majone, G. (1989) *Evidence, Argument and the Policymaking Process*. Yale University Press, New Haven.

Mannion, R., Davies, H. and Marshall, M. (2004) *Cultures for Performance in Health Care*. Open University Press, Buckingham.

Mannion, R., Goddard, M. and Smith, P. (2001) On the Limitations and Pitfalls of Performance Measurement Systems in Health Care. In *Quality in Healthcare: Strategic Issues in Health Care Management* (Eds. Davies, H., Tavakoli, M. and Malek, M.) Ashgate, Aldershot, pp. 158–169.

Marquand, D. (2004) *Decline of the Public*. Polity, Cambridge.

Marston, G. (2000) Metaphor, Morality and Myth: A Critical Discourse Analysis of Public Housing Policy in Queensland. *Critical Social Policy*, 20, 349–373.

McLean, B. and Elkind, P. (2004) *The Smartest Guys in the Room: The Amazing Rise and Scandalous Fall of Enron*. Penguin, London.

McNulty, T. and Ferlie, E. (2002) *Re-engineering Health Care: The Complexities of Organizational Transformation*. Oxford University Press, Oxford.

Meier, J. and O'Toole, L. (2002) Public Management and Organizational Performance: The Effect of Managerial Quality. *Journal of Policy Analysis and Management*, 21, 629–643.

Minister of State for Department of Health, Minister of State for Local and Regional Government and Minister of State for School Standards (2005) The Case for User Choice in Public Services.

Minvielle, E. (2006) New Public Management a la Francaise: The Case of Regional Hospital Agencies. *Public Administration Review*, 66, 753–763.

Moore, M. (1997) *Creating Public Value: Strategic Management in Government*. Harvard University Press, Harvard.

Murray, C. (1984) *Losing Ground*. Basic Books, New York.

Nettleton, S. and Burrows, R. (2003) E-scaped Medicine? Information, Reflexivity and Health. *Critical Social Policy*, 23, 173–193.

Newman, J. (2000) Beyond the New Public Management? In *New Managerialism: New Welfare?* (Eds. Clarke, J., Gewirtz, S. and McLaughlin, E.) Sage, London, pp. 45–62.

Newman, J. (2002) The New Public Management, Modernization and Institutional Change. In *New Public Management: Current Trends and Future Prospects* (Eds. McLaughlin, K., Osborne, S. and Ferlie, E.) Routledge, London, pp. 77–91.

Newman, J. and McKee, B. (2005) Beyond the New Public Management? Public Services and the Social Investment State. *Policy and Politics*, 33, 657–674.

Newman, J., Raine, J. and Skelcher, C. (2001) Transforming Local Government: Innovation and Modernization. *Public Money and Management*, 21, 2, 61–68.

Nicholson-Crotty, S., Theobald, N. and Nicholson-Crotty, J. (2006) Disparate Measures: Public Managers and Performance-Measurement Strategies. *Public Administration Review*, 66, 101–113.

O'Connor, J. (1973) *The Fiscal Crisis of the State*. Macmillan, London.

Oliver, M. (1997) *Whatever Happened to Monetarism? Economic Planning and Social Learning in the United Kingdom Since 1979*. Ashgate, Aldershot.

Ormerod, P. (1995) *The Death of Economics*. Faber and Faber, London.

Osborne, D. and Gaebler, T. (1993) *Reinventing Government*. Addison Wesley, New York.

Osborne, D. and Plastrick, P. (1997) *Banishing Bureaucracy: The Five Strategies for Reinventing Government*. Addison-Wesley, New York.

Osborne, S. and McLaughlin, K. (2002) The New Public Management in Context. In *The New Public Management: Current Trends and Future Prospects*, (Eds. McLaughlin, K., Osborne, S. and Ferlie, E.) pp. 7–14. Routledge, London.

Oswick, C. and Grant, D. (1996) Personnel Management in the Public Sector. *Personnel Review*, 25, 4–18.

Ouchi, W. (2003) *Making Schools Work*. Simon and Schuster, New York.

Ouchi, W., Riordan, R., Lingle, L. and Porter, L. (2005) Making Public Schools Work: Management Reforms as the Key. *Academy of Management Journal*, 48, 929–940.

Peckham, S., Exworthy, M., Greener, I. and Powell, M. (2005) Decentralizing Health Services: More Local Accountability or Just More Central Control. *Public Money and Management*, 25, 221–228.

Pemberton, H. (2000) Policy Networks and Policy Learning: UK Economic Policy in the 1960s and 1970s. *Public Administration*, 78, 771–792.

Pestoff, V. (2006) Citizens and Coproduction in Public Services: Childcare in Eight European Countries. *Public Management Review*, 8, 503–519.

Pestoff, V., Osborne, S. and Bransen, T. (2006) Patterns of Co-production Public Services: Some Concluding Thoughts. *Public Management Review*, 8, 591–595.

Peters, J. and Waterman, R. (1982) *In Search of Excellence: Lessons from America's Best Run Companies*. Harpercollins, London.

Pierson, C. (2006) *Beyond the Welfare State?* Polity Press, Cambridge

Polidano, C., Hulme, D. and Minogue, M. (1998) Conclusions: Looking Beyond the New Public Management. In *Beyond the New Public Management: Changing Ideas and Practice in Governance* (Eds. Minogue, M., Polidano, C. and Hulme, D.) Edward Elgar, Cheltenham, pp. 278–293.

Pollitt, C. (1986) Beyond the Managerial Model: The Case for Broadening Performance Assessment in Government and the Public Service. *Financial Accountability and Management*, 2, 155–170.

Pollitt, C. (1993) *Managerialism and Public Services*. Blackwell, Oxford.

Pollitt, C. (1985) Measuring Performance: A New System for the National Health Service. *Policy and Politics*, 13, 1–15.

Pollitt, C. (2000) Is the Emperor in His Underwear? An Analysis of the Impacts of Public Management Reform. *Public Management*, 2, 181–199.

Pollitt, C. (2003) *The Essential Public Manager*. Open University Press, Maidenhead.

Pollitt, C. and Bouchaert, G. (2000) *Public Management Reform: A Comparative Analysis*. Oxford University Press, Oxford.

Poole, M., Mansfield, R. and Gould-Williams, J. (2006) Public and Private Sector Managers Over 20 Years: A Test of the 'Convergence Thesis'. *Public Administration*, 84, 1051–1076.

Powell M. (1997) *Evaluating the National Health Service*, Open University Press, Buckingham.

Porter, M. (2004) *Competitive Advantage*. Free Press, New York.

Public Finance. (2007) PFI hospitals 'costing NHS extra £480m a year'.

Putnam, R. (1993) *Making Democracy Work: Civic Conditions in Modern Italy*. Princeton University Press, Princeton.

Quirk, B. (1997) Accountable to Everyone: Postmodern Pressures on Public Managers. *Public Administration*, 75, 569–586.

Rainey, H., Backoff, R. and Levine, C. (1976) Comparing Public and Private Organizations. *Public Administration Review*, 36, 233–244.

Rainey, H. and Bozeman, B. (2000) Comparing Public and Private Organizations: Empirical Research and the Power of the A Priori. *Journal of Public Administration Research and Theory*, 10, 447–469.

Rainey, H., Pandey, S. and Bozeman, B. (1995) Research Note: Public and Private Managers' Perceptions of Red Tape. *Public Administration Review*, 55, 567–574.

Rainey, H.G. (1989) Public Management: Recent Research on the Political Context and Managerial Roles, Structures, and Behaviors. *Journal of Management*, 15, 229.

Reichard, C. (2003) Local Public Management Reforms in Germany. *Public Administration*, 81, 345–363.

Rhodes, R. (1997) *Understanding Governance*. Open University Press, Buckingham.

Rintala, M. (2003) *Creating the National Health Service: Bevan and the Medical Lords*. Frank Cass Publishers, London.

Roberts, N. (2002). Keeping Public Officials Accountable Through Dialogue: Resolving the Accountability Paradox. *Public Administration Review*, 62, 658–669.

Ross, B. (1988) Public and Private Sectors: The Underlying Differences. *Management Review*, 14, 28–33.

Sabatier, P. (1988) An Advocacy Coalition Framework of Policy Change and the Role of Policy-Oriented Learning Therein. *Policy Sciences*, 21, 129–169.

Sanderson, I. (1998) Beyond Performance Measurement? Assessing Value in Local Government. *Local Government Studies*, 24, 1–25.

Sayer, A. (2005) *The Moral Significance of Class*. Cambridge University Press, Cambridge.

Schneider, S. (2005) Administrative Breakdowns in the Governmental Response to Hurricane Katrina. *Public Administration Review*, 65, 515–516.

Schofield, J. (2001) The Old Ways are the Best? The Durability and Usefulness of Bureaucracy in Public Sector Management. *Organization*, 8, 77–96.

Schwartz, B. (2004) *The Paradox of Choice: Why Less is More*. Harper Collins, New York.

Sheaff, R. (1990) *Marketing for Health Services: A Framework for Communications, Evaluation and Total Quality Management*. Open University Press, Buckingham.

Smith Ring, P. and Perry, J. (1985) Strategic Management in Public and Private Organizations: Implications of Distinctive Contexts and Constraints. *Academy of Management Review*, 10, 276–286.

Smith, J., Walshe, K. and Hunter, D. (2001) The 'Redisorganisation' of the NHS: Another Reorganisation Leaving Unhappy Managers Can Only Worsen the Service. *British Medical Journal*, 323, 1262–1263.

Spicer, M. (2001) *Public Administration and the State: A Postmodern Perspective*. University of Alabama Press, Tuscaloosa.

Spicer, M. (2004) Public Administration, the History of Ideas, and the Reinventing Government Movement. *Public Administration Review*, 64, 353–361.

Stewart, J. and Walsh, K. (1992) Change in the Management of Public Services. *Public Administration*, 70, 499–518.

Stillman, R. (1997) American vs. European Public Administration: Does Public Administration Make the Modern State, or Does the State Make Public Administration. *Public Administration Review*, 57, 332–338.

Stoker, G. (2006) *Why Politics Matters: Making Democracy Work*. Palgrave, London.

Sukel W. (1978) Contrasting the Private and Public Sectors. *Industrial Management*, 20, 2, 18–19.

Talbot, C. (2000) Performing 'Performance' – A Comedy in Five Acts. *Public Money and Management*, 20, 63–68.

Tallis, R. (2005) *Hippocratic Oaths: Medicine and its Discontents*. Atlantic Books, London.

Thomas, R. (1978) *The British Philosophy of Administration: A Comparison of British and American Ideas 1900–1939*. Longman, London.

Torfing, J. (2001) Path-Dependent Danish Welfare Reforms: The Contribution of the New Institutionalisms to Understanding Evolutionary Change. *Scandinavian Political Studies*, 24, 277–310.

Torfing, J. (1999a) Towards a Schumpeterian Workfare Postnational Regime: Path-shaping and Path-dependency in Danish Welfare State Reform. *Economy and Society*, 28, 369–402.

Torfing, J. (1999b) Workfare with Welfare: Recent Reforms of the Danish Welfare State. *Journal of European Social Policy*, 9, 5–28.

Turner, B. (1987) *Medical Power and Social Knowledge*. Sage, London.

Ventriss, C. (2000) New Public Management: An Examination of Its Influence on Contemporary Public Affairs and Its Impact on Shaping the Intellectual Agenda of the Field. *Administrative Theory & Praxis*, 22, 500–518.

Vigoda, E. (2002) From Responsiveness to Collaboration: Governance, Citizens, and the Next Generation of Public Administration. *Public Administration Review*, 62, 527–540.

Walsh, K. (1991) Citizens and Consumer: Marketing and Public Sector Management. *Public Money and Management*, 9–16.

Walsh, K. (1996) *Public Services and Market Mechanisms: Competition, Contracting and the New Public Management*. Palgrave, London.

Westergaard, J. (1999) Where does the Third Way Lead? *New Political Economy*, 4, 429–436.

Wildavsky, A. (1997) *The New Politics of the Budgetary Process*. Longman, New York.

Wilding, P. (1982) *Professional Power and Social Welfare*. Routledge and Kegan Paul, London.

Wilsford, D. (1995) States Facing Interests: Struggles over Health Care Policy in Advanced Industrial Democracies. *Journal of Health Politics, Policy and Law*, 20, 571–613.

Wilson, J. and Thompson, A. (2006) *The Making of Modern Management: British Management in Historical Perspective*. Oxford University Press, Oxford.

Wright Mills, C. (1956) *The Power Elite*. Oxford Press, Oxford.

Index